At the Fire's Center

At the Fire's Center

A STORY OF LOVE AND HOLOCAUST SURVIVAL

Jean M. Peck

UNIVERSITY OF ILLINOIS PRESS

URBANA AND CHICAGO

Publication of this book was supported by a grant from the Center for the Study of the American Jewish Experience, Cincinnati, Ohio.

This book is printed on acid-free paper.

Library of Congress Cataloging-in-Publication Data

At the fire's center : a story of love and Holocaust survival / Jean M. Peck.
p.   cm.
ISBN 0-252-02420-6 (acid-free paper)
1. Hornstein, Stephen, 1924–
2. Hornstein, Luisa, 1925–
3. Ornstein, Paul 1924–
4. Ornstein, Anna, 1927–
5. Jews—Hungary—Biography.
6. Jews—Poland—Biography.
7. Holocaust, Jewish (1939–1945)—Hungary—Personal narratives.
8. Holocaust, Jewish (1939–1945)—Poland—Personal narratives.
9. Hungary—Biography.
10. Poland—Biography.
11. Holocaust survivors—United States—Biography.
I. Peck, Jean, 1947–   .
DS135.H93A13 1998
940.53'18—ddc21
98-9060
CIP

Contents

Illustrations follow pages 44 and 186

Preface

WHEN RUTH ANN HORNSTEIN GOT MARRIED in August 1993, she felt the presence of five generations of family and friends. Her parents, Steve and Lusia Hornstein, and their best friends, Paul and Anna Ornstein, had good reason to be thrilled as they watched their children and grandchildren participate in the wedding ceremony.

Absent from the service, however, were Ruth's grandparents, great-grandparents, and dozens of aunts, uncles, and cousins. Their whereabouts were mostly unknown, but the manner of their deaths was knowledge borne every day by her parents and their friends the Ornsteins: the relatives of both families had all died half a century ago in Europe's ugliest years, that period known as "The Holocaust."

Today, though, for this joyous celebration, the two families reflected on what they had become: intellectually and financially prosperous, rich in love and friendship, respected and popular with their colleagues and many friends. Generous and good-humored, the Ornsteins and Hornsteins had established themselves as valuable resources in their community.

Years ago, however, the Ornsteins and the Hornsteins had seen death, heard it, smelled it, touched it, and marched through it to survive. They had circumvented their certain fate and through unimaginable roads and byways had finally arrived to assemble at this important life-cycle event.

The past has its way of coloring the future with its own hues and forgotten shades. As they watched Ruth Ann, the happiest of brides, float down the aisle, Lusia and Steve, Anna and Paul could not help thinking of where it all began, long ago, in Hungary and Poland, before the dark gray curtain descended on them and hope was nearly lost in fire and smoke.

Acknowledgments

GRATEFUL ACKNOWLEDGMENT FOR FINAN-
cial help in researching and writing this book is made to the University
of Cincinnati Medical Heritage Library Center, the Greater Cincinnati Holocaust Foundation, and the Center for the Study of the American Jewish
Experience at the Hebrew Union College–Jewish Institute of Religion. For
their faith in the project and their help in securing this financial support,
I thank Frank Harkavy, Sandy Thomson, Jeanne Bonham, and Henry
Winkler, president emeritus of the University of Cincinnati.

Jeanne Bonham's encouragement and sympathetic ear got me
through some particularly rough times. I also am grateful to Terry Susskind and Deborah Rieselman for reading the manuscript and offering
helpful and thoughtful criticism. Others contributed to this labor of love
in ways they may not know. I will always be grateful to Richard Friedman,
Michael Shapiro, Susan Glabman, Stuart Susskind, and my many friends
in Cincinnati for their love and support.

I also thank Judith McCulloh and Jane Mohraz of the University of
Illinois Press for their superb editorial direction and Robert Milch for preparing the index.

Of course, I offer my gratitude and appreciation to Anna and Paul Ornstein and Lusia and Steve Hornstein for their willingness to share their experiences with me. It is a privilege and an honor to know them.

I also thank my family—my daughter, Abby; my son, Joel; my mother; my father-in-law; my brothers and sister and their families; and my
extended family in Boston and Maine—for their constant support and
inquiries on the progress of the book. For the stories of her survival of
Auschwitz and the fire bombing of Dresden, I am grateful to my late moth-

er-in-law, Anna Koltun Peck. Sustaining me while I worked on this book were the lessons taught to me by my late father, Harry Marcus, forever my mentor and role model.

Finally, my eternal gratitude and love go to the most important person in my life, my husband, Abraham Peck, who knows too well the horrors and tragedies of the Holocaust and who sets an example for all of us with his kindness, generosity, humor, and decency.

Introduction

IN THE EARLY 1980S, A FEW YEARS AFTER MY husband and I moved to Cincinnati, we were invited to the home of Dr. Anna Ornstein. Dr. Ornstein was a psychiatrist of some repute, owing, in part, to her work with survivors—survivors in the broadest sense—of child abuse, crime, and the Holocaust. My husband, Abe, whose parents had survived World War II in various concentration camps, had become friendly with Dr. Ornstein, since she often spoken to a local children of survivors' group, of which he was a member.

While the guests chatted, I felt drawn to Anna, a beautiful, elegant woman with large, expressive eyes. She had an interesting story, some of which I already knew from my husband, who had told it to me as we drove across town to her home. Anna had been a young teenager growing up in a tiny village in Hungary when the Nazis marched in and prodded all the Jews into cattle cars—the eventual destination was Auschwitz. Somehow, Anna had survived, married, studied medicine, emigrated to the United States, and become a psychoanalyst. She and her husband, Paul, also a renowned psychoanalyst, were constantly in demand on the lecture circuit, not just in Cincinnati but across the United States and in Europe as well.

Many years later, in 1993, I read an account of her concentration camp experiences in an interview she gave to a local paper. "There's much more to her story than that," I thought. At the time, *Schindler's List* was about to appear in movie theaters, and Anna was in high demand. She had actually been an inmate of Plaszow, the camp depicted in the film. Because I was the editor of *Horizons,* the magazine of the University of Cincinnati, I assigned myself a story about Anna Ornstein. Since she was a professor at the University of Cincinnati's College of Medicine, her story would be timely and appropriate.

"If you're going to do a story on Anna," my husband advised, "you should include her husband, Paul, and Steve and Lusia Hornstein." "Who are Steve and Lusia Hornstein?" I asked. The Hornsteins are the Ornsteins' best friends, I was told, and all four of them survived the Holocaust in unique and chilling ways. I learned that Paul Ornstein and Steve Hornstein had been best friends in prewar Hungary and that their fathers and grandfathers had been close as well. The older generations of Hornsteins and Ornsteins had been leaders of the Jewish community in the small city of Hajdunanas, Hungary.

Paul had met Anna before the war. Even though they had managed to see each other only a few times, Paul wrote Anna beautiful, expressive love letters. He considered Anna his girlfriend and had every intention of marrying her as soon as she finished school.

Like his friend Paul, Steve Hornstein had dreams of becoming a doctor, even though admission to Hungarian universities was all but closed to Jews. Still, he managed to enroll as a special student at the University of Budapest and never lost hope of realizing his dream—even when the Germans invaded Hungary in March 1944.

Lusia Schwarzwald became acquainted with the other three in Munich just after the war. Lusia, born and brought up in privilege in Lvov, Poland, spent the war years hiding in Warsaw with false papers declaring her a Polish Catholic.

When my magazine article came out in the autumn of 1993, it drew such a positive response that the four agreed a book should be written about their experiences. So life-affirming, compelling, and richly textured were their stories that I eagerly offered to take on the project.

I sat down with Lusia Hornstein for my very first interview in May 1994. A few weeks later, I interviewed her husband, Steve. Then back to Lusia. Then Paul and Anna, together and separately. Two years later, I assembled a manuscript culled from eighty hours of interviews and nearly four hundred pages of material. I read their speeches, their published papers, and all the articles and stories written about them. I read Frank Hornstein's senior thesis, written while he was a student at Macalester College, containing interviews with his parents, surviving relatives, and the Ornsteins. I pored over Anna's Passover stories that she tells her children every year.

From my very first interviews with these four extraordinary people, I knew I would give my book a title from a Stephen Spender poem that we read at the memorial service on Yom Kippur. The poem is called "I Think

Continually of Those Who Were Truly Great." In it, Spender recalls the brave heroes who fought for their lives, who "wore at their hearts the fire's center." Clearly, the poem describes the survivors in this story.

What follows is an account of the darkest time in Jewish history and the emergence into light, shared with me by four of the best storytellers I have ever known. The events and dialogue I recount are based strictly on conversations with Paul and Anna Ornstein and Steve and Lusia Hornstein and were told to me as they recollected them.

At the Fire's Center

1   Hometowns

Hajdunanas, Hungary

In the small, flat, dusty city of Hajdunanas, a hundred and twenty miles from Budapest in Hungary's northeast corner, Stephen Hornstein and Paul Ornstein were considered two of the most promising Jewish teenagers. When the elders of the community considered the future in those uncertain economic and political times of the 1930s, they looked to these two outstanding young men to pave the way for the other young people of the town. Both were sure to take their places at the top, however precarious the world might be.

Born just a few months apart in 1924, Steve and Paul had been best friends since before they entered the neighborhood kindergarten. As toddlers, they played together at each other's homes and in the local synagogue, while their fathers and grandfathers discussed the weightier matters of the Jewish community. As the boys grew older, their days were structured around learning. Both attended the local cheder, or Jewish day school, where they studied Hebrew, scriptures, and the Talmud for two hours every morning, beginning at 6 A.M. Two hours later, they were at the elementary school, also run by the Jewish community, where they stayed until after lunch. By two o'clock, they were back at the cheder until dark. This educational regimen was followed every day except for the Sabbath, when they went to synagogue until noon. Even in July and August, they spent all day in Hebrew school. Still, as they became teenagers, they found time to socialize with other young people in Hajdunanas, attend an occasional movie, play a game of soccer, discuss their stamp collections, or just meet with their contemporaries in a local park after synagogue, where they would talk politics and Zionism until it was time to go home.

As teenagers, they were handsome, personable, and highly intelligent. Like the other Jewish boys from Hajdunanas, they came from solid Orthodox homes. All the Jews in Hajdunanas knew one another well, so it was not unusual that the friendship between the Hornstein and Ornstein families had actually begun two generations earlier. The boys' grandfathers had been best friends as well as leaders of the community, each proud of his prominent seat in the synagogue closest to the rabbi. A generation later, the boys' fathers were continuing the tradition of friendship and leadership, expecting nothing less from their sons as they watched the boys mature. Of course, Steve and Paul had plans for the future and could not wait to leave Hajdunanas and all its restrictions. Hungary, after World War I, was no place for young Jewish men with ambitions.

From the late nineteenth century until the end of the World War I, Jews enjoyed nearly full acceptance into Hungarian society. So well were they treated that they were able to convince themselves that their destinies and aspirations dovetailed with those of the ruling members of the empire—the politicians, aristocrats, and church leaders. Who could argue with that thinking? Jews were allowed every advantage Hungary could offer, including admission into Hungary's best universities. Armed with skills, knowledge, and professional status, the business and financial leaders of the Jewish community were permitted full access to all of Hungary's benefits and advantages.

Because of this relationship between the Jews and the country's ruling class, the Jews were willing to be fully supportive of those who allowed them to enrich themselves intellectually, financially, and spiritually. As long as both could see the advantages of mutual loyalty, each was eager to assure the other of its support. Nevertheless, the Jews were still viewed as a people apart; the aristocrats never really saw the Jews as their social equals. The relationship was much more shallow and precarious than either side wanted to believe. This was especially true for the Jews outside of the larger cities—the poor, uneducated Jews who refused to adopt the ways of the ruling Hungarian society. These uneducated "peasants" were visible proof that Jews were different and unworthy of the status granted them by Hungary's leaders.

When World War I ended with Hungary in economic and spiritual collapse, it was the end of the good life as far as the Jews were concerned. The aristocrats found themselves out of power, as a radical right wing took over. For a brief period, a Communist dictatorship took hold, dealing a swift blow to any inroads the Jews had made toward equality and progress.

The Communists saw the Jews as perpetuating two forbidden ideals: they practiced an organized religion, and they aspired to economic success.

Those Hungarians who had never had the power of the aristocrats had been hurt deeply by their loss of population and territory during the war. They saw how easy it was to blame the Jews for all that had befallen them. For one thing, a large proportion of the leaders in the new and hated Communist government were Jews by birth who had discarded their religious and ethnic identities. For another, successful and progressive Jews had been highly visible in Hungary as a class. Resentment ran high; the Jews were perfect scapegoats and symbols for all that had gone wrong during and just after the war. It was an ideal time for the rise of a new Hungary, with the kind of focus and leadership that would return the country to its former strength and status. Nothing could do that better than uniting against a common enemy—the Jews—who could be identified as friends of the former ruling aristocrats and the Communists.

To show they meant business, the Hungarians immediately adopted the *numerus clausus* act, the first country in Europe to do so. That law decreed that the Jews could make up just 6 percent of the total enrollment of Hungarian universities. For people of the book, who valued education and learning above all else and who saw university education as a path to success and respect, it was a staggering blow.

As Hungary's right wing flexed its muscle, the Jews adopted a "wait and see" policy, rejecting the help of international Jewish organizations willing to intercede on their behalf. Things would get better; this was an aberration; Jews were an important thread in the fabric of the country; these things were cyclical; a new government would soon be put into place.

Despite their hope that conditions would improve, the Jews watched warily throughout the 1930s as Hungary became friendlier with the Germans. When Germany adopted its anti-Semitic legislation, Hungary's laws began to mirror those of its friend and neighbor to the west. By the mid-thirties, Jews were no longer allowed to own property or work in certain professions, and they continued to be barred from higher education. All the progress of the Jews in Hungary was wiped off the slate of history as they descended swiftly from lives of comfort to existences filled with fear and trepidation.

As hope-filled and comfortable as life had once been, the 250 Jewish families of Hajdunanas found their circumstances singularly unpleasant after 1918. After the depression in the twenties, Jews were blamed for much of Hungary's economic woes. The townspeople took out their frustrations on their Jewish neighbors, and young Jewish men were regularly beaten at school while teachers and administrators looked the other way. Anti-Semitism was particularly virulent on Christmas and Easter. To escape the cries of "Christ killers!" and the pummeling fists of the non-Jewish youth, the young Jews were let out of Hebrew School early on those days, hoping to fool the waiting, blood-thirsty thugs.

It was not just the youngsters who felt the wrath of the local residents. Pogroms and desecrations were common, especially in the less sophisticated smaller cities and towns where Jews were a decided minority. By the early thirties, Jewish merchants, like their brethren in Germany, had lost their businesses and had been forced to give up their professions. Often, they turned to selling and peddling, but even then, they were allowed to trade only with other Jews.

Nothing dashed the hopes and dreams of the younger generation like the *numerus clausus* act, especially for such serious students as Steve Hornstein and Paul Ornstein, who saw a university degree as their way out of Hajdunanas and, ultimately, Hungary.

Yet despite this bleak picture, Hajdunanas could boast of a lively, vibrant, and close Jewish community. When Jews settled there in the early nineteenth century, they established small businesses and set up schools for their children and synagogues for their families. Though Jew and Gentile may have lived side by side as neighbors, each group was consigned to its own social and community life.

Steve and Paul came from big families. Steve had three older brothers, an older sister, and two younger brothers. Paul's family was not quite as large; he was the oldest child and had three younger brothers and a sister. Both families had once been quite wealthy, but when the Hungarian state went bankrupt in the depression of 1926, the Hornsteins and the Ornsteins suffered financial reversals and had to resort to new ways of earning money to support their families.

The Hornsteins had once been very rich—rich beyond wealthy. Steve's grandfather, Josef, had founded a straw hat factory that also made straw shoes and bags. Later, Josef's son Salomon expanded the business into a brick factory, the first steam-powered brick factory in Hungary. Its official name was, prosaically, the First Steam Brick Factory.

Straw and bricks were not the only means of support for Steve's family. Although Hajdunanas had no major industry, it was blessed with one of the world's most fertile soils. After the ice melted from the Ice Age, northeast Hungary was covered in rich black earth, and agricultural prod-

ucts for export became the region's lifeblood. Aside from the straw factory, Steve's grandfather also dealt in wheat futures, trading agricultural
products, especially grain. Steve and his many cousins often played in
those vast storehouses of wheat.

Steve's grandfather passed the business along to his sons, but by the
time Steve was five in 1929, his father had lost the factory. Economic chaos had descended like a black cloud over Hungary, and, financially, life
would never be the same for the Hornsteins. Salomon had been forced to
invest almost all of the business's capital in securities to help Hungary
recover from the war. But by 1926, the state was bankrupt and the securities were worthless.

Steve's father was not one to look back, so he became an insurance
agent. When that was not enough to provide for the needs of his large
family, he turned to selling merchandise door-to-door, often traveling to
distant villages. Poor though the family was in material possessions, it was
blessed with intellect and drive. Steve and his older brothers Karl and
Shmuel, all straight *A* students, tutored other youngsters who were studying to pass the entrance exam for admittance to the university. (Another
much older brother, Joel, was married and lived elsewhere in Hungary.)
The money they earned was willingly passed to their father to help support the family. Karl also prepared his brother Steve for entrance to the
"gymnasium," a high school and college combined that prepared students for university entrance. Steve, in turn, helped tutor his younger
brothers, Jerry and Henu. Ann, the only daughter, with whom Steve was
very close, was not groomed for higher education; she was expected to
help out at home.

Home was a refuge from the cruelties and ignorance of the outside
world. The family spoke Yiddish and, occasionally, Hungarian. Salomon,
though a stern and strict father, was primarily concerned with the welfare and happiness of his wife and children. Although he had known great
riches and then dire poverty, he was extremely generous to those less fortunate. He had high expectations of his children and asked that they attend to their studies, keep themselves clean and healthy, and help their
mother with the innumerable chores of running a large household.

Tobi Hornstein, Salomon's wife, was a shy and very religious woman,
completely dedicated to Judaism and her family. Remembered by many
as sweet and attractive, she worked very hard to attend to the needs of her
husband and many children. Tragedy lined her face; her second son had
died of tuberculosis at the age of eight. Still, she kept up her interest in the

children's education, often surprising them with detailed recollections of a book or a novel she had read in her youth.

Tobi's domestic abilities really shone on the Sabbath. She and the younger children worked hard to clean the house—the walls, floors, and furniture were soaped and scrubbed—and she would set the table with her best cloths and candles. The family would then gather around and enjoy the rich soup, meat, vegetables, and cake that Mother Hornstein had spent all day preparing.

After synagogue on Saturday morning, the family would visit Steve's paternal grandmother, who would have prepared some favorite cakes for the children. Then it was home to rest, at least for the adults. Steve and the other children were left to their own pursuits—which meant heading for the local park, where Steve would meet his crowd of friends, including, of course, his oldest and closest friend, Paul Ornstein.

Steve and his brothers were known as excellent tutors, helping the local Gentile boys pass the examinations they would need to enter university, something that would be denied to the Hornstein brothers simply because they were Jewish. To say that they were excellent students themselves hardly described their academic prowess. Steve was known as "Straight A," despite the anti-Semitism of some of his teachers. Of course, it did not matter what his grades were or how high he could score on the entrance exams for a place at the university in Budapest. He was a Jew, his brothers were Jews, and they would be denied. But they would not be thwarted.

Education was of the highest value to Steve's father. What mattered most to him was that his sons learn whatever they could of the world. This would mean sending them not to the local yeshiva, a Jewish school of higher learning, but to a Protestant gymnasium, since all public schools were under the auspices of the Protestant church. It also meant that Salomon would have to stand up to the disapproval and opprobrium of his friends and especially the local rabbi, who viewed that kind of decision with shock and horror. It was almost a betrayal for a Jewish father to send his sons to a Protestant school, a kind of religious crime, viewed as a snub to the entire Jewish community.

When the oldest son, Joel, had finished his primary school, he was sent, like other Jewish boys, to the yeshiva. But with his second son, Karl, Salomon braved the community's outright disapproval and contempt and sent him to the local Protestant gymnasium. As the first Orthodox Jew to send a child to a Protestant school, Salomon lost some of his insurance customers because of this rebellious act. Still, he held firm; when his third son, Shmuel, was ready, he, too, was sent to the gymnasium. When it was time for Steve, there was no question of his attendance at the same Protestant school. He entered there in 1938.

Steve began in the second academic year of the gymnasium, because his brother Karl had prepared him so well for the entrance examination that he was able to skip over the first year. Karl was a strict teacher, so strict that he would give Steve a slap on his hand if he incorrectly conjugated a Latin verb. Like Karl before him, Steve was at the top of his class. Still, the gymnasium was very different from the elementary school. Each day began and ended with a Protestant prayer. As a member of the school choir, Steve even found himself singing Protestant hymns.

Elsewhere in Europe, Nazism was on the rise, and although not a discernible presence in Hungary during the mid-thirties, Hungarians were well aware of its influence and acceptance. Perhaps the people of Hajdunanas were unaware of the deepening friendship between their government and the newly elected chancellor of Germany, Adolf Hitler. Nevertheless, Steve, as the only Jew in his class, found himself the target of the anti-Semitism of both teachers and students. He was regularly taunted and beaten by his classmates while the teachers ignored the situation.

The worst was in physical education class, where the sadistic teacher assigned Steve, one of his smallest students, to a boxing match with the biggest boy in the class. To the delight of the instructor and his classmates, Steve was beaten senseless by the bigger and stronger boy. Only when the teacher saw that Steve was seriously hurt did he stop the fight.

When Steve could take the abuse no longer, he went to see the principal of the school, who was one of his father's friends. The principal, a decent man who had not yet fallen prey to Nazi propaganda, announced to the school that anyone who hurt any Jew in his gymnasium would be subject to stringent punishment. Steve was safe for a while. He continued his study of Latin, German, French, natural sciences, and history, and he earned his tuition and that of his brothers by tutoring his classmates and other children.

For Steve's best friend, Paul Ornstein, life was continuing on a similar course. In Paul's home, just a five-minute walk from Steve's, could be found the same profound respect and love for learning. Even the financial, social, and religious circumstances were comparable to those of the Hornsteins.

Paul's grandfather had worked as the manager of a huge farm, but to ensure a future for Paul's father, Lajos, the grandfather moved to Hajdunanas and managed a lumber yard. A calm, cultivated, and thoughtful person, Paul's grandfather had been much loved by his family and friends. He was very proud of Lajos's endeavors to earn a Jewish and a liberal education. Paul's father attended a yeshiva and then studied on his own for the "matura" exam that would allow him to attend the university to study law. But the war of 1914 intervened, and Lajos served with distinction as a lieutenant. When the war ended, he returned to Hajdunanas and, calling on his business skills, grew prosperous from a bank he founded and served as president.

Lajos was a great friend of Salomon Hornstein, and the two became respected and knowledgeable leaders of the community. But as with Salomon Hornstein, the crash of 1926 wiped out Lajos. He then operated a retail store that sold flour, but as anti-Jewish laws progressively curtailed Jewish ownership of businesses, Lajos was forced to give up the flour store. He next worked as a tax expert and bookkeeper for several firms until the mid-1930s, when non-Jewish firms were prohibited by law from employing Jews. Every year, the restrictions grew more stringent, until his chances for employment were confined to only the Jewish community. Finally, Lajos ended up working as secretary of the Jewish community.

As time went on, men found it harder to support their families, and, of course, the women were restricted to the duties of the home. Paul's mother was also very religious, more so than her husband, but she was very practical and knowledgeable about business. When Paul's father could no longer support the family, Mrs. Ornstein managed to use her excellent skills with people to convince them to trade with her before taking their goods to the market. Her shrewd business instincts helped provide for the family.

Jewish sons were also called on to contribute where they could. Paul, like his friend Steve, tutored his classmates or younger children in their neighborhood. Paul's three brothers and sister were still quite young and were just beginning school themselves. Paul earned enough money tutoring to help support his two younger brothers who were attending a Jewish school in the nearby town of Debrecen.

Paul attended the same gymnasium as Steve but was a grade ahead of him, because Steve had been sent to a kind of prep school in a neighboring town for a year after elementary school. Paul's father, a self-educated man in law, history, literature, and Jewish history, wanted to be sure his son received the best education available. Unlike Salomon Hornstein, Lajos was not the least bit concerned about the reaction from the Jewish community. He was an active and ardent Zionist, always occupied with raising money for the kibbutzim in Israel or arranging meetings with other Zionists from neighboring towns. His activities had earned the condemnation of the rabbi and several of his colleagues, who reacted by withholding business from him. Nonetheless, Lajos felt he had to take the long view and see that his son got the best education possible. His friend Salomon had already paved the way to secular education by sending two of his sons to the gymnasium.

Although the curriculum at the gymnasium lasted for eight years, Paul left after the fifth. His plan was to go to the rabbinic seminary in Budapest, even though he was not sure he really wanted to become a rabbi. In fact, Paul could not remember a time when he did not question his belief in God. He was skeptical, even cynical, when it came to Bible stories and legends. But, like his father, Paul loved Jewish history and Jewish philosophy, and since he had no hope of acceptance to any university in Hungary, the seminary was his only chance for education. What really interested him, if the truth could be told, was psychoanalysis and the study of medicine. Both Paul and Steve hoped that somehow they could study to become doctors.

In the months before Paul was to take the train to Budapest, news of further trouble for Jews in Germany reached Hungary. Travelers from the west had told them some awful stories of Jewish property being destroyed and Jews being dragged from their homes and beaten. Still, the Jews of Hajdunanas were skeptical of these tales, even though this was not the first time they had been directly warned. In Hungary's larger cities, Jews who did not have Hungarian citizenship were being deported to Poland. Hungary was making no secret of its support of Hitler.

One evening, Lajos was host to a German Jew who was traveling through Hungary trying to raise enough money to finance his trip to Palestine. Paul was allowed to listen as the man addressed about a dozen Jewish elders of Hajdunanas and described his experiences in Germany. Although the Hungarian men were as financially generous to the traveler as they could afford to be, they were not so charitable after his departure. That the Germans were violently anti-Semitic—yes, that they could believe. But the rest of his tale? Preposterous! What a tragedy, the men told their wives, that this German Jew had to resort to such a story to get to Palestine.

Yes, the news of the German Kristallnacht, November 9, 1938, a night of government-sponsored terrorism against Jewish homes and businesses, had made its way to Hajdunanas. Yes, the anti-Semitic laws in Hungary would try to thwart them. But they would survive the restrictions, and the German army would meet defeat. Since all of Hungary's crops were being exported to Germany and since Germany was so dependent on Hungary's goods, Hungary was safe. The Jews were safe. Though they knew that whole communities in Germany had ceased to exist, it was not going to happen in Hungary. If Jewish communities actually were threatened, the Jews would leave as soon as they could for Palestine.

In the summer of 1939, before he left for rabbinic school, Paul filled out the papers and forms that would pave the way for him to emigrate to Palestine. He sent the papers to London, but he never heard a response. He considered it a foolish endeavor anyway. He was only fifteen years old, and at that age, he could not imagine leaving Hungary without his family.

On the evening of August 31, 1939, Paul said goodbye to his parents, brothers, and sister and boarded the overnight train that would take him to Budapest, where he would begin his studies at the rabbinic seminary. It was quite a heady experience for a fifteen-year-old to travel and to study on his own in such a big, sophisticated city as Budapest, but he had relatives there who could look after him—and soon, his sister, Judith, would arrive to begin her studies as a dental technician. Budapest was a world away from Hajdunanas and, as Paul would discover, a world away from the rest of Europe.

Szendro, Hungary

Unlike Hajdunanas, the small Hungarian village of Szendro in northern Hungary was quite attractive, with several clear rivers flowing down from the surrounding Carpathian Mountains. About fifteen kilometers from the border with Czechoslovakia, Szendro was an agricultural hamlet of four thousand people, mostly peasants. The town had no electricity or running water. In the winter, deep snow covered the unpaved streets; as the snow melted, the town was blanketed by mud. Hajdunanas was a thriving metropolis in comparison, for Szendro had no high school, no library, not even a hospital.

As in all the small cities and towns of Hungary, life was difficult for the forty Jewish families of Szendro. Because the townspeople were uneducated and primitive, anti-Semitism was rife, aided and abetted by the anti-Jewish laws of the country. The heads of Jewish families were restricted in how they could earn a living, and Jewish children, beyond a few grades of elementary school, were educated at home. Girls were not expected to pursue higher education at all.

In Szendro, Jewish friends and neighbors enjoyed close relationships, and Jewish identity was positively emphasized in their small religious community. This was especially true in one of the more sophisticated and wealthier homes in the village. That home belonged to the Brünn family—the parents, Sophie and William; two sons, Andrew and Paul; and the youngest, everyone's darling, Anna.

Born in 1927, Anna was a singing, dancing sprite, a girl of boundless energy, always at the center of her group's games and fun. She was the first to organize a spring or summer outing for her friends and the last to come indoors when the weather turned cold. With her lively dark eyes and chestnut hair in two neat plaits, she had a special way of drawing people to her, an uncanny talent for empathy and compassion. To her, Szendro was a land of many natural wonders, though her parents found the town backward and confining.

While the Brünns may have taken up physical residence in Szendro, culturally they were miles apart from the other citizens of that city. The Brünn house had no electricity or running water, but it did have comfortable furniture, expensive carpets, and, most important, books piled high on shelves, great volumes written in German and Hungarian. Although Anna Brünn and her two older brothers attended the local Szendro Jewish school, most of their education took place in their home under the tutelage of the two best possible teachers: their mother and father.

Anna's father and her uncle had inherited their father's building equipment business that sold lumber, cement, equipment to assemble sewer pipes, tiles for roofing—whatever one needed to build a house. In addition to the main store, another satellite operation was situated about fifteen kilometers away. This store was run by Anna's father but unhappily so; he was known for his lack of business acumen.

William Brünn had earned a teaching certificate and, with his love of books and learning, knew that education was his true calling. But he could not give up the family concern that his father had worked so hard to establish, until all his efforts became moot and the anti-Jewish laws decreed that Jewish men could not own businesses. Spiritually weakened by a situation over which he had no control, William had to ask for help from his wife, fifteen years younger, whose natural drive and endless energy he could not help but envy.

Although Anna attended school, she received most of her education at home. Sophie taught her French and algebra, but even more important, she impressed upon her daughter that studying and learning took precedence over everything else. Anna took this lesson to heart, because it was reinforced by example. She and her brothers often found their mother sitting on the floor, a book in one hand, a dust cloth in the other.

Anna was aware of the restrictions that applied to Jews, but, like the other Jewish children of Szendro, she walled herself off from this reality, creating a universe she knew but did not know. Jewish families of the town implicitly made a decision: be aware and wary, but try to maintain some semblance of normalcy. Because the Jewish community was so much smaller than the one in Hajdunanas, anti-Semitism was more direct and hurtful, especially from a child's point of view. The restrictions were not subtle. For example, Jewish children were not allowed to use the local community swimming pool during the summer. The children knew why, but it was more expedient for them to pretend that they could have just as much fun swimming in the local river.

With her mother preoccupied with helping her father, Anna took over the household chores. She worked hard to please both her parents, especially her father, approaching her housework with zeal and vigor. By age nine, she knew how to cook and bake bread, and she would take the chickens she raised to the *schochet,* a man whose job was to slit the throats of the chickens so they would be killed in the kosher and humane way. When she brought the chickens home, she would rinse them thoroughly and kosher them with salt. Then she would make chicken soup for the family.

In addition to developing her culinary skills, Anna took special pleasure in washing and waxing the kitchen floor until it sparkled the way her father liked it. She had great compassion for this sensitive man, who had taught her about opera by humming the arias for her. Although the house had no electricity for a record player, the rooms were filled with song. Anna and her brothers learned music from the voices of their parents.

By 1939, when Anna was twelve, she had grown used to the harassment suffered by her parents and the other Jewish adults in the village. She learned to accept as commonplace the officials who would come to her home and intimidate her father for minor and insignificant transgressions, such as not keeping a certain level of fresh water in a rain barrel in the unlikely event that the water would be needed to douse a fire. These annoyances were increasingly becoming a fact of life in Szendro.

The air was filled with enough worry already. Because Szendro was so close to Czechoslovakia, Jewish refugees from that country were crossing the border seeking safety in Hungary. Although their home was without a radio, Anna knew all about Hitler, who was training his greedy eye on Austria. Anna's parents were frightened for their relatives in Vienna and worried about the future of their sons. Would Paul and Andrew be sent to forced labor camps or taken for the Hungarian army? Anna's mother's debilitating migraine headaches increased in intensity the more she heard about Hitler and his atrocities.

Despite her youth, Anna could not help being concerned. She worshipped her brothers, thought they had supernatural qualities. Her older brother Paul was very much like her mother, practical and realistic. Anna would watch as he assessed a situation and then acted on it. Paul knew that he had no chance at higher education in Hungary, so he dropped out of school and learned a trade.

Andrew, three years older than Anna, was more like her father, a dreamer and philosopher. Yet he excelled in the exacting subject of math. Both boys were adored by their mother, just as Anna was an especial favorite of her father. All three children were made to feel that each brought a special gift to the family. Each experienced a childhood in which education and Jewish identity were strongly emphasized, tempered with their parents' love and respect.

Although the war clouds from the west seemed to be moving toward Hungary as fast as the rumors from Austria and Czechoslovakia, Anna's parents tried their best to see that their daughter's life would proceed on course. Because there was no high school in her town, Anna was being tutored for an exam that she had to pass to enter the Jewish gymnasium for girls in the town of Debrecen. If all went according to plan, she would attend school and room with an aunt, who lived within walking distance of the academy. Anna had secret ideas about becoming a doctor, and even though wishes like that rarely came true for Jewish girls, who had no hope whatsoever of attending the university, she allowed herself to indulge in the luxury of these dreams.

Lvov, Poland

Lvov, Poland, part of Galicia in eastern Poland, might as well have been on the other side of the world from Hajdunanas and Szendro, Hungary, for all it had in common with those two shtetls. As Poland's third largest city, with a population of 330,000, Lvov could boast of wonders and attractions Hajdunanas and Szendro would never know: a symphony orchestra, an opera house, theaters, and restaurants. Its citizens were divided into three groups: Poles, Ukrainians, and Jews, each with its own culture, heritage, and customs.

Well known in the Jewish community was the Schwarzwald family, a large, wealthy, extended clan of grandparents, aunts and uncles, brothers and sisters, grandchildren, and many cousins. They were supported by several firms specializing in the export of wood to countries all over Europe.

Norbert Schwarzwald owned one of the firms, and every year, it grew and prospered. He leased forests in Poland and cut wood, especially for matchsticks and beer and wine barrels. It was the Schwarzwald firm that supplied wood to Faber for pencils. His business took him everywhere on the Continent and to England. Travel was so much a part of his life that, as a young man, he had boarded a train in Lvov and disembarked in Vienna just to meet a pretty girl, whose picture someone had sent him. The beautiful face that lured him to Vienna belonged to Frieda Mayer, who became his wife in 1921.

Norbert Schwarzwald's business acumen made his family very wealthy. He and Frieda owned a large apartment house at 5 Bernsteina Street, just on the edge of the Jewish section of the city. They had knocked out the walls of three separate flats and made one grand apartment on the upper floor. Norbert's office was on the same floor; Frieda's parents, Schulim and Sabina, lived across the hall. Sabina stayed with the Schwarzwald children when Norbert and Frieda traveled, so the living arrangements were most convenient. Of course, Frieda had hired several maids—usually, Ukrainian girls—to help with the cleaning and laundry. Sabina also ran the kitchen to make sure it was strictly kosher.

Norbert's father and his second wife and his sister and her family lived in the building next door and were frequent visitors. Other family members lived close by, sharing Sabbath weekends and holidays together as much as possible.

Norbert cut an impressive figure—tall, well-spoken, and beautifully dressed. Frieda, though matronly, was a beautiful and stylish woman. Although she was never really comfortable in Poland, with either its language or its customs, she was very cultured and sophisticated; she read widely and spoke several languages. Her fluency in German was particularly notable.

Despite Frieda's discomfort in Lvov, the Schwarzwalds lived very well. Their home was furnished with the best money could buy, and since money was no object, the apartment was well known in Lvov for its luxury. The bathroom with its marble fixtures and special gas tank for hot water was the talk of the city. The Persian carpets and custom-made furniture (both in the apartment and in Norbert's office) made the home a Lvov showplace.

For all their possessions and achievements, however, nothing made Frieda and Norbert prouder than their three children. The two boys, Julek and Milek, were smart and handsome, each destined for greatness, whether running the wood export firm or in one of the professions. The middle child, named Lusia for her paternal grandmother, was a girl with great talent for languages and music. Like her brothers, she was at the top of her class, popular with her friends, and expected to succeed in any endeavor. Though her parents hoped she would make the piano her life's work, Lusia, who greatly admired the family's pediatrician, had a secret yearning to study medicine.

The Schwarzwalds had plenty of money for travel, to visit Frieda's relatives in Austria or to spend the summers in the mountains. When four-year-old Lusia needed a mastoid operation, the family embarked on the overnight train to Vienna, where a world-famous doctor performed the procedure. In June after school let out, the entire household would be packed up—clothes, bedding, kitchen wares—and moved along with the family to a house in Jaremcze, a resort city in Poland's Carpathian Mountains. Even the Ukrainian maids would go along.

Frieda and her mother carefully supervised the crating of the kosher kitchen's pots and pans for the annual summer excursion, because the Schwarzwalds were Orthodox, though not as religiously strict as others in the community. Frieda, however, was an ardent Zionist, a staunch member of several Zionist women's groups. She was always urging Norbert to sell the business and move to Palestine. Norbert would explain patiently that one could not simply liquidate a business just like that; he did, though, hold out some promise that one day they would leave, at least for the sake of the children.

Lusia and her brothers were active Zionists as well. Her older brother, Julek, with whom she was very close, had definite plans to leave Poland when he could and emigrate to Palestine. The children were already learning Hebrew in school and knew all the Zionist patriotic songs.

Lusia, born in December 1925, attended a private school for girls, the Jewish Society for Grammar and High School, modeled on the schools in Palestine. Several of her cousins were in the upper grades. Her brothers attended the boys' school. Classes in the lower grades were taught in Hebrew. Because her father conducted business in German, and since Lusia's mother was from Vienna, Lusia learned German as well. At home, the Schwarzwalds spoke Polish; the grandparents, Polish or Yiddish. Because the maids were Ukrainian, the children also picked up some of that language.

Although Lusia Schwarzwald lived a world away from the small towns of Hungary, one experience for Jews across Europe was universal: anti-Semitism. Sheltered though she was, her parents could not shield her from the stories of Jews being taunted or beaten on the streets. Jewish students at the Lvov polytechnic and at the university suffered not just threats and intimidation but also savage beatings. As Hitler's roar sounded closer and closer, news of the beating death of two Jewish students at the hands of particularly anti-Semitic Polish fraternities reached the ears of the local Jewish community. When Frieda Schwarzwald heard about these episodes, she and Norbert began to consider sending their children to universities outside Poland. Polish universities had the same *numerus clausus* for Jews as universities elsewhere in Europe, but the Schwarzwalds still had hopes for higher education for their children. Julek had plans to attend Brighton University in England to study architecture; Frieda wanted Lusia to go to the conservatory in Vienna to pursue a degree in music. By 1938, however, Hitler had already taken over Czechoslovakia and Austria; Jews from those countries were fleeing to the east and desperately seeking sanctuary in Poland.

By the late thirties, politics was on everyone's mind. Rumors and stories of violence against Jews in Germany to the west had reached the ears of the Jews of Poland. Fear hovered over them as they went about their daily business. At night, the Schwarzwald family would gather around the radio and listen to Hitler's ravings in German. When Hitler marched into Austria in 1938, Frieda sobbed in fear for her family in Vienna. It was with a mixture of relief, surprise, and consternation that the Schwarzwalds returned from their summer holiday in the Carpathian Mountains to find Frieda's aunt and uncle from Vienna waiting for them. Like other Jews in Austria, they had walked over the border into Poland to seek refuge with their Lvov cousins.

Family members who had been living in Czechoslovakia had also returned to Lvov. Lusia's cousin Leon, a physician, and his wife, Gerdie, fled

Prague as soon as Hitler marched into that country. Leon and his wife joined Leon's brothers, Salo and Samek, who both worked in the Schwarzwald family business. Although Norbert and Frieda were happy to have their extended family back among them, their arrival also brought fear and anxiety.

Poland was stuck. Its citizens knew that Hitler was on the move, first to Austria, then marching into the Sudetenland of Czechoslovakia, with his eye trained on the Polish corridor. That corridor divided Germany from Prussia, which belonged to Germany. The corridor itself belonged to Poland and was that country's only access to the Baltic Sea. While Hitler's army marched on and anti-Semitic propaganda filtered through to Poland, many Jews made plans to get out. By that time, however, it was almost too late.

Horror stories of the plight of German Jews reached the city of Lvov, carried there by many of the German Jews themselves, who had either been deported from Germany or had escaped. Lusia, who lived down the block from the Jewish Community Center, a beautiful building with famous stained-glass windows, met many of these refugees when she went to the community center to deliver food and clothing collected for the refugees. The leaders of the Lvov community were also asking families to take in some of the displaced people from Germany, and the Schwarzwalds obliged. Now living with them were the five members of their own family, Frieda's parents, and a German-Jewish couple and their son. Yet the apartment was big and lavish, and the Schwarzwalds were thankful that their own family was together.

Collecting clothes for the refugees who had fled or been forced out of Germany was a good way for Frieda and her family to keep busy. Lusia, however, was quite puzzled when she helped distribute the clothing; the German women, instead of expressing gratitude, had nothing but disdain for the Polish Jews' generosity.

"Bei uns in Deutschland . . . ," Lusia heard them say over and over again, as they disgustedly picked through the clothes the Jews of Lvov had donated to them. "The way it was for us in Germany" was a phrase that began to sicken Lusia, who was not used to having her generosity scorned and derided. What were they talking about, she wondered: "Bei uns in Deutschland"? They had just been thrown out of their precious Deutschland, and now they had the nerve to look down on the Jews of Lvov.

No matter what their nationality, the Jews in Poland were stuck. They could not go west; Hitler was already there. They could not go east; the

Russian border was closed, and the Russians were nearly as hated as the Germans. In eastern Poland, where the Schwarzwalds lived, the anti-Semitic Ukrainians were already siding with the Germans. Frieda begged Norbert once again to wrap up his business affairs and make plans to leave for Palestine. Norbert again demurred, but told Frieda he would begin to look into it as soon as he returned from his next business trip in August 1939.

Trying to hold on to some semblance of normalcy, at least for the children's sake, Frieda again supervised the yearly summer packing of the house on Bernsteina Street. With nearly all of the household goods except the heavy furniture, Frieda, her children, and the Ukrainian maids boarded the train for the mountain resort and a summer of swimming, hiking, and relaxation. Other members of the vast Schwarzwald clan would meet them there, along with several of their friends. Norbert would try to join them. His last stop would be Brussels, and if he could, he would make every attempt to spend a few days in the mountains with his family. If not, he would see them when he returned to Lvov.

Away from the city, the family enjoyed a pleasant few months. Frieda, of course, was worried about her husband on his extended trip abroad, but she tried to shield the children from these concerns. The family had rented a villa close to the Prut River, where they could swim and hike. All the villages in that part of southeast Poland were summer resorts, and the Schwarzwalds had friends or family in each one. They would take a horse-drawn carriage and visit back and forth. Thankfully, Hitler, with all his threats, seemed far away.

Norbert did join them on August 28, 1939, just before they were to return home. When they had settled back in Lvov, Norbert told his family some frightening news that served to confirm what everyone already expected: war was imminent. Although this seemed indisputable, considering what was in the newspapers and on the radio, Norbert had heard it from someone who could speak with authority. While on business in Antwerp, Belgium, he had met with Frieda's nephew, who implored him not to return to Poland. The nephew had just escaped from Vienna. Norbert informed him that he had no choice: his entire family was in Lvov.

Returning to the house on Bernsteina Street, the elder Schwarzwalds tried to proceed with business as usual. On September 1, the children would be starting the school year and would need new clothes and school supplies. As was the custom in Poland, Julek, Lusia, and Milek would first go to synagogue for a special blessing that heralded the start of the academic year, just as their non-Jewish counterparts would attend church for a similar service.

Talk of war was everywhere. By now, Frieda knew it was too late to pack up and leave for Palestine. Refugees from the west had fled to Poland; relatives who had escaped from Vienna and Prague were living with the Schwarzwalds and other family members. Norbert did not want to frighten the family, but he made sure that the bomb shelter in the large cellar was properly stocked with blankets and food, enough for everyone in the building.

The older son, Julek, went to bed on August 31 with plans to protect his finances. Even though he knew he had to be up early the next day for synagogue and the first day of school, he decided he would rise early, go to the bank, and withdraw his bar mitzvah money. He had saved most of it; if war came, he figured, the family might find it useful.

Lusia, too, prepared for school. She could not ignore her parents' fears, but at thirteen and a half, she ached for her life to return to normal. Trying to generate some enthusiasm for the year ahead, she carefully laid out her new clothes: a navy blue wool dress with short sleeves and a white collar, meticulously made to measure, as befitted the lucky daughter of a prominent family.

2   Lvov on Fire

NOT THE RADIO, NOT THE NEWSPAPERS, NOT the rumors, not the refugees from Germany, not even the travelers who brought the news from across the border—nothing adequately prepared the Poles for the screaming air raid sirens, the panic in the streets, and the reeling chaos as German war planes rained upon Poland bomb after bomb on Friday, September 1, 1939. In her new navy blue school dress, Lusia somehow managed to elude her frantic parents and race the four blocks to the bank in search of her beloved older brother, Julek, who had gone there earlier that morning to retrieve his bar mitzvah money. That errand proved a fortuitous one, for the Schwarzwalds would live partially on the boy's funds in the weeks to come.

As Lusia and Julek ran home from the bank, they passed several engulfed and burning houses. The fires had found their way indiscriminately around the neighborhood; some buildings were perfectly intact, while others were consumed by the inferno. Displaced people wandered everywhere, desperately seeking shelter. The streets were full of dust and debris.

Although children had been trained in the use of gas masks at school, nothing prepared them for the fear and hysteria of that day. The unremitting noise and the relentless bombing were enough to reduce a once-civilized population to primitive behavior, where survival was all that mattered.

Luckily for Lusia and her family, the Schwarzwald basement had been declared an official air raid shelter, and all the families in the building had been assigned part of a large "room." The building's janitor had constructed a bed in the Schwarzwalds' corner where the entire family could sleep. Norbert and Frieda had had the presence of mind to stock the shelter with plenty of food and blankets.

Luckily, too, the raid had begun early enough in the morning so that everyone was still at home. When Lusia and Julek arrived breathlessly back at 5 Bernsteina Street, they found their parents and younger brother, Milek, their grandparents, and their aunt and uncle in the basement of the house, huddled against the noise and fear of the German's relentless bombing. Candles lit the dark interiors, for, of course, electricity had been cut off. Water was also scarce; during the next three weeks, Lusia and her family would dash upstairs when necessary, to wash or use the toilet, but they were usually too frightened to do so. The air raids no longer warned of an impending attack; the noise of an approaching plane was the only harbinger of a raid.

The close quarters in the basement began to fray the nerves of the thirty-five people who had taken shelter there: the various tenants of the building, their maids, and other household employees. Although everyone had brought down as much as they could—water, food, mattresses, and blankets—life in the basement was desperate and depressing. The alternative, of course, was worse. Once in a while, on the pretense of running upstairs to the apartment for clean clothes or to use the bathroom, Lusia would dare step outside, just to breathe some fresh air. Just as quickly, she would retreat to the relative safety of the cellar. What she witnessed in her brief forays outside were fires burning everywhere and people, forced from their destroyed homes, wandering the streets begging for food or shelter.

For three and a half weeks, the residents of Lvov—if they were among the fortunate ones—subsisted in their shelters, wondering what the Germans had in store for them. They knew, of course, from the radio and newspapers that several days before the German attack, Germany's foreign minister, General von Ribbentrop, had signed a nonaggression pact with Russia's Josef Stalin, agreeing that Germany and Russia would not attack each other. The plan was that Germany would then conquer and divide Poland, giving the Russians the eastern part of the country.

Three weeks after the first screaming air raid, the skies over eastern Poland fell suddenly silent. The Russians, who had been waiting by quietly as the Poles were bombed into submission, then marched into the country and took over. They were a bedraggled, sorry-looking phalanx of warriors. Lusia, watching from a window, actually felt sorry for this ragtag army, which had its rifles and tea kettles lashed to wagons by string instead of leather straps. The Polish army, with its fine horses and disciplined soldiers, had actually made Lusia proud. But these Russians looked like a joke. What they portended was not, however.

≋

Communism had been outlawed in Poland prior to 1939, but now, under the Russians, that ideology became a way of life for everyone in eastern Poland. Lusia and her brothers resumed going to their Jewish school, but now classes were taught in Yiddish instead of Hebrew. Hebrew, the language of Palestine, and Zionism, an ideology in direct opposition to Communism, were outlawed by the Russians. Almost immediately, the Russians organized rallies at the schools and throughout the city, extolling the virtues of peace and prosperity through Communism.

This new way of life quickly imposed its grip on the Schwarzwalds' world. Norbert's business was soon nationalized; Polish Communists—including some Jews who had become enamored of the movement—were put in place as the heads of banks and schools. Lvov had no place now for wealthy Jewish businessmen, no matter how generous they had been to those less fortunate. Julek and Lusia helped their father burn the papers that contained the financial transactions of Norbert's wood export business.

Norbert had left some money with business friends in England and Switzerland, money that the family could use after the occupation was over. "Memorize these names," Julek ordered Lusia, as the two children helped their father destroy some of the papers from his desk. "They might be able to help us some day." She idolized her big brother and would do whatever he commanded. Dutifully, she committed the names and addresses to memory.

One early morning, a few weeks after the Russians took over, the Schwarzwalds heard a knock. The family was in nightgowns and pajamas. With trepidation, Norbert answered the door, as his family watched with a mixture of fear and curiosity.

An officer in the Russian secret service—the NKVD—pushed his way into the apartment and ordered the family to get out immediately. The Russian then padlocked the door and sealed the apartment. The Schwarzwalds—with no clothes, no money—were able to stay with relatives in a nearby apartment.

Lusia and her brothers were unable to go to school, because they had not been allowed to take clothes with them. For two weeks, they existed in this limbo at their cousins' house, their imaginations running wild with fear. Would Norbert be arrested and sent away, the fate of many other wealthy business people the family knew? Would they all be ordered east to Russia, to some forbidden territory, and the boys taken for the Russian army?

Frieda and her children had faith in Norbert, who was clever and resourceful. Yet every time he left the cousins' apartment, they panicked, afraid they would never see him again. But one day, after two weeks of exile from their home, Norbert gathered his family and told them they could go back to 5 Bernsteina Street. Without telling his wife, he had gone to the army's headquarters and bribed the Russian officer who had initially ordered them to leave. The Schwarzwalds were allowed to return to the apartment, which, they were happy to see, remained exactly as they had left it. Nothing had been removed or touched in any way.

Their relief and happiness were short-lived, however. Norbert confessed that he had agreed to give the Russian officer and his wife a room in the lavish Schwarzwald flat in exchange for permitting the Schwarzwalds to return home. Now, home was no longer the refuge it once had been from the madness outside.

Still, life settled into an odd rhythm. The children returned to school, although thirteen-year-old Lusia could not hide her anxieties—her grades dropped precipitously. The privacy and security she craved as a teenager had been taken from her. Her parents could not hide their worry and concern about the future. Norbert, it was evident, would have many more dealings with the Russians—meaning more bribes, more compromises.

This was just one more headache the beleaguered family had to cope with now. Norbert, without his business, was forced to look for work and did manage to find a job as an accountant to help him eke out a living. Actually, Norbert felt that the family could live on the jewelry and gold pieces that he had hidden away, but under the Russians, everyone had to have a job. The household (exclusive of the Russian couple) also managed to subsist on Julek's withdrawn savings from which they borrowed heavily. Fortunately, Norbert had invested in gold coins before the war, and these also kept the family in food and necessary bribes. Frieda willingly began to sell off her impressive collection of jewelry, piece by piece, to help the family survive.

The Russian occupation took its toll in many ways. One Sabbath evening, as the family was preparing to celebrate the end of the week, Lusia's grandfather—Frieda's father—lurched into the Schwarzwald kitchen and collapsed on the floor, dead of a heart attack. Frieda's father was only seventy-two years old; Frieda was his youngest—and favorite—child. The family often joked that although she was a grown, married woman, her father would not turn off his light at night until he knew that Frieda and Norbert were back home from an evening out. The grandfather was the first of many casualties of the war; his was the first funeral thirteen-year-old Lusia had ever attended.

With her grandfather gone and with strangers living in the house, life for Lusia and her family became even more drear and depressing through the cold winter of 1940. To the Russians, anyone who was not a Communist posed a threat. To keep people in a state of uncertainty, the occupiers had a habit of rounding up heads of household and sending them to jail—or worse, out of the country. With their loathing for anything bourgeois, they singled out the German refugees, the wealthy Poles, and anyone who had been active politically. Because Norbert Schwarzwald had been a successful, wealthy businessman, he knew he was constantly in danger of being arrested and sent away.

That Norbert was a host—of sorts—to a high-ranking officer in the NKVD offered him some protection, but he knew that the Russians were always watching him. He asked the janitor to build a hiding place for the family's valuables, the silver and crystal they had accumulated over the years. Like other wealthy Poles, Norbert had bought American gold dollars with his Polish zlotys. Now he hoped his investment in the gold coins would see the family through the Russian occupation and help get them safely out of Poland. The coins, along with his wife's vast jewelry collection, had to be hidden away.

Although he could try to hide their wealth, he could not make himself inconspicuous. One day, on a cool spring evening in 1940, the NKVD came and took Norbert away. Lusia was out at the time; when she returned home, her mother and grandmother, quaking with fear, told her the news.

If Frieda had known of Lusia's whereabouts when Norbert had been arrested, her fears would have been heightened to hysteria. While owning property and displaying any signs of wealth were strictly forbidden by the Russians, so was any kind of anti-Communist activity, and that included Zionist meetings. That was where Lusia had been at the very moment the Russians had knocked on the door for Norbert.

Frieda herself had always been an active Zionist, but those forbidden activities stopped as soon as the Russians moved in. She was now careful about the people with whom she associated. Her two older children, however, found it exciting and exhilarating to take part in something so strictly forbidden. Julek introduced Lusia to some friends of his, about five or six young people, who had formed a Zionist cell. Julek was part of another cell. Knowing how close she had come to arrest herself, coupled with the anxiety about her father, Lusia could barely comfort her distraught mother and grandmother.

Two days later, the doorbell rang. Norbert, looking unkempt and disheveled, was standing there, an NKVD officer at his side. Brushing past his astonished wife and children, Norbert began showing the Russian where he could find the crystal and the silver. "Take it," Norbert urged him. "You can have it all."

But the Russian officer was more interested in the vastness of the Schwarzwald apartment. He looked around, opening closets, poking into cupboards, and pronounced it all to his liking. Norbert motioned for his family to keep silent as the officer inspected the premises, a prospective and eager tenant.

"We will still have plenty of room," Frieda whispered to Lusia in an attempt to comfort her. "I am sure your father has a good reason for this."

While he was jailed in the notorious Brigitki prison, so close to Bernsteina Street that the Schwarzwalds could easily see into its yard from their rear windows, Norbert had cleverly befriended the Russian officer by lending a willing ear to his complaints about the shortage of satisfactory housing in Lvov. Norbert assured the Russian—who of course needed no such assurances—that his family would love to have the company of the Russian officer and his family. If he could somehow arrange for Norbert's exit from the prison, he would be glad to introduce him to his wife and children (he carefully left out the other tenants of the flat) and let him see for himself the wonders of the hot water heater in the bathroom, the polished wood floors, the marble fixtures, the spacious kitchen with its many modern conveniences.

The next day, the Russian officer, his wife, and their two small children moved into the Schwarzwalds' apartment. Now living at 5 Bernsteina Street were the five Schwarzwalds; Frieda's mother; the first Russian officer Norbert had bribed when the family was ordered to vacate their home, and his wife; and the four newest tenants. The German refugee family, for whom the Schwarzwalds had provided a safe haven, had been ordered by the Russians to move out. As the Schwarzwalds' living space dwindled so did their freedom and security.

Still, the arrival of the new Russian family had its advantages, even as the wife cheerfully cooked ham and lobster in the Schwarzwald's kosher kitchen alongside Lusia's shaydl-wearing grandmother. The Schwarzwalds were willing to bear this assault on their religious laws in exchange for a commodity not even Frieda's jewelry or Norbert's gold coins could ensure them: information.

The wife of the second Russian officer, a very friendly woman, proved of utmost value to the Schwarzwalds. The Russians were known to conduct *razzias,* or roundups, where soldiers would come to the door of a home in the predawn hours and order everyone to leave. Although this had already happened to the Schwarzwalds when they were roused from their beds and ordered to vacate the premises, now they had the advantage of advance warning. The wife of the second Russian officer, while in the kitchen steaming her shellfish or honeying her ham, might sidle over to Frieda, who was boiling some potatoes, and whisper, "It would be best if you didn't sleep at home tonight." Forewarned, the Schwarzwalds would find space in friends' basements or in empty stores, whose shopkeepers had agreed to let them stay after they had closed up for the day. Lusia never actually slept, always conscious of the scurrying sounds of rats and mice. While the *razzias* were frequent and the Schwarzwalds were evidently on a list of "undesirables," they managed to avoid deportation to the east.

By the fall of 1940, when the school year began, the Schwarzwalds had endured many changes in their lives. Because the Russians were slowly sapping their financial reserves, the Schwarzwalds had to resort to the black market for food and fuel, especially wood to heat the huge apartment. They had to grow used to sleeping away from their apartment several times a month, huddling in friends' basements or in shop pantries; living on the proceeds of what they could sell of their crystal, silver, and gold; helping Lusia's aunt and uncle make paper shopping bags that they could exchange or sell for other goods; always watching for signs of the next Russian *razzia;* witnessing friends being taken away and shipped, presumedly, east to Siberia; and enduring a complete upheaval of a way of life whose memories were too painful to bring forth and examine.

The school curriculum had changed again. Where once Lusia and her brothers had studied Hebrew, literature, art, and humanities, now physics, biology, and chemistry were taught in their place. In the fall of 1939, the Russians had banned Hebrew as the language of instruction and instituted Yiddish; now, in September of 1940, the schools were ordered to teach in Ukrainian.

The teachers coped as best they could, not just with the new language but also with the revised curriculum. Lusia and her classmates were now drilled in the history of Russia and the many uprisings of the peasants and the workers' revolutions against the czars. They were taught that the Poles were fascists and that the world would be saved through Communism. Peace and prosperity would come to all through Communism.

At least once a week, Lusia and her friends attended mandatory rallies that extolled the virtues of the Russian way of life. At first, as a young impressionable teenager, she could not help but be caught up in the rhetoric: "Long live the revolution! Long live Stalin! Long live the people!" Her parents were horrified, but Lusia soon realized it was all propaganda.

The one activity that kept her life on as even a keel as possible were her music lessons. Of course, under the Russians, she was no longer allowed private instruction, but Lusia was enrolled at the conservatory, where she attended classes in piano and music theory. If nothing else, the Russians knew something about music.

With her music, her secret Zionist cell activity, her schoolwork, and her friends, Lusia's life outside of 5 Bernsteina Street proceeded as agreeably as possible. Inside was another story. Her mother's nerves were on edge with constant worry about her husband. A fog of depression had descended over her with the deaths of her parents, for her mother, too, had died earlier in the year. Norbert was at his wits' end as well. What could he do to help his family? Why hadn't he heeded the warnings and advice of friends and relatives and tried to escape when he had the chance? Now there was no chance. Germany had made allies of all the neighboring countries, notably Hungary and Rumania. To the east was Russia, and he hated the Communists. At night, he would huddle by his forbidden shortwave radio and listen as the BBC brought news of Hitler and the havoc he was wreaking to the west. Still, he could not help thinking that the Germans would be preferable to the Russians. The Germans were cultured people. At least they were civilized.

All through the winter of 1941 and into the spring, the Schwarzwalds existed in this new situation, too busy trying to cope to mourn for their old way of life. The children, being teenagers, had their friends, their school, their many activities. The parents, however, lived on life's edge, watching and waiting for what could happen next.

Lusia, now fifteen, was finally allowed to go out for the evening with her friends without an adult along to chaperone. On June 21, 1941, she dressed to attend an outdoor concert of classical music with her friends. With the usual admonitions ringing in her ears—be careful, don't walk home alone, come in on time—she left her parents sitting in one of their two rooms, hunched over the forbidden shortwave radio. The music from the upcoming concert was already playing in her head.

Despite the sense of foreboding that hung over the city, summer was still a time of freedom as far as Lusia and her friends were concerned. Although there were no more trips to the Carpathian Mountains, she and her friends found plenty to keep them busy. She could still enjoy the ballet, Yiddish theater, and concerts in the park.

As a bright and aware teenager, however, she could not be sheltered from the concerns of her parents and their friends. The Jews of Lvov sensed that another attack was imminent, because people who were living close to the border reported that the Germans were massing huge armies there.

But Lusia and her friends put those thoughts of out of their minds as they enjoyed the concert in the hot, muggy June evening air. Just being out alone—unchaperoned—with a whole group of teenagers gave her a sense of freedom she had not felt in two years. If only the night would never end!

When she returned home, she found Norbert just as she had left him, hunched over his beloved and forbidden shortwave radio. Lusia and her mother knew there would be real trouble if he were ever caught. But on this night of freedom, Lusia had no fear. She felt only gratitude. The family was together, they still had two rooms in the large apartment, there was enough to eat. The summer stretched out before her, with more concerts, more ballet, more opera. How exciting it was to be a teenager! Someday, the war would end, and Poland would be Poland again.

Lusia had not just been bitten by this heady sense of freedom—she had also been bitten by hundreds of mosquitoes at the outdoor concert, and she awoke in the predawn hours, itching in agony. When she saw the huge welts all over her body, she burst out crying, loud enough for Norbert to hear her from her parents' room next door.

Lusia's new bedroom was part of what once had been the Schwarzwalds' spacious dining room. She slept on a daybed that Norbert had used in his study. Now her father came into her room to comfort her, applying cool wet compresses to her welts. She urged him to go back to sleep, but he would not leave her side. It was not often these days that he got a few moments of his teenage daughter's precious time, so he sat on the edge of the small bed while she told him all about the concert and her other plans for the summer that stretched ahead.

Norbert let his daughter do most of the talking while he seemed to be listening; he was a man with much on his mind. Rumors were everywhere that the Germans would soon break their nonaggression pact with Russia and invade Poland—and everyone had heard the stories of the fate of the Jews of Germany. Norbert Schwarzwald hated the Russians, hated the way they had taken everything from him, everything that he had worked so hard to build. The Germans—well, he had done business with them, had traveled there many times. The Germans knew about music, about art—they were cultured, civilized people. It could not be any worse for Lvov or for the Schwarzwald family if they fell under the Germans.

While the father and daughter sat talking, dawn seemed to break brilliantly with a sudden burst of sunlight. But it was not the sun at all—the bright light was followed by a deafening explosion, then one after another. Suddenly, the sleeping city was wide awake. If the first German bombing on September 1, 1939, had been relentless, then this one, on June 22, 1941, was intolerable and seemingly endless. Chaos reigned everywhere, as the Schwarzwalds, the Russian families, and all the refugees who had taken shelter in the large apartment house fled once again to the basement of 5 Bernsteina Street.

"Run!" Frieda shouted to Lusia and Julek, pulling young Milek down the stairs to the cellar. "Don't stop to look out!" she cried, as she caught Julek trying to see out the window on the landing.

Again, the city was on fire, but this time, it was different. Two years ago, when the Germans bombed Lvov into submission, they had not entered the city. They had merely handed over all of eastern Poland—including Lvov—to the Russians. This time there was real fighting. The Germans were not relying on bombs alone; they were shooting people in the street, Poles and Russians alike. Lusia managed to escape the basement for one minute to look outside; the sky was bright red. The whole city seemed to be on fire; the noise and screams from the bombs, guns, and a panicked population created a scene of total chaos.

In the midst of all this turmoil, one of the Russian officers who was sharing the Schwarzwald apartment approached Norbert in the basement shelter. "Come with us quickly," the officer whispered. "I have a car standing in front of the house for you and your family. We will take you with us to Russia."

Norbert barely considered the offer. Frieda, although she had always begged Norbert to get them out of Poland, refused as well. Both of them knew that the Germans would never let a car full of Russians and Jews through the streets. They would be killed on the spot.

Huddled in the basement, trying not to show the children their confusion and fear, the family endured the onslaught. Again and again, they reminded each other that they were still alive, they were together, and they would weather this new crisis. The bombing would not go on forever.

The elder Schwarzwalds were partially right. By June 29, quiet again descended on the city, and, gingerly, the family made its way up to the apartment. Gone were the Russian families; the house was theirs once again. But there was no time for rejoicing, since nothing lay ahead but worry and uncertainty. These fears were punctuated by the once-illegal shortwave radio on which the latest German allies—the Ukrainians—took great pride in broadcasting this welcome to their new liberators: "We will meet the Germans with baskets full of Jewish heads!"

The parents gave up trying to hide their fears from Julek, Lusia, and Milek. The children would have to grow up fast and share the burden of endurance with their parents. That Julek, the elder son, was now considered a man was no longer in dispute, especially when at 10 A.M. on June 30, 1941, Ukrainian militiamen knocked on the door of the Schwarzwald apartment and ordered Norbert and Julek out of the house immediately. Frieda, Lusia, and Milek cowered against the apartment wall, too stunned to speak.

As Norbert and Julek Schwarzwald were led away from their home, Frieda literally collapsed. All day long, she moaned in pain and fear, as she, Lusia, and Milek listened to the sounds of gunfire from the streets. They knew that the Germans were ordering the roundup of Jews, arresting them, imprisoning them, deporting them, even killing them.

Miraculously—it could only be a miracle—Norbert returned that evening, looking frightened and haggard. Always a quick-thinking, resourceful person, he had hidden in the prison bathroom all day and simply walked away during the evening. But what about Julek? Where was he? He would come back, Norbert told them, comforting Frieda, who was half hysterical. Wherever he was, they would let him go soon.

Thousands of Jews were shot or beaten to death in the hundreds of German pogroms that continued well into July 1941. Then, even more frightening, came Petlura Days, named for a Ukrainian nationalist who had murdered many Jews and had then been killed by a Jew in Paris. Usually, Petlura Days were celebrated by rallies and gatherings, but this time the celebration was aimed at retribution against the Jews. Looting and rioting by the Ukrainians were sanctioned and encouraged by their new German friends.

From the small surrounding villages, the Ukrainians descended on Lvov. With the Germans standing by, they raided and ransacked Jewish homes. Forcefully, they entered the Schwarzwalds' apartment, yanking open drawers and cabinets and roughly going through their contents. They rifled through the two large armoires in Lusia's parents' bedroom, emptying them of coats, suits, and dresses. They wrapped their booty inside bedsheets, tying the ends with a knot, and dropped them out the windows to their accomplices waiting in the street below.

Within an hour, the apartment was stripped of all of its silver, dishes, linen, and clothing. If the Ukrainians left anything behind, it was because Norbert and Frieda had had the foresight to hide it or because the Ukrainians, in their wild frenzied orgy, simply did not notice it.

"Why are they doing this?" whispered Milek to his father. "Shh," cautioned Norbert, who knew what could happen. He had spent one frightening day in a German prison and was not looking forward to more. "Just be quiet, and they will leave soon."

The family huddled in a corner of the room and looked away. From their third-floor window, they could see the Ukrainians massed in the streets. Jews were being pulled from their houses and marched along the roads amidst the shouting and shooting.

Frieda was cowering on Norbert's shoulder. Lusia's legs were shaking with fear. Milek tried not to stare in wonder at the laughing Ukrainians. What horror would the family experience next?

When the Ukrainians set off for their next victimization, Frieda begged Norbert to do something. "We will build a hiding place," he said, trying to calm her. Everyone he knew was building hiding places, although secretly he wondered what good it would do. The Germans always knew where to find people. But to soothe his wife's nerves and keep the children calm, he negotiated with the renters on the second floor of the apartment house for the use of their dining room.

With the help of the same janitor who had constructed a hiding place for Frieda's jewelry in the ceiling of the Schwarzwalds' bathroom, Norbert built a false wall in his neighbor's dining room, wallpapering over it so it would look just like the rest of the room. He constructed a false door with such accuracy and precision that no one could detect it. Still, the whole idea of a hiding place was more psychologically soothing than anything else. When the Germans came calling, they did so without warning; the Schwarzwalds would have to run downstairs and assemble in the hiding place. Even the children knew that the idea was not really practical.

By August 1941, the Germans had ordered the Jews of Lvov to set up a *Judenrat,* or council, at the Jewish Center, which for the Schwarzwalds was conveniently located at 10 Bernsteina Street. The *Judenrat* set up an *arbeits-amt,* or work committee, because the Germans were constantly asking for workers. The Germans communicated to the Jews through the *Judenrat* whenever they needed a work detail or, more likely, whenever they needed money.

The Germans were always demanding money from the Jews. Lusia and her family were constantly trying to scrounge up Russian rubles, since this was still the local currency. The Germans also asked for fur coats for their men at the Russian front, so the Jews came to the Jewish Center bearing their furs. The Ukrainians had stolen Frieda Schwarzwald's fur coats, so she had none to give, but the Schwarzwalds retrieved gold from their hiding place when the Germans demanded money. If the Germans did not get it, they threatened to take more people away.

Norbert could always pretend that he was happy to hand over more of his hard-earned money to the Germans, since he hoped he could exchange gold for information about his son, Julek, however small a scrap. But it was Frieda who actually tried to strike a bargain with the Gestapo in exchange for any news of Julek, news that would bring her some relief from her constant anguish.

In the late summer, Norbert cautiously answered a knock on the door. Without ceremony, three Gestapo men entered the apartment, eyed its few remaining contents, and pointed to Lusia's grand piano. Lusia inhaled sharply as the men went about planning its removal.

As the Gestapo officers carried out the piano, the bench, Lusia's books, and sheet music collection, the leader spoke to Frieda. They talked about Goethe, about Schiller, about other German writers and poets. "Please," she begged, "take anything you want, but bring me news of my son." The German, with his eye on the exquisite custom-made cabinet that Norbert had built for his office, promised that when he returned for that item, he would bring a message from Julek.

He returned for the cabinet, but he had no news. Next time, he promised. When he came back for the Persian carpets, he still produced no news of Julek. "You'll hear from him soon," said the Nazi, as he and his cohorts rolled up the Schwarzwalds' rugs. Frieda's knowledge of German literature had been for naught.

In August, the Germans communicated to the Jewish Council that all Jews were to buy, then wear, white armbands with the Star of David in blue and a red number underneath. Anyone caught without this identification could be killed outright. Not that the Germans needed a reason; people were being shot on the street without cause or warning.

In September came a further frightening command: all Jews were to move to a separate Jewish quarter that the Germans had created in the worst part of the city. Jews had to flee their own homes as they searched for housing in a part of town few had ever visited. They were then ordered to buy the new hovels and slum dwellings. As the Jews moved out of their homes, Germans, Poles, and Ukrainians moved in.

Fortunately for the Schwarzwalds, the new Jewish ghetto was so large that their apartment house was at the very edge of it, and they were allowed to remain in their home. The Germans set up a checkpoint to the area where the Jews had been forced to move and meticulously examined each person who tried to go in or out of the new Jewish quarter. If someone was old or looked sick, the Germans would take him or her away, destination unknown but suspected.

The Germans set up a concentration camp called Janowska near the Jewish cemetery. One of Lusia's uncles was arrested on the street and taken there. When the Germans used the camp inmates to build an extension to Janowska, they told the Jewish forced laborers to use tombstones from the Jewish cemetery as building matcrials.

Next to the Janowska camp, the Germans opened a factory, where slave laborers were to sew uniforms for the army. A new decree was announced, ordering that all Jewish boys and girls aged fourteen through sixteen had to work as slave laborers in the factory.

In her white armband with the blue Star of David, Lusia said an implicit goodbye to any sort of life she had previously known. She was fifteen years old. That same lucky teenager who had meticulously laid out the navy blue dress for the first day of school only two years ago now had other things to think about.

3   Hungary, Friend of Germany

THE HUNGARIAN NEWSPAPERS TOLD ONE story, but the forbidden BBC out of London told another. How long could Hungary remain an ally of Germany? How long would the Hungarian Jews be "safe?" In Hajdunanas, Steve Hornstein, still a student at the Protestant gymnasium, knew that the Jews of Hungary were hearing only the partial truth about the war to the west. It was no secret that Jews living in Hungary without benefit of Hungarian citizenship were being deported to Nazi-occupied Poland by the Hungarian authorities and never heard from again. Jews with Hungarian citizenship began to feel less secure every day. Unless they fled Europe, their lives could be in great danger.

But where could they go? There was fighting to the east; Germany, having already conquered Czechoslovakia and Austria, lay to the west. Rumania, like Hungary, was already a German ally. The Jews of Hungary were stuck, as if frozen to their coveted black Hungarian soil. The more they found out, the more they felt doomed.

Although the Jews of Hajdunanas seemed able to go about their business, their livelihoods were becoming severely restricted. Salomon Hornstein, Steve's father, who had once been quite wealthy, was now forced out of the insurance business and reduced to selling household items—brushes, cleansers, and towels—from a suitcase that he carried on trips out of town. His pride would not allow him to go door-to-door in Hajdunanas. When he returned on the Sabbath, he was weary and haggard from the week's toils and had little money to show for his efforts.

As the oldest son living at home, Steve Hornstein did not shirk his financial responsibilities. With Karl at veterinary school in Budapest and Shmuel at the rabbinic seminary in the same city, Steve, like his older brothers, was expected to contribute to the family's economic well-being.

To help out, he used the excellent teaching skills learned from his brothers to tutor the neighborhood children, readying them for the gymnasium entrance exams. He also tutored his younger brother Jerry, with whom he was very strict. "Pay attention!" he would command Jerry, who could usually think of many other places he would rather be than under the relentless thumb of his older brother.

Steve was busy with his own schoolwork, too, maintaining, to the consternation of his classmates, a straight *A* average. It was Steve who set the curve at school, and the others resented it. As the only Jew in the class and easily one of the best students, he stood out. His classmates often let him know how they felt about it, taunting him and threatening him with their fists.

Steve could withstand this torture, because he was confident that he had a future. That future would take him to Budapest, where he would join his brothers and his best friend, Paul Ornstein, as a special student at the university. Because of the *numerus clausus,* Steve knew that there was no hope for him to matriculate at the university as anything *but* a special student. His high marks and good standing gave him the confidence he needed, and he knew he could get good written recommendations from some of his teachers and from a local doctor who was his mentor. Steve saw a set road ahead of him: he would go to Budapest, get admitted as a special student, study privately with a few sympathetic professors who did not care that he was a Jew, take the necessary exams, and then apply somewhere for medical school. Perhaps by the time he was ready to take that step, he could emigrate to Palestine and attend medical school there. Or even—this was too much to hope—the anti-Semites in Hungary would be defeated somehow, and Steve would be allowed to pursue his dream of becoming a doctor in his own country, surrounded by family and friends.

This plan was endorsed by his parents and his two older brothers Shmuel and Karl. Karl was Steve's idol. Seven years older than Steve, he was considered the most brilliant, most artistic, most gifted boy in the family. Any pursuit of Karl's was always undertaken by his younger brother. Karl was the goalie for the city soccer team; when Steve took up the sport, he also elected to play goalie. Karl helped tutor Steve for his exams so that Steve could enter the gymnasium. He was a strict but loving teacher, and Steve was happy just to be in his presence, to bask in his aura.

Karl had no desire to become a veterinarian and was actually shocked that he had been admitted to the college. He had applied only at the behest of a student he had tutored for the college's entrance exam. The student had cajoled Karl into applying to the veterinary college so that Karl would be available to coach him through his difficult science subjects. Still, Karl knew it was his one chance at any higher education.

Karl disliked the veterinary college for more reasons than his lack of interest in veterinary medicine. The students of the school were notoriously anti-Semitic, and Karl found it best to keep to himself, attend his classes, and do his work. Except for the student from Hajdunanas whom he continued to tutor, Karl did not interact with any of the Gentile students.

Anti-Semitic feelings at the veterinary college were stoked by the Hungarian Nazi party, as they were at universities all over Hungary. One day, the Gentile students at the college decided to prevent the handful of Jews from attending classes. A brutal fight broke out, and the Jewish students were beaten mercilessly. Karl, who was punched and kicked to the floor, looked for his friend, the pupil he had helped to pass the entrance exams for the veterinary college. Before he could spot him, he felt a staggering blow to the back of his head. When he turned to face his assailant, he cried out in surprise: the young man who had dealt the blow was the very student Karl had so patiently and thoroughly prepared for the entrance exams.

When Karl was visiting Hajdunanas for the holidays, he related this story to his parents and younger brother Steve. This was even more confirmation that their world was becoming smaller. Soon Steve would finish his schooling at the gymnasium and head for Budapest as a special student to study with that handful of professors who cared more about his mind than his religious beliefs. But if someone who owed his future to Karl could turn on him like that, what could they expect from the larger, uncaring world?

The war in Europe soon pervaded what was left of the tranquility of the Hornstein family early in 1941. Steve's oldest brother, Joel—married and living elsewhere in Hungary, far from home—was drafted into the Hungarian militia, an auxiliary to the regular Hungarian army. Joel was consigned to forced labor, digging ditches and doing other heavy work for Hungarian soldiers in northern Hungary, close to the Russian border. During that particularly cold winter of 1941, the Hornsteins learned that Joel had died from starvation and exposure. He left behind a wife and two children. Not one person drafted into his unit survived.

More than ever, it was not a good time to be a Jew in Hungary, certainly not when that country was cozying up to Hitler. In exchange for its agricultural know-how and the excellence of its black soil, Hungary was being allowed—for a time—to escape Hitler's wrath. For how long could the Jews count on that? Every day seemed to bring new trouble, new reasons to examine their very limited options, the outside chance of escaping and fleeing to Palestine. Hungary, however, was landlocked, literally between lands that Hitler had already claimed. There was no way out.

On September 1, 1939, Paul Ornstein, age sixteen, stepped down from the overnight train from Hajdunanas to Budapest to begin the next phase of his life as a rabbinic student at the seminary in the capital city. He left behind his younger siblings and his parents, with all their worries and concerns about life in Hungary now that Germany had declared war on Poland. Even though Hungary was one of Germany's allies, it was still bad news for the Jews. It meant that the Hungarians would try to appease the Germans and put more pressure on Jews by carrying out the anti-Jewish laws that forbade them to own property, work in certain professions, or gain acceptance at universities.

This was one reason why Paul had decided to enroll at the rabbinic seminary in Budapest. Hajdunanas and the gymnasium there held no future for him. At least in Budapest, he knew he could tutor other students and make enough money to help pay the tuitions of his younger brothers Zoli and Tibi, who were attending a Jewish gymnasium in Debrecen. Soon, his younger sister, Judith, would move to Budapest to study to become a dental technician. Paul would try to get home to Hajdunanas as often as he could, at least for the Jewish holidays.

Paul came from a religious home, where the family strictly observed the rules governing daily Jewish life and the Sabbath. During his first days at the rabbinic seminary, he was shocked to find that the attitudes of his classmates were quite casual about riding the streetcar or turning the lights off and on during the Sabbath. Paul had long ago lost his belief in God, but the rituals and traditions of the religion were still of utmost importance. When he overheard some of his fellow students making plans to attend a movie on Friday night, he was completely shattered. But what could he do? It was either the rabbinic seminary or nothing; all avenues to higher education were closed to him except for this one.

Paul knew by now that he wanted to study to become a doctor, but how would he be able to do that? Certainly not in Hungary, not with the *numerus clausus* laws. Even if he could get admitted to the university, he would not be able to pay the tuition. At least the rabbinic seminary was free. Going elsewhere was hardly worth thinking about, certainly not in Europe—Hitler was everywhere. If only he could somehow get to Palestine, but every gateway to Palestine seemed blocked. The rabbinic seminary would have to do for now.

News from Hajdunanas came through letters that family members painstakingly took time to write. Paul often saw Shmuel, the brother of his friend Steve, since Shmuel was also a student at the seminary, and they would share any tidbits they had gleaned through letters from home. Paul found life in Budapest tedious and lonely. Still, he settled into a rhythm of going to classes, studying, tutoring, and taking a few breaks to go home for Rosh Hashanah, Passover, and a couple of weeks in the summer. Then, all too soon, the academic year would resume again.

In letters from home, Paul learned that his father, Lajos, had lost his job working as an accountant for the two flour mills because Gentiles were forbidden to employ Jews. Lajos wrote that he was able to earn a small living by arranging for citizenship papers for Jews in danger of deportation, thanks to his ability to negotiate with the authorities. Between these negotiations and some under-the-table money from the mill owners, Lajos was able to feed his family.

Lajos could not do so, however, without the help of his eldest son, Paul. Fortunately, Paul was finding plenty of opportunity to earn money in the capital. The cosmopolitan Jews of Budapest wanted their children to be educated in secular studies as well as in Hebrew. Paul found as much work as he could handle, tutoring in Latin, Hungarian, and even English. In English, he was often only one or two lessons ahead of his pupils. Paul was such an excellent teacher and so sought after as a tutor that he was able to support himself and earn most of the tuition money needed by Zoli and Tibi at the Jewish gymnasium in Debrecen, forty kilometers from Hajdunanas.

Always thinking and planning, Paul continued his studies at the rabbinic seminary with the hope that someday he could leave Hungary and study to become a doctor. Someday, however, seemed very far away. When Paul left Budapest in June 1941 for the summer in Hajdunanas, talk of war was everywhere. The Jews of Hajdunanas felt hopeless and frightened. The times were becoming more uneasy and more uncertain, even as families went about their daily routines and Sabbath rituals. Paul would walk the long block to Steve Hornstein's house, and the two friends would sit and talk about their futures and their plans. Whatever lay ahead for them, however, they knew would not be in Hungary. If Jews were being run out of Germany, what would happen to the Jews of Hungary if the Germans won the war? Would they be reduced to beggars, living in the streets? Would the Germans strike a deal with some other country and deport all the Jews there, where life might be even worse?

Paul was also dismayed to learn that during his year in Budapest, his father had been taken away to a forced labor camp in the Carpathian Mountains, in what had previously been Czechoslovakia. Although Lajos had been released and returned home shortly thereafter, the experience had been frightening for the entire family.

The Jews of Hajdunanas were too afraid to look upon this incident as a harbinger of things to come. They tried to convince themselves that since Hungary was an ally and a valued supplier of agricultural products to Germany, what was happening in the rest of Europe was not going to happen to them—at least not for now. Nervous and uncertain, the community went about its daily affairs, sometimes hungry for news from the rest of Europe and at other times refusing to believe what they were hearing.

Yes, they were becoming increasingly impoverished. Yes, they could hear the news on the BBC from their illegal shortwave radios. But if they would just sit tight, not make any demands, all this might blow over. Anyway, what choice did they have? Palestine was blocked by the British. The United States was turning Jews away. Immigration to Canada depended on having family who would take responsibility for penniless relatives. Even Australia limited immigration for Jews. The rest of Europe was at war. No one wanted them, which sent a clear signal to Hitler that he could do whatever he wanted. No one would care.

In December 1941, Paul and his friends at the rabbinic seminary were heartened to hear that the United States had entered the war. Endlessly, they debated what that country's declaration of war on Germany would mean for Hungary. Paul could not wait to get home to Hajdunanas to see what his friend Steve Hornstein would have to say about this new development.

He and Steve spoke constantly about Hungary's future and their own. The visit to Hajdunanas passed much too quickly. Paul's mother had cooked and baked his favorite holiday foods for Chanukah. As usual, the eldest son's visit home had been treated as something really special.

Paul made plans to leave for Budapest on December 24, 1941, a trip that would take about eight hours. He would have to make one stop, in the city of Debrecen. Since it was Christmas Eve, all the shops and restaurants would be closed. Paul already had a good idea how he could spend the hours of the train's layover, though.

Paul's father had taken a trip to Debrecen in the autumn and had stopped to visit his cousin Piri. He was particularly charmed by the young girl who was living with Piri while she attended the Jewish gymnasium there. "If you have a chance," Lajos told his oldest son, "stop by and say hello to my cousin Piri and the beautiful young girl who is staying there with her. I think you'll like her."

Paul stepped off the train at 7:30 P.M. at the Debrecen station. As he expected, the darkened streets were deserted. The city's citizens were home with their families, preparing to celebrate the holiday. It was not safe for a Jew to be out on the streets on Christmas Eve, but his father had told him how to find Piri's apartment. He walked there quickly.

In the little village where the young girl named for Anna Karenina was growing up, the actual fighting of the war seemed far away. But uncertainty for the Jews of Szendro, Hungary, was much closer. Sometimes Anna Brünn would hear her parents and other adults whispering, the name Hitler always spoken with a mixture of vehemence and fear. Whatever real news they had from the west was through rumor or the contraband radio.

As elsewhere in Hungary, life for Jews in Szendro was becoming more difficult. This Anna knew and accepted as fact, but for the most part, she was able to retreat into her daydreams, where she could know but not know. There she was protected from thinking about such incidents as when the police came to arrest her father for not keeping enough emergency water in his rain barrel or when he was suspected of hiding money or secret information in the rear ends of cows and sending the animals across the border to Czechoslovakia. Preposterous as these accusations were, Anna's father would be taken to the local police station, where he would have to stay overnight before being released. Anna, who loved her father dearly and worried about him because he was not as emotionally strong as her assertive mother, became nearly sick with fear.

Still, the family was together. On holidays, her two brothers, Paul and Andrew, would come home from their gymnasium in the nearby city of Miskolc, and Anna and her mother would clean the house thoroughly until the floors shone—not an easy task, since dirt and dust were constantly being dragged in from outside. She and her mother would cook her brothers' favorite foods—the chicken soup they loved, the cakes for a special treat.

Anna and her parents would meet the brothers' train with great excitement and anticipation. They would rush home and change into their holiday clothes and walk over to Anna's grandmother's house—her father's mother—where the children would receive a special blessing. Anna, petite though she was, had to bend down so this tiny woman could place her hands on her granddaughter's head and recite the blessing, "May you be like Ruth, Rachel, and Leah."

Then at home, Anna savored the family's togetherness, just as they savored the holiday meal, with Anna's mother and her brothers deep in conversation. Sometimes an argument would ensue as they debated the relative merits of this political philosophy or that one. Voices could be raised, but never in anger. It was merely that all three wanted to get a point across, and each had been blessed with the gift of rhetoric.

As 1941 unfolded, the Jews of Szendro, like those in Hajdunanas, clung to the very dailiness of their lives, hoping that if they pretended everything was ordinary, maybe everything would be. For a while—despite the harassment of the heads of households, despite an increase in the frequency of Sophie's migraine headaches, despite the growth of the rumor mill—everything seemed almost as normal as life for a Jew in Hungary could be.

By the time Anna was fourteen years old in 1941, she had gone as far she could go in Szendro's educational offerings for her. She had graduated from the one-room schoolhouse. Her parents had taken her as far as they could in instilling in their beautiful young daughter an appreciation of art, literature, and music. Anna and her two brothers had learned about opera from listening to their parents sing the arias. But in that small town of 3,500—where people and cows drank from the same central well and where there were only two grocery stores, a bakery, and a tobacco shop—the elder Brünns knew that they had to give Anna more. They would have to send her away to the Jewish gymnasium in the nearby city of Debrecen.

Debrecen would be the perfect place for Anna. With other young people in her classes, this lively, energetic fourteen-year-old would thrive. She was so quick, so intelligent, so hungry to learn what the world had to offer that to keep her in Szendro, however much it pained her parents to send her away, would be a great disservice to this young girl of many talents.

What made the idea of sending her to Debrecen seem even more fitting was the presence of Anna's aunt Piri, her mother's half-sister, a young woman who could really use Anna's company and her help. Piri's husband had been conscripted into a forced labor camp at the border between Russia and Hungary, and she had just given birth to a new baby. Anna could live with Piri, help her around the house, and still attend her classes at the gymnasium. This satisfied the Brünns, who knew that Anna would be safe and well-chaperoned. It pleased Piri, who greatly enjoyed young Anna's company, and Anna, who adored her aunt Piri and the new baby.

Besides, 1941 was a good time to leave Szendro. The anti-Semitic overtones of the town were growing louder and louder. Jews now had to report to city hall once a week and were being accused of all kinds of crimes against the state. Anna and her mother worried when Hungarian police came to the house and arrested Anna's father on one trumped-up charge or another, especially since they were aware of William's delicate psyche. He simply was not as strong as the two women he most adored. Because of this frequent harassment, Anna's father grew increasingly depressed and relied more on the advice, know-how, and strength of his more formidable wife.

So when Anna left on the train in the autumn of 1941, she feared for what she was leaving behind but excitedly anticipated what lay ahead for her. While she was reluctant to leave the warmth and assurance of her lovely home, a house built on the ruins of a burned-out castle, she could barely resist daydreaming all the way to Debrecen about her classes, her new friends, and her future. She also harbored the secret hope that life for Jews would be different in Debrecen, that she would be able to leave behind the worries and concerns that intruded on her family's life and were causing her mother's headaches to worsen and her father's fear and depression to deepen.

By the time Paul Ornstein found his cousin Piri's apartment, it was already eight o'clock, dark, and cold. He knocked loudly and stood in the hallway, shivering, waiting for someone to answer. He knocked again; perhaps no one was home. But where would two Jewish women and an infant go on Christmas Eve?

Inside the apartment, Piri was nursing her baby. Anna was already in bed. She had worked hard all day, studying her school subjects and then cleaning the kitchen and scrubbing the bathroom. Anna enjoyed physical labor, getting a great deal of satisfaction from making a floor shine, a kitchen or bathroom sparkle. This was a woman's job in the household, and at home, her parents had praised her liberally for her efforts. Her father was always especially pleased with her work. Lying in bed, Anna thought of her parents now, longing to see them, hoping that she could soon get back to Szendro to spend some time with them and her two brothers.

She was just drifting off to sleep when she heard the knocking at the door. "Don't answer it," Piri whispered to her. "They could be looking for Jews." Anna knew what Piri really feared: it might be someone bearing unwanted news of her husband at the Russian front.

Anna slipped out of bed and buttoned herself into Aunt Piri's long, flowing bathrobe. She tiptoed to the front door and held her finger to her lips. She pressed her ear to the door to listen, expecting to hear a clue to the caller's identity. When she heard nothing, she called out, "Who is it?"

"It's Paul," answered a young man's voice. Anna was puzzled. She knew several boys from school named Paul, one or two who had even walked her home and carried her books, but none of them would come calling after dark on Christmas Eve. No Jew would be out on the streets at this time of night without a compelling reason. She looked over at Piri and shrugged. "Paul who?" she called. "Paul Ornstein from Hajdunanas," he replied. "It's my cousin's son," cried Piri. "Let him in!"

Anna unlocked the door and held out her hand in greeting. She was about to introduce herself when the dark-haired, handsome young man took her hand and kissed it. Shocked by this gesture, Anna drew back and went to sit down. Only then did she realize that Paul must have mistaken her for Piri, since she was wearing her aunt's bathrobe. Still, she could not help being overwhelmed by this hand kiss from such a good-looking— and older—boy. She was, after all, only fourteen, and he was a very mature and sophisticated seventeen.

Paul sat and talked to Piri about topics on which Anna had barely a passing knowledge: philosophy, religion, world literature. Though he was handsome, intelligent, and polite, he seemed way too old for her. As Paul and Piri talked, he would turn to Anna, as if encouraging her to contribute an opinion, but she was too much in awe of his knowledge of the subject matter. Still, she felt that he was definitely interested in her, although she had little to add to the conversation.

After an hour's visit, Paul got up to return to the train station so that he could continue his journey to Budapest. "I hope to see you again," he said to Anna, this time shaking, not kissing, her hand. She swallowed hard and nodded. This Paul was quite different from the Pauls at the gymnasium who vied to walk her home and carry her school satchel. She had never met anyone quite like him.

After he left, she peppered Piri with questions. How were they related? Did that make him Anna's relative too? No, Piri assured her, it did not. How well did Piri know him? Did she think he would come back again? Could Piri remember the names of the philosophers and writers they had talked about?

Piri answered Anna's questions until she was too tired for any more. But Anna could not get Paul out of her mind. She was still thinking about him the next day when, straightening up the apartment, she came across a pair of men's gloves that could only belong to last night's visitor.

"His hands must be freezing," said Piri. "We must send these to him immediately." "Why would he forget his gloves on a freezing night like last night?" asked Anna. "Maybe he left them here on purpose," said Piri mischievously. "What do you mean, 'on purpose'?" Anna asked. But Piri was already in the other room taking care of the baby.

A few days later, Anna received a letter from Paul Ornstein, saying how much he had enjoyed meeting her. He also asked her to send his gloves back to him at the rabbinic seminary in Budapest. This she did, but first she placed a note in the finger of one of the gloves, saying that she had enjoyed meeting him, too. Anna knew that it was a long way from Debrecen to Hajdunanas, even longer from Hajdunanas to Szendro, so she had no hope, really, that they would ever have a chance to meet again. Besides, a smart, handsome Jewish boy like that probably had lots of girls interested in those writers and philosophers he had spoken about so passionately at Aunt Piri's house on Christmas Eve.

The Brünn family, 1920, in front of the L-shaped house in Szendro, Hungary, where Anna would spend the first seventeen years of her life. Her grandparents are in the middle of the front row; her father, William, is at the far left; and her mother, Sophie, is sitting in front of her father. Most of the family died in Auschwitz.

Anna, age fourteen, with her brothers, Paul (left), nineteen, and Andrew (right), eighteen. The brothers did not survive.

Anna, age fourteen, in Szendro.

Paul and Anna, August 3, 1943, when he surprised her by riding his bike to visit her in Szendro.

Paul Orstein's mother, Frieda, who died in Auschwitz.

Paul (far right), age twelve, with his sister, Judith, ten, and brothers Tibi and Zoli in Hajdunanas, Hungary. Paul was the only one to survive.

Paul on his way to visit his girlfriend, Anna Brünn, in 1943.

Paul in Budapest, 1943.

Steve's parents, Tobi and Salomon Hornstein, in Hajdunanas, Hungary, 1943.

Steve's oldest brother, Joel, who was killed in a forced labor camp on the Russian front before Hungary was invaded.

Steve's sister, Ann, holding a nephew. Ann died in Auschwitz, along with her parents and brother Henu.

Steve (top), sixteen, clowning with friends.

Steve, age sixteen, wearing the cap that was part of his gymnasium uniform.

Lusia Schwarzwald's maternal grandfather, Shalom Meyer, circa 1937.

Lusia's maternal grandmother, Sabina Meyer, circa 1937.

Lusia's mother, Frieda, probably taken in the mid-1930s.

Lusia, eighteen months old, with her older brother, Julek, while vacationing at a resort in the Carpathian Mountains. Julek was arrested early in the war and was never heard from again.

Lusia, age four, in Vienna.

Lusia, age twelve, at her sixth-grade graduation. All girls were required to wear a sailor collar for the picture.

4   *The Lvov Ghetto*

SWOLLEN WITH HUNGER AND LACK OF PRO-
tein, the Jews of Lvov were forced to live—exist, really—at the bidding and
whims of their German masters. Subjected each day to beatings, arrests,
humiliation, and fear, the Jewish population suffered severe bouts of anxiety and panic, as people were arrested off the streets of the city and transported to places unknown. Lusia, her twelve-year-old brother, Milek, and
her parents tried to wrap themselves in the warmth of their dwindling
family, but fear took its toll. Huddled in the corner of their dining room
at 5 Bernsteina Street, with blankets strung up to give them some meager
privacy from the others living there, the family prayed for news of their
son and brother Julek and for any scrap of information that would give
them some peace of mind.

Norbert, with his hidden stash of money, his knowledge of German, his
resourcefulness in the community, and his ability to understand the broad
view and possible implications of any situation, was able to keep the family functioning. Frieda, however, was often at the brink of collapse, totally
devastated by the lack of news concerning her older son. Lusia tried to be
cooperative, volunteering for the constant work details demanded by the
Germans. She also felt responsible for looking after her younger brother. It
was not exactly a burden, but something she felt obliged to shoulder if it
would relieve the weight of the stress on her parents' shoulders.

In early December 1941, as was his weekly habit, Norbert left after Friday night dinner to attend services in the little synagogue located near the
Jewish Community Center on Bernsteina Street. Frieda, fearing for her
husband's safety, hated to watch him go, but Norbert found that the familiar prayers and chants of the service freed his mind for a while, allowing him to think what to do next. On this Sabbath evening, after the ser-

vice was long over and the late autumn night had darkened the streets, Frieda felt the familiar panic begin to well up. Norbert had not returned. Something must be wrong. He knew better than to worry her.

"Perhaps he's meeting with some people," Lusia suggested hopefully. She knew that secret meetings among Jews were strictly forbidden, but she wanted to convince herself as well as her mother that Norbert would soon return. "Even if there's trouble, you know he'll find a way to get out of it. He always does."

Lusia was half right. There was trouble. A few hours later, their doorbell rang. A Jew, a man they did not know, was standing there. "They took him away," the man whispered. "They picked him up off the street and took him away." Lusia and Frieda did not have to ask who "they" were. Mother and daughter collapsed against each other, totally dissolved by this latest news. Now what would become of them?

A few days later, a Polish man rang the Schwarzwalds' doorbell and handed Frieda a letter from Norbert. Shaking, she tore open the envelope, scanned the letter's contents, and cried out in relief. He was alive! He was healthy!

"I am in a forced labor camp not far from Lvov," Norbert wrote, "and I am all right and well treated. Because I know German so well, the camp commandant has given me an office job and actually lets me sleep on a cot in the office! So instead of working at hard labor, I am in charge of the camp's books. Please do not worry."

Every ten days or so, Norbert was able to send a similarly encouraging letter to his family. Just knowing that he was all right and working inside made the late winter of 1941 easier to bear for the small Schwarzwald family. They knew very well that if Norbert could maneuver his way from digging ditches or other forced labor into an accounting job in a warm office, he would soon be negotiating his release from the camp altogether. That small ray of hope made their lives a bit easier to bear.

As the Schwarzwald family dwindled in size, Lusia's responsibilities grew. In her grief and despair, Frieda could barely function; she lived for every letter from her husband, every scrap of good news she could obtain. There was little good news to grab on to. The Germans were becoming more relentless in their demands for money, household goods, and workers. At one point, the Germans ordered the *Judenrat* to round up two thousand Jews to shovel snow. Lusia quickly volunteered. There was no more school to go to, no more music lessons to attend. She found that keeping

physically busy was a good way to avoid thinking about the family's pre-
dicament and the unknown future.

After the back-breaking work of shoveling, Lusia would return exhausted to 5 Bernsteina Street to help her mother sew. They were not mending
shirts or darning socks. Lusia and Frieda spent the evenings surreptitiously
sewing Frieda's jewelry into their clothes. They removed the diamonds
from Frieda's ornate brooches and bracelets and stitched the gems into a
secret panel in her girdles; they sewed the diamonds from her earrings into
her bras. Gold rings and pins were stitched into the cuffs of Lusia's blouses.
Other precious stones were hidden in nightclothes. They felt lucky to have
the jewelry to use as bargaining chips. And who knew? Perhaps they could
use it to buy Norbert's release. That small ray of hope was all that sustained
them through the waning months of 1941 and into the cold, cruel winter of the next year.

The Schwarzwalds subsisted on the crumbs of hope contained in
Norbert's letters. He was doing well, he wrote: it was warm in the commandant's office; his knowledge of German had saved him; life was not so terrible. He hoped he would be released soon. Huddled in the small corner
of the dining room in what had once been their own vast and luxurious
apartment, Frieda, Lusia, and Milek were grateful that their husband and
father was alive. All around them, people kept disappearing, never to be
heard of again.

In late February, they received another letter, but the handwriting on
the envelope did not look like Norbert's. When Frieda opened it, she
looked puzzled. This letter was written in Yiddish; Norbert's letters were
always written in German. She and Lusia began to read it together. "I re-
gret to inform you that your husband, Norbert Schwarzwald, has died of
typhus," said the letter. "But please be assured that he was given a Jewish
burial wrapped in a prayer shawl."

Frieda felt she could not sink any lower. What would happen to them
now, a woman alone with two children? How would they stay alive? What
hope did they have now that Norbert was dead? At least she had her jewelry; at least she had the children to comfort her. Still, she did not know
how she would carry on in the face of all the dangers and uncertainties
that awaited them. Sixteen-year-old Lusia mourned her father by wearing
a black apron in the Jewish custom. She thought of him constantly but
barely had time to cry, so busy was she trying to prop up her mother and
keep her from total collapse.

In March of 1942 came yet another decree from the Germans: the part of the Jewish quarter that included Bernsteina Street was to be emptied. This decree coincided with a massive *aktion,* or raid, lasting almost three weeks. Ten thousand to 20,000 of the 160,000 Jews of Lvov were taken away, transported to Belzec, a death camp not far from Lvov that began its mass extermination program that month. Lusia knew people who escaped from the trains by pulling up the floorboards and jumping free. Some were caught and shot. Others were lucky enough to survive, at least for a while.

A new part of Lvov—a very poor section where Lusia had never visited—was now designated the Jewish ghetto. Frieda had managed to buy at great expense a little wagon to hold whatever household goods and clothes they could take with them. Lusia and her twelve-year-old brother took turns with their mother pulling the heavy cart through streets and fields for what seemed like hours but was probably a distance of only about five miles. Finally, they arrived at a small farmhouse, where they were to share living quarters with four other families. The three-member Schwarzwald family was assigned one small corner of a room, containing one metal bed and a closet. The families shared a kitchen and an outhouse. Lusia, friendly and sociable, immediately set about getting to know the other families. She became friends with most everyone, including a dentist who lived on the other side of the farmhouse.

Frieda, through her connections with people Norbert had known, was able to secure work and work papers for herself and her children. Milek, at twelve, was tall for his age and was able and willing to work. Children, like the old and infirm, who were unable to contribute to the economy were considered a liability and were taken away by the Germans.

A German entrepreneur whose name was Kremin set up a plant near the new Jewish ghetto and employed thousands of Jews to work in his warehouse sorting glass, metal, paper, and cloth that had been collected from war rubble and from old clothes and uniforms of soldiers and prisoners of concentration camps. Each area of the warehouse was designated by whatever was being sorted there. Lusia, her mother, and her brother, along with about a thousand other Jews, worked sorting cloth.

The warehouse that the Schwarzwalds worked in twelve hours a day was filled with big metal tables covered with heavy netting, a little coarser than window screens. On each table were piled sacks of rags of all sizes and shapes. The worker's job was to sort out the rags, making separate piles of cotton, wool, and rayon and placing them in baskets. Lusia knew that some of the rags—soiled with blood and other unspeakable fluids—came from German or Russian soldiers from the front or from Jews in concentration camps. Many of the rags were crawling with lice. This was not surprising, since typhus had already felled many people in the ghetto.

The workers were not allowed to sit down in that unheated warehouse. As Lusia's fingers became numb, she tried not to think about where the rags came from, of whose clothing they had once been a part. She wore gloves with the tips cut out of them to make the sorting easier, but her fingers bled from the cold. Her feet were frostbitten as well. It was an unbearably cold winter, those early months of 1942, and the weather, hard work, lack of food, and strain of survival took its toll on the Jews of the Lvov ghetto.

In August of 1942, another big *aktion* took place; more Jews were rounded up and deported. Lusia's mother, only thirty-nine years old, looked haggard and frail. Lusia feared that the Germans would think her mother too weak to work and would take her away, too. Frieda held on as best she could, but her spirit had died with her husband's death and her son's disappearance.

During the fall of 1942, Lusia became fearfully ill with a high fever and painful sore throat. If the Germans discovered a Jew home in bed and unable to work, that person was either transported out of the ghetto or shot. Sick Jews were useless to the German cause; what was worse, they could spread their disease throughout the ghetto. A Jew with a fever was a huge risk.

The fever finally subsided, but Lusia was still so sick that when she drank water, it came out her nose. One of the residents of that crowded farmhouse was a dentist that Lusia had befriended. "Very sore throat, high fever," he mused. "You have paralysis of the soft palate." What Lusia and the dentist did not know was that those were symptoms of diphtheria.

She was young and determined, and she felt confident that she could rise above this illness. What other choice did she have? To give in would leave her mother and brother on their own. Her mother was too depressed; her brother was too young to take proper care of her. The law of the ghetto implicitly stipulated that if you could move, you went to work. If you could not go to work, you would suffer the consequences. So Lusia went to work, standing up at the metal table for twelve hours sorting bloody rags.

Because of her youth and strong immune system, she finally recovered. That she had also lost several teeth since moving to the ghetto seemed minor compared with what she had just suffered. Thankful for her good health, Lusia tried her best to concentrate on just living for that day. She made every attempt to put her old life out of her mind. Someday this would end, she told herself. That was what they talked about as they stood around the metal tables and put the cotton rags into one bin, the wool into another. Someday this would end.

One morning during the late summer of 1942 when the Jews were working, the Gestapo came and ordered them onto trucks. "Schnell!" they shouted. "Quickly! Run to the trucks!" Lusia held the hands of her mother and brother so they would not be separated. "Where are we going?" Milek whispered to Lusia. "Shh," she cautioned him. "Just don't wander away once we get there. We have to stay together."

By the afternoon, the Jews were all sitting on a grassy field outside of the grounds of the Janowska concentration camp. They sat there through the night, wondering what would become of them. They whispered back and forth, consulting each other, planning strategies to stay alive.

Lusia could see inside the camp. She tried as hard as she could to look for her uncle, her father's brother-in-law. She had heard that he was a prisoner there. To see him alive would give them some bit of hope that if they did become inmates of this camp, they, too, would have a chance to survive. Still, she was prepared to be "selected out" and never see her small family again.

As dawn broke and the sun warmed the shivering Jews who had lived through the night of terror, an SS commandant ordered them back on the trucks. It appeared that Kremin, the German who owned the factory, had convinced the SS that he needed these workers to further the war efforts. Where else could he find such cheap labor? Where else could he find such willing workers who could labor through the most trying conditions? Evidently, Kremin had put forth a persuasive case, because by that afternoon, the Jews were back at work. And they had their lives.

Staying alive became the chief preoccupation of the Schwarzwald family and their fellow inmates. People were being shot right in their own living spaces. Every day, people were loaded onto trucks and taken away. They were dying of disease and starvation. But so far, the Schwarzwalds were alive. They had not been transported away. They had not been shot. This was not happening to them. It was happening to someone else. As long as they could stay together and stay healthy, they could survive— maybe even escape one day.

Plans to escape were hardly new to the Schwarzwalds. Before Norbert was arrested, they were going to make an attempt with another family to cross over the border into Hungary. If they could get across the Carpathian Mountains into Hungary, they might be able to get all the way to Palestine. A man Norbert knew was supposed to come and help them. The escape was to cost a great deal of money, but the man—a Ukrainian—never showed up.

Another scheme had the Schwarzwalds' escaping Poland and being smuggled through Siberia and into China. Again, this plan fell through. After Norbert was taken away, Lusia, desperate for help from someone, went to visit one of the family's former maids. She removed her armband to do so, since a Jew caught in that forbidden part of town would be shot on the spot. But the maid sent her away, saying there was nothing she could do for them.

Lusia knew, of course, that escaping the Lvov ghetto was nothing more than a dream. For one thing, they now had absolutely no contact with the outside world. For another, all they ever did was go to work in the morning, return twelve hours later, try to scrounge up some meager portion of food, and make plans for that moment's survival. Any ideas that anyone had for escape were futile—and foolish.

Late in 1942, Milek turned thirteen. Like other Jewish boys his age, he recited the prayers and performed the rituals that led to his bar mitzvah. Somehow, Frieda managed to find a cake on the black market, and they celebrated this usually festive event by sharing this meager dessert with their friends. How far they were from 5 Bernsteina Street. Lusia tried to dismiss from her mind the thoughts of what Milek's bar mitzvah should have been like. Her grandfather, her father, her brother Julek—all handing the torah down to the youngest male of the family. They were all gone now, and Milek's bar mitzvah, as far as she was concerned, was no cause for celebration.

In the fall of 1942, another big *aktion* took place. The SS took over the ghetto and the plant. They made the Germans who employed Jews buy houses for their workers. Kremin, the owner of the plant, bought a few places and crammed his thousands of workers into them. The little farmhouse, where four families had shared a room, a kitchen, and an outhouse, seemed a palace compared with where the three Schwarzwalds were now consigned. Each person living in the apartment was allowed two square meters of living space. The Schwarzwalds shared a small area in the triangle-shaped kitchen of the house, huddled and cramped next to the stove. They had one cot to share.

Other changes loomed large in their lives. Suddenly, they were required to march by fives to and from the factory. In the Lvov work camp,

Jews wore white armbands with a red star of David. They also wore the letter *A* for *arbeiter,* or worker. In addition, Lusia and her family now had to wear a small metal badge with an *R* on it for *rustung,* indicating that they worked for armaments or that they were involved in important labor.

Conditions worsened through the winter months and into 1943. The days were long and cold; the workers were marched to work six days a week at 7 A.M. and then marched back at 7 P.M. They never saw daylight. They were given some thin soup and a piece of bread to eat while they worked, but no other nourishment. All the while, the Ukrainian police, collaborating with the Nazis, checked on them constantly to make sure no Jews were lollygagging at home in their meager quarters. Jews also served on police details, and they checked, too.

A new commandant was appointed to oversee the camp, a man obsessed with cleanliness. The windows of the factory had to be scrubbed, as well as the windows of the Jews' pitiful tenements. Residents of the camp were assigned to wash the sidewalks. Lusia scrubbed the stairs of her slum dwelling until they were spotless. After twelve hours of work in the factory, the slave laborers came home to spend hours with pails and brushes, cleaning their quarters.

The commandant wanted the Jews to clean and scrub, partly to make their meager lives even more miserable but also because disease was rampant in the ghetto. Typhus was everywhere. At first, the three Schwarzwalds were spared the agony of this disease, until one day, one of Norbert's cousins, who was also a camp inmate, showed up in the cramped house, where among them, they had six square meters of space. The man was very sick with typhus and had no one to take care of him.

This task fell to Lusia and her mother, but making him well was futile. There was no medicine, no nourishing food to help bring down the high fever, the uncontrollable shivering, and the dementia that was setting in. Norbert's cousin died in that little kitchen. Fortunately, Jews were still allowed to say the prayers over the dead, and Norbert's cousin was buried in a Jewish ceremony.

As terrible as that experience was, something worse happened: Milek came down with typhus in January 1943, probably caught from his relative. Lusia had managed to drag herself to work when she was sick, but it was much too dangerous to try to move Milek. He soon fell into a coma.

Lusia and Frieda panicked. They could not both go off to work and leave Milek alone. What if he came out of the coma and his mother and sister were gone? What if something worse happened? The women decided that one of them would stay behind while the other went off to work.

They were aware of the danger. If the SS found a Jew at home and not at work, that person had better have a very good reason for being there. Taking care of your dying son or brother was not a good excuse. Besides, a sick person who could not work would be shot on the spot.

The plan was that they would cover Milek with the heavy feather quilt, leaving just a little room for air. If they heard noises, whoever was watching him would cover him up completely. He was so thin and emaciated, no one could detect a body in the bed. Lusia and Frieda were well aware that during the Gestapo's periodic checks of the residences, they would poke their bayonets into the bedding to make sure no one was hiding at home.

After seven days in a coma, Milek's fever broke. Miraculously, he recovered before the Gestapo checked the house, before the guards even noticed he was missing. Without medicine, without any heat in the house, without any food for nourishment, Milek's young body managed to rally. Soon he was back at the warehouse sorting rags.

Milek's illness was so frightening to Frieda, she decided that her children were going to have meat to eat, no matter what. Many things the Jews wanted were available on the black market, and Frieda had her jewelry to sell. One Sunday, when she called Lusia and Milek for lunch, the children were shocked to find meatballs waiting for them.

"Where did you get this?" Lusia asked. It tasted a bit sweeter than meat she remembered eating before the war. "What is it?" "Never mind," said Frieda. "Just eat it." The children ate with relish. Anything was better than their usual fare of watery soup and cold potatoes.

Later, Frieda confessed that kosher or not kosher, her children were going to eat a real meal. If that real meal happened to be horse meat, well, God would forgive them. Milek and Lusia stared at each other. They had just eaten horse meat? Their grandmother would be spinning in her grave! But actually, it had tasted pretty good. "You must have paid a fortune for it," Lusia said.

The horse meat episode was one break in the tedium of their lives. They were now sharing their small apartment with thirty or forty people. Still, many mornings, the SS would come to the apartment and take someone away.

Their work routine was the same. Frieda, Lusia, and Milek would rise at 6 A.M., dress, and assemble by the gate of the camp. Soon, the patrols would arrive and march them by fives to the factory. Along the way, Poles and Ukrainians lined up along the path, jeering and throwing rocks at the marching Jews. Lusia tried to hold her head high, but she could barely contain the tears of humiliation. Was it not enough that she had lost everything—her father, her brother, her home? Were they not satisfied that she was dressed in rags, freezing and working as a slave? Why did they have to stand at the side of the road and jeer as they passed?

The Nazis had a method of selection every morning. If they did not like the way someone looked, they would pull that person out of line and send him or her away. Everyone tried to appear healthy and clean, but how could you wash your face without a piece of soap? How could you appear well-nourished with nothing to eat? Lusia wondered how long it would be before it happened to her.

It was even worse when they were marched back at the end of the day. Exhausted and worn out, the Jews were searched by the guards to make sure no one was smuggling in the bread they had received during the day or any food they had managed to buy from the Poles or Ukrainians. Sometimes, as with Milek, a sick family member would be unable to make it to work that day, and the thin slice of bread would be all he or she would get to eat. If a person was caught smuggling, however, he or she would be shot at once. Lusia witnessed this many times.

Marching out, working long hours, marching back, coming home to scrub the floors and clean the windows. Then to bed, only to begin the same routine the next day. Everyone was miserable and depressed. At the sorting tables in the factory, the women talked of nothing but food—how to cook a roast, bake a pie, stuff a chicken. Everyone was starving. There was no food, and no one talked about anything but food. In this way, they managed to nourish their aching hearts and emaciated bodies.

One evening in winter, as the Jews collected by the factory gates to march home, they knew that something was different. The sky was completely red, as if buildings were burning. As the Nazis marched them through the gates into the camp, they saw with horror that every ten meters or so, a dead Jew was hanging from a tree. Not only had the Germans shot these people, but they had burned their houses as well. Later, they learned that a Jew had killed an SS man, and the hanging bodies that lined the streets were a warning and retaliation for this act. The bodies hung there for days, a sick, sad reminder to the Jews—as if they needed reminding—not to anger their masters.

One day, when Lusia was standing at the rag-sorting table, an SS woman with thigh-high boots and a whip commanded silence in the room. They were looking, she said, for someone to wash windows at Commandant Kremin's house. Much to Frieda's dismay, Lusia immediately volunteered. What could be so bad about washing windows in the warm house of the commandant? It would certainly get her out of the factory for a day.

Lusia and another young woman were led by a German (because Jews were not allowed out on the streets alone) to the commandant's apartment house. There, they were given a bucket of soapy water and clean rags and told to get to work. Lusia was not an expert window washer, but how hard could it be? The house was warm, and the smell of cooked vegetables wafted upstairs from the kitchen. Maybe she could get something to eat. She could not begin to express her gratitude for this day.

Commandant Kremin and his family lived on the second floor of the apartment house. On the third floor lived Fräulein Hoepke, who had given Lusia the window-washing job. Stern and strict, the SS woman missed no opportunity to scream at and slap Lusia that first day when she felt the teenager's work was not up to par. Lusia was terrified of her; her voice was harsh, her fist was menacing, and her leather whip was a constant threat.

Across from Fräulein Hoepke, on the third floor, lived a family of Jews named Sonderling, who were from Katowice, a mining town near the German-Polish border. The Sonderlings, somehow, had obtained Bolivian passports; Jews who had passports from countries not at war with Germany were allowed to live outside of the camps and ghettos. Mr. Sonderling ran the business of the factory for Commandant Kremin.

Lusia was able to observe all this as she went from apartment to apartment washing windows. When she was finished—or when Fräulein Hoepke told her she was finished—she was almost sad. The work had not been difficult, the apartment house was pleasant, and the Ukrainian cook in the kitchen had called Lusia downstairs for a meal of vegetables and bread.

As Lusia and the other woman prepared to leave with their SS escort, Fräulein Hoepke confronted her. "You," she said pointing at both of them with her whip. "You come back tomorrow."

The next day Lusia and her friend returned and washed more windows. Again, they were called down to the kitchen and given a meal of whatever the cook had on the stove. As they prepared to leave, Fräulein Hoepke stopped them at the door. "Come back tomorrow," she said.

So it continued every day. Lusia would march in the column of five with her mother and brother to Kremin's plant, where a Nazi guard would come for her and escort her to Kremin's apartment house. Some days she washed windows. Some days she did Fräulein Hoepke's laundry. Never to the SS woman's satisfaction, of course; once when she found a run in her stockings, she slapped Lusia so hard with her open hand that the young girl fell down. Lusia was terrified of Fräulein Hoepke and tried to stay out of her way as much as possible.

Other times, Lusia scrubbed the floors. Always, the Ukrainian cook would call her downstairs to the kitchen and give her a meal of whatever she was cooking for the day. One day, much to Lusia's surprise, the cook gave her a hard-boiled egg. "Take it home," she whispered to Lusia, placing it carefully in her palm. Lusia quickly hid the egg in her underwear. An egg in the camp was like gold. Her mother and brother had not seen a hard-boiled egg since—Lusia could not remember the last time.

Soon this became a daily occurrence. Just after she had eaten her meal, Lusia would be stopped by the Ukrainian cook and handed a piece of bread, an egg, or some fruit. Carefully, she would hide her prize in her bra or panties. To be caught with these items would mean certain death. Then, at the end of the day, guarding this bounty as carefully as possible, she would walk with her guard back to the factory, where she would join her brother and mother on the march home.

To get out of the rag-sorting place was wonderful enough; the extra food for her family was an added bonus. But best of all the Sonderling family befriended her. Mr. and Mrs. Sonderling could not help liking Lusia, a young girl so bright, so engaging, so well mannered. They were quite impressed by this young girl working as a maid, who had obviously been destined for a better life. When they were able to, they would invite Lusia into their apartment on the third floor and give her a cup of tea. Sometimes they would offer her a sweater to wear and take home. Lusia told them about her situation, about how hard it had been without her father and brother Julek.

"Do you have Polish papers?" asked Mr. Sonderling. "No, we don't," said Lusia, wondering how on earth she could get her hands on false papers. "You really should have them," said Mr. Sonderling. "You don't know what the future will bring. Perhaps I can help you."

Lusia went home and told her mother. Her friendship with the Sonderlings was a blessing; they had no one else to give them advice. Many of Lusia's cousins who had helped counsel and give them moral support after Norbert died had fled Lvov on false Polish papers. The only relative they had remaining was a man named Salo, her father's cousin, who also lived in the camp. But Lusia did not know Salo very well.

Frieda gave Lusia the gold needed to purchase the false papers. Lusia smuggled the gold into the apartment house when she went to clean and gave it to Mr. Sonderling. A few days later, he handed Lusia something that looked like a passport, a form of identification that a Pole would carry. There were papers for her brother and mother, too.

Now they had false papers, but they had nowhere to go. Every day brought on the same terror, as the small family marched to work and back. When the guard took Lusia to Kremin's apartment house, she had no idea whether she would find her mother and Milek at the end of the day. The Germans were killing people to reduce the Jewish population of Lvov, which once was as high as 160,000, counting the German refugees, but was now about 10,000. Daily the rumors flew that the camp was to be liquidated. Lusia and her family knew what happened to Jews once a camp was liquidated. They were sent to other camps to be gassed, or they were murdered right there. They knew this because some of the Jews who had been selected for transportation to other camps had managed to escape and return. When they came back, they brought with them the terrifying tales that made all the Jews' attempts at existence seem futile.

Then, one day in April 1943, the Germans held another big *aktion,* where they pulled many Jews out of the columns as they were marching to work. One of them was Frieda Schwarzwald. Lusia cried out but had to keep marching or she, too, would have been pulled from the line.

When the guard came to take her to the apartment house, Lusia was almost sick with anxiety. She could not wait to get to work and talk to the Sonderlings. They advised her to flee. The next person to be pulled out of the marching columns could be Milek or Lusia herself. Even Fräulein Hoepke, who heard what had happened to Frieda, advised Lusia to go away. "Why don't you just leave?" she told Lusia, while she busily wrapped a package for her family in Berlin. Fräulein Hoepke always took care to show Lusia as little compassion as possible.

Through her tears and fears, Lusia scrubbed floors and washed windows that day with a vengeance. What was she to do? Where would she go? Would she be able to take Milek? Two Jews wandering the countryside—it was impossible. But if the horrible Fräulein Hoepke was telling her to leave, then she knew the fate of the Jews in that work camp.

Back in their cramped living space that night, she sat comforting Milek, wondering what to do. She was only seventeen, but the weight of the world was on her shoulders. Perhaps she could go to her father's cousin Salo for help, but she felt odd about doing that; she did not know him all that well. Anyway, he had his own survival to think about.

Still, donning a scarf against the chilly night, she left the apartment and went looking for Salo. When she found him, she sat down and cried and told him the story. He could not help feeling sorry for this young girl all alone with her young brother. He remembered Lusia from the old days at 5 Bernsteina Street, where he had always been warmly welcomed by her parents.

"You should go away," he advised her. Everyone was telling her this. "Where should I go?" Lusia implored him. "What should I do?" Salo paused a long time before speaking. "I am going to do something I shouldn't," he said. "My two brothers, Leon and Samek, are in Warsaw with false papers. I'm going to give you their address." Now Lusia and Milek had a place to go, but how would they get there?

The next day at work, she confided in the Sonderlings. She had an address, but how would she get there? She had the false papers that said she was a Polish Catholic, but she was afraid to travel by herself.

"We know someone who can take you," whispered Mr. Sonderling. "Tomorrow come to work and bring your brother with you. Just know that you will not go back."

Lusia barely slept that night. Would she and Milek be safe? What if they were caught trying to get to Warsaw? Jews were not supposed to be traveling on public transportation. What if she got to Warsaw and could not find her cousins' apartment? What if they refused to let her in? It was terribly dangerous for her to even know their whereabouts, much less show up on their doorstep with her younger brother, begging for help.

When morning finally came, Lusia and Milek dressed hurriedly. She made sure to take with her the jewelry and gold so meticulously sewn into the pockets of her underwear and clothes. She told Milek that he was not to say a word, that she would do all the talking.

The two of them marched in the column of five to the factory, but when the guard came to take her to Kremin's apartment house, she told him that she had been asked to bring a helper. The guard looked Milek over for a minute and then motioned for him to follow his sister.

When they arrived at the apartment house, Milek was immediately whisked away and hidden in the attic. If he had been found in the apartment house, the Sonderlings would have been severely punished. For helping the two Schwarzwalds escape, they could be killed.

Lusia spent the day working, scrubbing floors, polishing woodwork, and washing walls and windows. She could barely keep her mind on her tasks, so nervous was she about her approaching escape. The Sonderlings had already told her that a *volksdeutsche,* a woman born in Poland of German heritage, had agreed—for a sum of money—to travel with Lusia on the train to Warsaw. Lusia would have to pretend to be this woman's Polish maid. The woman's brother would take Milek to Warsaw as soon as they heard from Lusia that it was safe to do so.

When the German guard came to the apartment house to escort Lusia back to the factory at the end of the day, he was told that she had already left. To actually do so would have been foolish and dangerous, and no Jew would wander through the town to the factory alone. But the guard mercly shrugged and left the house.

Lusia stayed hidden in the attic until it was dark outside. She gave Milek some money, a hug, and a kiss and told him she would see him soon. She then descended the stairs, dressed in some clothes the Sonderlings had given her—and without her armband. From all outward appearances, she was no longer a Jew. She was a Polish maid.

As she passed the kitchen on her way downstairs to meet her *volksdeutsche* companion, she saw the Ukrainian cook looking at her. For a moment their eyes locked. The cook's gaze traveled to Lusia's armbandless sleeve. If the cook cried out, it could bring the ferocious Fräulein Hoepke running from her third floor apartment, and that would be the end of the escape. It would also be the end of Lusia, for surely she would be killed for trying something so dastardly. She held her breath. The cook looked away and went back to her pots and pans.

In the hallway downstairs, the *volksdeutsche* woman nodded at her to follow; soon the two of them were on the street. It was the first time in years that Lusia had been outside without her armband. The two silently boarded a streetcar and headed for the railroad station. The *volksdeutsche* bought two tickets, while Lusia tried to keep her eyes trained on the ground. Still, she could not help noticing how crowded the station was with Poles and German soldiers. No Jews were to be seen, of course.

Lusia and the woman boarded the train and sat in a compartment marked for Germans. Each compartment had two benches and a rack above for suitcases and parcels. The woman spoke freely with the German soldiers in the compartment, but Lusia was playing the part of a Polish

maid, so she had to pretend that she could not understand German—
which of course, she understood all too well. It helped to look out the
window or stare at the floor. She hoped that no one could tell how much
she was shaking with fear.

The trip took the whole night. As dawn broke, the train passed Lub-
lin, and Lusia could make out the buildings and barracks of some sort of
camp high up on a hill. She saw what looked like prisoners milling about
on the grounds.

The soldier sitting across from her pointed out the window. "See that?"
he queried her. "That's the place where they put the Jews. Jews are scum."
He searched her face for a reaction, but Lusia shook her head, indicating
that she did not understand. She knew then that what she had seen was
the death camp Majdanek.

"I can recognize a Jew a mile away," the soldier boasted. Lusia shrugged
in feigned ignorance, but her heart was pounding. What if he knew? What
if he denounced her? But the soldier must have been satisfied that she was
an illiterate Polish maid, for he no longer tried to engage her in conversation. Lusia prayed that no one would look at her, because the pounding
of her heart would surely give her away.

Finally, the train arrived at the Warsaw station. She and her escort disembarked and walked toward the streetcar. Lusia kept her eyes on the
ground. The *volksdeutsche* asked if the car went to Franciszkanska Street;
hearing an affirmative answer, she and Lusia boarded.

Franciszkanska Street was in a poor section of town, previously a part
of the Jewish ghetto. When the two women found the address, Lusia
cringed at how run-down the building appeared. Still, they mounted the
rickety steps to the third floor, found the apartment, and knocked on the
door.

It seemed a long time before someone answered. Then the door
opened a crack, and Lusia's cousin Leon looked out. If she expected to be
greeted with open arms, she was mistaken. When Leon saw Lusia, he recoiled in horror. "What are you doing here?" he whispered angrily. "How
did you know how to find us? Who is this woman?" he asked, indicating
the *volksdeutsche*. "Don't you realize you could get us killed?"

Lusia started speaking in rapid Polish, trying to explain all that had
happened to her.

"Go away!" Leon hissed at her. "You will bring us nothing but trouble!"

5   The Shattering of Peace in Hungary

FROM THE MOMENT HE MET ANNA BRÜNN on Christmas Eve 1941, no other girl existed for Paul Ornstein. From her very first note to him—the one she stuffed into the finger of the gloves he had left behind in her aunt Piri's apartment—he was thoroughly smitten. She was only fourteen years old, and he was a worldly man of seventeen, a rabbinic student in the cosmopolitan city of Budapest, but she was beautiful and sweet-natured, lively and intelligent. All this was instantly apparent from the moment he saw her, even though his impromptu visit at the apartment of Anna's aunt Piri had not given Anna any time at all to dress or brush her hair.

Her youth may have seemed an obstacle to this young love affair, but Paul Ornstein was a young man used to dealing with problems and overcoming challenges. Somewhat headstrong but never wavering when a decision had to be made, he assessed a situation, made a plan of action, and forged ahead. His friends considered him something of a dreamer, but they could not argue with his determination. As he pondered all sides of a situation, he also considered the possibility of defeat, but that never deterred him for long. If he chose not to act because he might not succeed, he would never act at all. Paul had such faith in his own abilities, intellect, and emotional strength that success nearly always seemed to him the most probable outcome.

Of course, there were circumstances beyond his control, situations about which he could do nothing. That his father could barely make a living, for example, because of the anti-Jewish laws that prohibited Jewish men from working in certain professions and that kept Gentile firms from employing Jews—those laws Paul could not change. But he could tutor students in Budapest and relieve his father's financial burdens by sending a good portion of his earnings to his brothers, Zoli and Tibi, who, like Anna, were attending the gymnasium in Debrecen. He could also help his sister, Judith, who was studying in Budapest to be a dental technician. Fortunately, no tuition was charged to students at the rabbinic seminary, so beyond his meager living expenses, Paul did not need much. His self-esteem and self-respect were intact, fostered by his parents' and siblings' faith and confidence in him and his own strong belief that whatever he endeavored—with hard work as well as determined focus—would be realized. It simply never occurred to him that Anna Brünn would not fall for him as hard as he had fallen for her. He never considered the possibility that his pursuit of this animated, energetic, and interesting young girl would come to naught.

As soon as he received the note Anna had stuffed into one of the fingers of the gloves he had left behind at Aunt Piri's, Paul sat down to compose a letter to Anna. But what to say? Should he write simply, inquiring after her health, her schoolwork, and her activities in Debrecen? Or should it be something deeper, more meaningful, where he would confess his true feelings for her?

Putting pen to paper, Paul composed a masterpiece, full of references to Baudelaire and Voltaire. He wrote of his studies, what they meant to him, and how he was not sure that he wanted to study to become a rabbi but that he did love Jewish history, philosophy, and literature. He confessed to Anna that he would really like to study medicine, but for right now, it was impossible, what with the *numerus clausus* act, keeping Jewish enrollment to just 6 percent of the entire university population. Perhaps there would be another way, when the anti-Semitic government was out of power.

One thing Anna and Paul had in common was their ardent Zionism, which had been fostered in their homes and at their schools. Both of them had hopes of emigrating to Palestine. Paul had spent four weeks during the previous summer at a camp in the Hungarian mountains, where young people were prepared physically, spiritually, and intellectually for life in Palestine.

Now that love had entered his life, Paul found his situation in Budapest more tolerable. Although he was still conflicted about studying for the rabbinate, since he knew his true calling was medicine, his situation no longer felt desperate. With Anna, anything would be possible.

Yet, to realize these possibilities, he and Anna would have to leave Hungary and begin life elsewhere. If only there were a way out. The Germans had blocked every escape route. They had annexed Austria and Czechoslovakia, invaded Poland, and were at war with the Russians to the east. There was nowhere to run. Food in Hungary was now rationed, since whatever crops grew in the rich Hungarian soil were harvested and transported to Germany.

By 1942, life had become less tolerable for the Jews, although they were still permitted to live in their own homes, earn whatever living they could, and attend their own schools. Germany, however, was exacting more from the Hungarians in terms of adherence to their restrictive policies toward the Jews. The anti-Semitic government in Hungary was only too happy to cooperate with the German allies.

Stories about the fate of the Jews from Germany and Poland made their way to Hungary via travelers and escapees from those countries. The Hungarian Jews were well aware that whole Jewish communities had disappeared in Germany and Poland, but they were somehow convinced that this would not happen to them. For one thing, their country's alliance with Germany raised a protective umbrella over them, shielding them from the war clouds of Europe. For another, Jews were still allowed to practice their religion relatively unmolested. Jewish students were still beaten by thugs, and teachers often looked the other way when a Jewish student was jumped, but the idea that they would not survive never occurred to the Hungarian Jews. It was too preposterous to believe that the Germans had in place a systematic plan to murder all the Jews of Europe. Wasn't the whole world watching? The Hungarian government, despite its already severe anti-Semitic laws and regulations, would protect them. At any rate, any government, however harsh, was certainly preferable to being in the hands of the Russians—that would be unthinkable. Better to follow the laws and lie low. The German army had already suffered some defeats, especially now that the United States was in the war. It would all soon blow over.

Anna Brünn was much more politically naive than her friend Paul, but she was aware of the increased suffering of her family. In her small town, the forty Jewish families were more visible than in the larger towns and cities and therefore easy to single out for harassment. On her visits home to Szendro from school in Debrecen, Anna could see the toll this was taking on her parents.

Her father was becoming increasingly depressed; it was like him to react to the harassment with passivity, to retreat to his books and private thoughts. Anna felt deeply for him. She adored her father. She also felt her personality was much like his. She, too, shied away from confrontation;

she was a sweet-natured, giving child, whose greatest joy was to try to please those around her.

Her mother, in contrast, felt it was important to get feelings and thoughts out into the open, the better to solve problems and reduce conflict. Sophie was good at assessing a situation and formulating a plan of action, while her husband, William, would withdraw from this challenge—a challenge his formidable wife would just as gladly embrace.

Still, Anna felt totally comfortable with both of her parents. She willingly practiced the lessons they taught her about Judaism, respect for learning, love of family, and hope for the future. She felt so close to her mother that when she received one of those extraordinary letters from Paul Ornstein, with its literary and philosophical references, she gladly read it aloud to Sophie and asked for her comments. Sophie, too, was impressed by the breadth of knowledge of this articulate young man.

Paul and Anna could communicate only by letters. The Brünn family did not have a phone; neither, for that matter, did the Ornsteins in Hajdunanas. To speak by telephone, both parties would have to agree on a specific time for the call, which would then have to be placed from a post office in one city to a post office in the other. Even if those arrangements were successful, the telephone lines were not always reliable, so letters passed swiftly between Szendro and Hajdunanas during the summer, Paul's filled with sophisticated quotes and passages about young love, Anna's more shy and sedate. She was just a young teenager, still discovering the world.

After his initial visit to her in December of 1941, Paul saw her again when he went home for Passover in the spring and again in June when he returned to Hajdunanas for the summer. During July of 1942, when Anna was back home in Szendro, Paul made an unexpected five-day bicycle trip from Hajdunanas to see her. When Anna saw him coming through the front gate, she ran to her mother in nervous ecstasy. "Paul's here!" she shouted to Sophie, tugging at her sleeve. "What should I do?" Anna was just barely fifteen years old, and while she had many young boys vying for her attention, none had embarked on an arduous bicycle journey during a hot and muggy summer just to visit her.

For the first time, Paul met Anna's parents and her brothers, Paul and Andrew. The young people went swimming and picnicked by the river. At night, they listened to the town's gypsies play their music at one of the gypsy weddings so frequent in the summer. The merriment would continue long into the night, and parents often had to come drag their children inside, so mesmerizing were the sounds of the gypsies' fiddles.

Too soon, however, the visit ended. "It's obvious that he's in love," Sophie commented to her daughter as Paul waved goodbye and cycled off down the unpaved road. "You'd better take that young man seriously."

"But I'm only fifteen," Anna replied. "Maybe I'm not ready for all that attention." Still, for the remainder of 1942 and throughout 1943, Anna continued to delight in his infrequent visits and weekly letters. She answered them immediately; as before, Paul's letters were ardent and full of references to love and romance, while Anna's were more demure. "Somehow," said Sophie, knowingly, after listening to Anna read a passage from one of Paul's letters, "I think this is the man you will marry." "I've got plenty of time to think about getting married," said Anna. "I've got years to think about it."

For Steve Hornstein, 1942 would be the last year he would spend living at home in Hajdunanas and the last year he would attend the gymnasium. Like his friend Paul Ornstein, he was aware that life for Jews was becoming more restricted, but he never suspected the worst—not even when a cousin who had been thrown out of Poland came to Hajdunanas and said, "We are lost. They will kill us all."

Steve's father, the president of the Hajdunanas Jewish community was incredulous. "Are you crazy?" he asked his cousin. If Salomon Hornstein, a learned and educated man, did not believe the stories of his own cousin, then why should anyone else?

Steve was busy with his tutoring responsibilities, his studies, and, since Hungary was an ally of Germany, his civil defense chores. Every male at the age of seventeen was assigned to two kinds of civil defense work and issued an identification card that specifically stated these duties. One of Steve's weekly assignments was to climb the one hundred steps to the top of the tower of the Protestant church in the town square and look out of each of the four windows of the tower in search of enemy planes from the United States, England, or Russia—any country at war with the Germans.

Steve's role was to alert the town of Hajdunanas by ringing the church bell if any such planes were spotted. Early on, Steve realized that by the time he rang the church bell after spotting an enemy plane, the town would surely be doomed; the bombs would have already done their damage. Still, Steve dutifully climbed into the bell tower each week to fulfill his assignment.

His other civil defense chore was performed with Paul, who came home from the rabbinic seminary that summer. The two of them were assigned to monitor the region's harvested wheat for an entire day and night at a large farm on the outskirts of town. The piles of wheat were highly combustible, and the Hungarian government feared that if the enemy dropped incendiary bombs on the area, the entire crop would be destroyed. Part of Paul's and Steve's job was to water the wheat during the day and stand guard over it at night.

Working outdoors during the Hungarian summers was more a gift than a chore, and Steve and Paul actually looked forward to this assignment. Once in a while, an older fellow was put on the same detail. He was most impressed with the intellectual prowess of the two younger fellows. To pass the time, he would give Paul and Steve a topic to debate, and if the two could sustain the argument at a reasonable, logical level for a prolonged period of time, they would be rewarded with a small gift of money. A memorable topic that had them debating back and forth one long night until sunrise was the advantages of city life versus country living. Paul and Steve kept the topic going for their own amusement as well as to pass the time on that warm summer evening when they could not help feeling a bit foolish about standing guard over some piles of wheat. What were they to do if the enemy actually dropped a bomb? But Jewish boys were in no position to point out to the anti-Semitic Hungarian government that its methods of defense were a waste of time and effort.

The summer before Steve left for Budapest was filled with performing his civil defense duties, tutoring his students, talking and debating with Paul, and helping his youngest brother, Henu, with his studies. Henu often made it clear that he would rather be outside kicking a soccer ball or meeting with his friends, but Steve felt it was his duty to tutor Henu, just as his brother Karl had helped prepared Steve for his exams.

Steve also spent whatever free time he could with Dr. Sreter, the general practitioner who lived next door. Dr. Sreter was Steve's mentor, the person who encouraged Steve to study medicine no matter how arduous that long road might seem. In the summer, when the doctor's wife and twin daughters were away on holiday, Steve moved into the doctor's house and helped him with his patients. He was the kind of physician who treated every sort of ailment, from sore throats to stomach aches to fractures. Dr. Sreter taught Steve everything the boy was willing to learn; during the year, Steve showed his appreciation for the doctor's counsel and patience by tutoring his daughters. It was because of this man that Steve knew he had the skills and the knowledge to become a doctor.

The autumn of 1943 brought great promise for Steve. He had graduated with straight As from the gymnasium in Hajdunanas in the spring, and that autumn he said goodbye to his parents at the railway station and boarded the train for Budapest. He planned to enroll in courses at the university there—not officially, of course—because as a Jew, he would not be eligible. But he would try to convince a few sympathetic professors to allow him to audit their classes in chemistry and physics, since these were the most important courses during the first year of medical school. Somehow, somewhere, Steve was determined to get to medical school.

Steve's older brother Shmuel, who, like Paul Ornstein, was studying at the rabbinic seminary, helped get Steve a room in the Jewish students' guest house supported by the Jewish community of Budapest. Steve lived there at minimal cost and helped defray his other expenses by tutoring students from high school and at the college level. Shmuel was also secretary of the Jewish Students Union and helped establish a laboratory in the basement of the Budapest Jewish Institute for students who were not officially enrolled at the university but were taking classes nonetheless. With his housing and educational needs looked after, Steve thrived in Budapest.

This was where Steve could shine, where others looked up to him as a leader. While his friend Paul Ornstein was considered a bit of a dreamer, more impulsive, more willing to make a decision and forge ahead, Steve was known as someone more contemplative. He was proud of his presence of mind and his ability to weigh all sides of a situation, to put himself in another's place and see how that person might react. This ability to think quickly and immediately find the right thing to do had always been his strength.

By 1943, Karl, the brother Steve most admired, had already graduated from the veterinary college at the University of Budapest and had developed a vaccine that prevented cows from contracting a very contagious form of tuberculosis found in cattle. Word of this vaccine spread quickly throughout agricultural Hungary, and Karl was summoned by the official veterinarian of the farm of Governor Miklos Horthy, the regent of Hungary, to continue his work at Horthy's large farm in eastern Hungary. This was a very prestigious position, not just for a young man but for a Jew.

Yet trouble was brewing. What were once imperceptible shifts in politics and allegiances were now seismic changes that were felt by all the Jews of Hajdunanas, especially Salomon Hornstein, the president of the Jewish community. Restrictions on Jews became more severe with each passing day, as Hungarian Nazis took over positions in the local government, the police department, the army, and the schools. The Germans were making more demands on their Hungarian allies for food and materials for their troops at the front lines and for stricter compliance with their anti-Jewish laws, now that Italy had dropped out of the alliance with Germany.

Nonetheless through the autumn of 1943, life proceeded on course for Steve. He took courses as a special student in the science curriculum at the university and tutored students. His younger brother Jerry was also in Budapest, training to become a jeweler and a watchmaker. The three Hornstein brothers got together for holidays and other important occasions. Steve also found time in his busy schedule of studying and tutoring to visit with Paul, who was talking about marrying Anna Brünn. Steve had never actually met Anna but felt he knew her since Paul talked about her so much. During the winter holiday, Paul visited Anna, while Steve, Shmuel, and Jerry remained in Budapest, celebrating Chanukah together. Endlessly, they debated the future of Hungary. Would the country be drawn into the fighting? Now that the Allies were making some progress, the Germans could not possibly hold out for long.

In January 1944, with the holiday season over, the residents of Budapest settled in for the harsh Hungarian winter. Paul Ornstein returned to the city, carrying with him dozens of pictures of Anna Brünn that he gazed at lovingly to help pass the time on the long train ride. He composed a letter to her, telling her all about his weeks at home in Hajdunanas, reminding her to look for his brothers, Zoli and Tibi, at the Debrecen gymnasium. He did not know when he could see her again; perhaps when he came through Debrecen on his way home for Passover.

The winter of 1944 was cold and dreary, lit up only by the heated debates and discussions among the students of Budapest. Rumors of a German invasion were everywhere. The rabbinic school was rife with stories of the ferocious Nazi soldiers. Were the rumors true? To believe them meant that the situation in Hungary was hopeless, that soon the country would have no choice but to capitulate. Then what would happen to the Jews? To believe that a German invasion was inevitable was an acquiescence to certain confusion about their future. Would they be rounded up and deported? To argue and believe in the other side—that Horthy could continue to appease Germany with Hungarian labor camp workers and agricultural support—was much more palatable, because it meant the Jews could stay alive. The debates continued throughout the winter.

By mid-March, Steve, Jerry, and Shmuel were making plans to go home in a few weeks for the Passover holiday, but before they could leave, Steve wanted to take care of a nagging toothache. He arranged an appointment for March 17 at the dental department of the Jewish Hospital in Budapest, and while sitting in the waiting room, he happened to look out of the window that overlooked a small railroad depot for freight trains only. What he saw puzzled and then frightened him. Men were unloading long lines of German freight cars filled with new military trucks. It could only mean one thing: the Germans were going to invade soon, and when their soldiers arrived in Hungary by train, the trucks would be waiting for them.

As soon as he could, Steve rushed to find Jerry. Together they went to Shmuel's place to seek his advice. Should they all go home to Hajdunanas to be with the family for Passover? What if they remained in Budapest? Perhaps Steve was wrong, maybe those trucks were for the Russian front, perhaps the German soldiers would just be coming through Hungary on their way to Russia? The rumor mill was churning at an unbelievable speed by now, with students rushing about the city, packing up their rooms, talking, debating, deciding what to do.

On March 19, 1944, there was nothing more to talk about. What the Hungarian Jews had dreaded for some time became a reality when Adolf Eichmann, one of Hitler's closest henchmen, arrived in Budapest. Eichmann was a very successful Nazi officer, having already fulfilled Hitler's promise by making most of Europe's great nations *judenfrei,* or free of Jews. He had liquidated the Jewish populations of Germany, Austria, France, Belgium, Holland, Russia, Poland, Rumania, the Baltic states, Yugoslavia, and Albania. Now, his mission was to do the same for Hungary.

Overnight, with the active help of the Hungarian Arrow Party, Hitler's army occupied Budapest. A reign of terror descended over the 250,000 Jews of Budapest, one-fourth of the capital's population. Eichmann brought the gendarmes from the countryside to help the Arrow Party and the Budapest police. This vehemently anti-Semitic group, which had been in charge of policing outlying areas, was known for its physical abuse and incarceration of Jews on false charges. It was these gendarmes who had made life so miserable for the Jews in small cities like Hajdunanas and in villages like Szendro.

With armed and uniformed Nazis—both German and Hungarian—on every street corner, the three Hornstein brothers discussed what to do. Since Shmuel was the director of the Jewish dormitory, he felt he had to stay in Budapest to take care of matters there, but he urged Steve and Jerry to return to Hajdunanas right away. Packing up a few belongings, the two Hornstein brothers threaded their way through the mass of people clogging the streets of Budapest and reached the main railway station. Jerry went inside to stand in line for the tickets to Hajdunanas, while Steve stayed in the lobby to assess the situation.

One thing he noticed was that at each entrance to the train tracks were representatives of the Budapest police department, detectives in civilian clothes, a uniformed German officer from the Gestapo, and one or two other soldiers from the German army. Each person attempting to pass through these portals was being asked for identification, and what interested the guards who were checking these documents was whether the person was a Jew. Gentiles were being allowed through to board the trains, but the Jews were being told to step aside.

Steve thought quickly. Did he have any identifying papers that did not state his religion? All identification documents in Hungary—citizenship papers, passports, driver's licenses, student passes—indicated religion. Except for one document—his civil defense card, the one issued to him so he could climb the bell tower of the Protestant church in Hajdunanas and look for enemy planes or guard the stacks of wheat at the farm during the summer. Mercifully, even Jews were capable of these "high-level" assignments.

Jerry was allowed to buy the tickets, but he could not pass through to the trains. All his identification showed that he was a Jew. Jerry stepped out of line, handed Steve a ticket, and told his older brother to try to go through. When the Hungarian policeman and a German Gestapo officer looked at Steve's document that showed his name was Hornstein, they held up their hands for Steve to wait.

"That's a Jewish name, isn't it?" asked the Hungarian guard, looking the card over for a religious affiliation. "You must be a Jew."

Steve glared at the guard and the German Gestapo officer in righteous indignation. "Hornstein is a German name," he said imperiously. "Would you entrust an important job like civil defense to a Jew?"

The Hungarian policeman contemplated that challenge for a moment and translated for the German officer. Finally, they agreed that no government in its right mind would want Jews defending it, and they waved Steve through. When he looked back before boarding the train, he saw his brother Jerry off to the side of the platform, standing with a group of other Jews who had been detained. Steve hesitated for a moment, but Jerry motioned for him to go on. Fear for his younger brother's safety kept Steve awake all night on the trip home to Hajdunanas. He dreaded explaining Jerry's absence to his parents.

Paul Ornstein was in class on Sunday, March 19, 1944, at the seminary when the door opened and three men dressed in German uniforms walked in. One man introduced himself as Adolf Eichmann and announced that the Germans would be taking over one of the rabbinic school's buildings to use as a transit camp for those people who were to be deported. The students were frightened. Paul looked out the window during this presentation and saw the German tanks rolling through the streets of Budapest.

Back in the Jewish students' dormitory that night, the young men had much on their minds. Many of them were just a few months away from certification; would they be allowed to continue? Would the seminary remain open? Would the Hungarians just lie down and allow the Germans to roll over them? What about their safety? What about their families? How could they contact them? Debating and arguing back and forth, the discussion lasted long into the night.

It became evident that the Germans were going to allow the rabbinic students to live in the dormitory as long as they had the school building in which to detain some of Budapest's most prominent Jews before deportation to a town called Kistarcsa. The students were told that their exams would still be given as scheduled, but they were so thoroughly demoralized and worried about the future that they did not want to study.

The students were forced to help the Nazis process the Jews and run the transit camp. In defiance of German authority, the rabbinic students were able to smuggle messages to the detainees' families in Budapest.

The students might have just as well been detainees themselves. Jews were not allowed to travel out of Budapest on their own; everywhere were stories of whole villages being rounded up. Paul was frantic about his parents in Hajdunanas and Anna in Debrecen. Although rare contact with his parents by telephone was possible, there was no way he could get in touch with Anna or even send a message. What would become of her?

≡

In the late afternoon on March 19, 1944, the students of the Jewish gymnasium in Debrecen had just concluded their Zionist Youth Group meeting held on the school building's second floor. The meetings always ended with some exuberant singing and dancing, the students throwing their hearts and souls into the energetic and noisy hora, a kind of national dance of Palestine. The students felt that they had not given the dance its all unless the floor was literally shaking. As usual, Anna Brünn was at the center of the fun, the lustiest singer, the liveliest dancer of the bunch.

Amidst this frivolity, a somber-faced school administrator entered the room and clapped his hands for quiet. The students fell silent, immediately suspecting bad news. But what could it be? Was a classmate ill? Was a parent in the hospital?

With his voice cracking, the school administrator told the students that the Germans had invaded Hungary and had ordered all Jews to remain where they were. They were not to try to travel anywhere. Jews were expressly forbidden to use public transportation.

Scared and shaking, Anna ran home to Aunt Piri's apartment. She wanted desperately to go to her parents in Szendro, but Piri would not hear of it. It was far too dangerous. The Germans were everywhere, and rumor had it that they were rounding up Jews.

The next day, German tanks rolled into Debrecen, and German soldiers filled the streets. Anna had previously promised to tutor a seven-year-old girl who lived nearby, and as she walked home from the lesson at dusk on Monday, she tried to melt into the buildings so she would not draw the attention of the German soldiers. Anna could not help noticing how young they were—about her age—but how cruelly they behaved. They delighted in linking arms and shoving elderly people off the sidewalks.

When Anna let herself into the flat, a frantic Aunt Piri hurried her niece into the bedroom and ordered her under the bed. In a city rampant with rumors, Piri had heard one particularly frightening tale: the Germans were rounding up young girls and transporting them to the front to "entertain" the German soldiers. Anna obediently slid under the bed, quaking in fear.

Later that evening, Anna was spirited away to the janitor's apartment, where, it was assumed, a man could offer her more protection than young Aunt Piri. Anna stayed at the janitor's flat, never venturing outside until that Friday, when a young boy knocked on Aunt Piri's door asking for Anna Brünn.

"Who is it?" Piri asked nervously. "It's Tibi Ornstein," came the answer. "My father sent me to take Anna home to Hajdunanas." Tibi was twelve years old, but like his older brother Paul, he exuded confidence and self-assurance. He had learned that the Germans had not yet occupied the countryside, so Hajdunanas was still considered safe.

Reluctantly, Piri let Anna go to the train station with Tibi. Although Jews were not supposed to travel, the Nazis had not yet set up roadblocks or guards at all the railway stations. Tibi and Anna were allowed to board the crowded train to Hajdunanas.

All the way home, Tibi stood protectively by Anna's side, as she sat precariously in the train compartment. By the time they arrived in Hajdunanas, the Sabbath had already begun. Lajos, Paul's father, had taken the youngest child, six-year-old Lacika, to synagogue. Paul's mother was waiting for her husband's return and for Tibi to bring Paul's girlfriend, whom the Ornsteins had never met, to their home.

When Anna first greeted Paul's mother, she felt immediate empathy for her. She saw before her a beautiful woman with lines of worry and concern etched into her face. She looked tired, as if she had lain awake for many nights worrying about her sons, wondering what war would mean for them. Although Zoli and Tibi were home from Debrecen, they had not had any word from Paul in Budapest.

Mrs. Ornstein saw how tired Anna looked, so she served her some chicken soup and suggested she go right to bed. That soup had eggs shirred into it—how could Mrs. Ornstein prepare such a wonderful meal when food was rationed? Anna immediately relaxed, enjoying the warmth of the kitchen and the family that had reached out to gather her in.

The next day was the Sabbath, and Anna joined the Ornstein family on their long walks and visits to their friends and relatives. Everyone seemed to know her; evidently, Paul had spoken of her lovingly and often. But now the discussion was consumed with news from the larger cities and the possibilities that lay ahead.

The next day, Anna arose early and watched as Paul's mother built a fire in the kitchen. Eager to help, she was thrilled when Mrs. Ornstein asked her to do some sewing for Paul so she could send him a package of clothes. This signaled to her that Paul's mother had accepted her as the girl her son loved. At that moment, she felt very close to Paul's mother and to his family.

The citizens of Hajdunanas knew that the arrival of the Germans was imminent, so when Anna said she wanted to go home to her own parents, the Ornsteins had no choice except to let her go. Since the trip to Szendro was thought to be too dangerous because the Germans had no doubt set up blockades on the Tisza River, Anna agreed to return to Debrecen to see what her aunt Piri would advise. On Monday morning, Paul's father took her to the train station. They walked through fields of corn and wheat instead of on the roads of the city, lest the Germans detect them and thwart Anna's travels. Holding Lajos's hand as they hurried toward the station, she could feel his fear and tension. Anna knew how concerned he was for his family's future. When she boarded the train and watched Lajos from the window, she knew this visit had been something special, that life in Hungary would never be the same.

Fortunately, the Germans had not set up any checkpoints yet between Hajdunanas and Debrecen, so Anna was able to make the trip back to Aunt Piri's with no fear that her documents would be subject to scrutiny. In Debrecen, however, everything was chaotic. German soldiers were everywhere, soldiers who looked no older than Anna herself. She realized then that all the young German men were at the front, and these teenagers had been charged with leading the invasion.

Five or six students from the gymnasium in Debrecen lived near Szendro, and one of them contacted Anna at her aunt's and asked if she would like to try with them to get home. Quickly, she agreed. She knew she would feel safe there. But how would they get past the document checkpoints? Every identification paper they had said they were Jews.

On the appointed day, Anna said a tearful goodbye to Aunt Piri and headed for the train station with her five young friends. Buying tickets was no problem, but boarding the train would entail significant risk. The students put their plan into action.

Because the soldiers guarding the train station were so young, they were happy to banter with people their own age. So when the group from Szendro with their contagious laughter caught the soldiers' attention, they were eager to join in the fun. When the soldiers finally moved on, a boy from the group who had boarded the train when the soldiers were distracted, signaled that it was safe to board.

Still, they knew they would have to show their identification papers when the train reached the roadblock on the bridge over the Tisza River. The group was aware of the fate of a Jew discovered on the train: instant death. Still, the same plan went into effect. Guards at the checkpoint, like the ones at the station, were the same age as the Szendro teenagers. The guards were so taken with their new young friends that they gave their papers only a cursory glance. The students, however, were prepared; they kept their thumbs over the stamp that said "Jewish." The rest of the trip was uneventful.

When Anna ran up the walk to her house, her parents were shocked but relieved to see her. At least they knew the whereabouts of this one child; their two sons, Paul and Andrew, had been sent some weeks earlier to forced labor camps.

Anna found Szendro's Jewish community sick with fear. Everyone, including her parents, was trying to obliterate the word *Jew* from all identification documents. Anna was too exhausted to think about the Germans and their cruelties, real or imagined. She climbed into her mother's bed and slept the most peaceful sleep she had had in weeks. Too soon, her waking hours would become a nightmare.

6 Lusia:
Underground in Warsaw

LUSIA, SOBBING, TREMBLING, PLEADING, half hysterical with the loss of her mother, frantic over the whereabouts of her brother, fearing for her own life and the future—whatever future lay in store—begged her cousin Leon to let her into the apartment on Franciszkanska Street in Warsaw. Because it was too dangerous to let her stand out in the hallway where she could be spotted, Leon grabbed her and whisked her inside. She was so relieved to be off the dangerous streets of Warsaw that she put her head in her hands and cried. As best she could, she poured out her story, going back to what seemed like years ago, as she explained how her father and brother had been arrested on the streets of Lvov, how the family had been told of Norbert's death, how her mother had been selected out of the marching line in the work camp, how Salo—Samek and Leon's brother—had taken pity on her, a seventeen-and-a-half-year-old girl left alone to care for her younger brother. Just telling the story unburdened Lusia tremendously. It was a relief to be out of that camp, to be among relatives.

When she had calmed down, Lusia was able to take stock of her surroundings. The shabbily furnished apartment was on the top floor of the building, and though she was forbidden to look out of the windows, she could confirm her first impression: they were in a very poor, run-down part of the city. The flat was small and cramped, and she could see why Leon had been so reluctant to admit her. Already living there on false Aryan papers as Polish Catholics with Polish names were Leon and his wife, Gerdie; his brother, Samek; their mother, Anna; a young woman named Krzysia; and another couple that was also using the apartment as a hiding place.

Lusia had known Leon and Gerdie since 1939, when they had returned to Lvov from Czechoslovakia after Hitler had annexed that country in the

Anschluss. Leon, in his early thirties, was a physician, and Samek, in his late twenties, had been in business for himself in Lvov. They all lived in a house about two blocks from the Schwarzwalds. They were several years older than Lusia, and she immediately felt protected and safe with them.

Before coming to Warsaw, Samek had been ordered to work for the German army at the Janowska forced labor camp. One night, a German officer warned him that the next day all the Jews would be sent away to a concentration camp. The German officer liked Samek and arranged for false travel papers for him; Samek was able to escape early the next morning. He contacted some people he knew in Warsaw who steered him to the apartment on Franciszkanska Street. He immediately sent for his brother, sister-in-law, and mother.

Lusia's main concern now was not just her own safety but also her brother's. It took some convincing for Leon and Samek to agree to allow Milek to come to the apartment—the more people who knew where and who they were, the easier for them to be denounced and handed over to the Germans. He would be another mouth to feed, one more person to look after, and a child at that—but Lusia had jewelry with her that could buy them food, shelter, time, and protection. After a hurried and hushed conference of whispers and gestures, Leon and Samek relented. Lusia, at the first available opportunity, went to a working phone and called the woman who had accompanied her to Warsaw to say it was safe to bring Milek to the apartment.

She waited all that week for Milek to arrive. Every footstep brought both fear and hope: fear that it would be the Nazis on a search for Jews, hope that it would be a messenger with news of Milek or with Milek himself. But her brother never appeared. Every few days Lusia would call her former escort, only to be told to wait, have patience, that he was on his way. The woman's brother had picked up Milek as promised and taken him on the train—that was all she knew. Lusia would just have to be patient. Lusia waited throughout May 1943, but Milek never arrived.

With her brother very much on her mind, Lusia tried to adjust to her new surroundings. Samek and Leon managed to get new false papers for her that said her Polish name was Marysia and that she was the sister of Samek—his Polish name was Gustav. Soon, she found herself answering to that name as if it had been hers for years.

One thing that she had noticed immediately was the acrid smell of smoke, as if a nearby fire had been left to smolder. She could also hear gunfire not too far away from their apartment. "What is that?" she asked Leon. "Are the Nazis trying to burn the city?"

Leon explained that just before she had arrived, the Jews in the Warsaw ghetto had mounted an uprising and were still holding out in small pockets before they were forced to surrender. The Jewish ghetto was not far from where the Schwarzwalds were now hiding. Lusia could not help feeling a mixture of pride and sorrow as Samek told her the story. When would this war ever end? And who knew what the outcome would bring? Would all this effort at hiding and disguise be for nothing? Would the Nazis kill them anyway?

Now that so many people were either living in the apartment or knew that they were there with false papers, Samek and Leon decided they needed a hiding place. Because the flat was on the top floor of the building, they paid the Polish janitor's son to help construct a hidden room for them under the eaves. The janitor was privy to their story, knew they were Jews in hiding, and still risked his life to do their shopping and keep their secrets. The group had to pay him for his services, of course—Lusia used the jewelry given to her by her mother in the early days of the war—but it was a huge risk to him, nevertheless.

The two Schwarzwald brothers watched warily as the janitor assembled his materials for the hiding place with the help of his son. Samek did not trust the janitor's son; now it was one more person who knew that the Jews were there. Despite Samek's misgivings, the janitor and his son were paid for their work. The hiding place did give the group a feeling of safety and security.

Still, Samek was suspicious. He could not put his finger on it exactly; something was just not right about the janitor's son. "I think we ought to move," he told the group one night. "Move?" Gerdie asked her brother-in-law incredulously. "Where do you think we can go?" "I know a place," said Leon, who had many contacts in the city. "Samek is probably right about the janitor's son. He may have already told the Gestapo where we are hiding."

Thanks to his connections, Leon rented another apartment for them, but they could not go there until that night. What could they do in the meantime? They certainly could not go out together; although they had false papers, some of them looked more Jewish than Polish and, as a group, would certainly arouse suspicion. Still, Samek insisted that they vacate the apartment right away; he felt it was too dangerous to stay there a minute longer. At the last moment, the other young couple that had been sharing the apartment elected to stay behind. They felt safe, especially with the new hiding place. But Samek was adamant and ordered the rest of them out of Franciszkanska Street.

That morning the six of them dispersed, but Krzysia and Lusia, the two teenagers, wanted to stay together. Until that night, they had nowhere to go and nothing to eat. Fortunately, it was a sunny August day, so it was not unusual for people to be outside, running errands or shopping for whatever scarce supplies could be found in the meager Warsaw marketplace. As the two youngest people in the apartment, the girls had formed a firm friendship and felt they would be safe in each other's company.

They walked through the streets speaking Polish quietly, taking care not to make eye contact with anyone passing by. After hours of what seemed like aimless wandering, they were tired and hungry, so they headed for a nearby church. Benches ringed the church's entrance, so they knew this would give them a chance to sit down. If the benches were occupied, they would simply go inside the church and pray.

"I'm not going into a church to pray," said Krzysia. "I'll sit there, all right, but I'm not praying." "Yes, you are," whispered Lusia adamantly. "You can't just sit there. Why else would we be in church?"

They had all learned the Catholic prayers in the apartment on Franciszkanska Street, because a good knowledge of Catholicism and its rules and rituals was an important part of their identity. After all, they were carrying papers that said they were Polish Catholics. Lusia knew the rosary by heart, the stations of the cross, and even the custom of putting hay under the tablecloth at Christmas time to show respect for Jesus Christ, who had been born in a stable. If the unthinkable happened and they were caught and questioned, it was of vital importance to their authenticity to appear conversant and knowledgeable in their adopted religion. Jewish men were easy to identify; maybe a Jewish woman could fool the Gestapo by solid grounding in her new identity.

Just as Lusia and Krzysia were about to enter the church, two youngsters, no more than six years old, ran up to them, pointing and taunting. "Jew!" they cried, loud enough so that bystanders turned around. "You're Jews!"

Lusia grabbed them by their arms. "Stop that this instant," she hissed at them. "I'll turn you over to the police if you say that again!" The two boys, frightened by this young woman whose tenacious clutch showed she meant business, wriggled free of her grasp and ran away. The sound of her own heartbeat throbbed loudly in her ears.

"I'm ready to pray," whispered Krzysia with great relief.

They stayed in the church a long time, praying to God and fingering their rosaries. When no one was in earshot, they whispered together, plotting a strategy for traveling by streetcar early that evening to their new address. Traversing the city took much planning.

The two teenagers stayed in the church most of the day, but finally left when they felt people were becoming aware of their presence. They had no food with them and no money to buy any, so they continued to walk around, eyes cast downward, whispering to one another only when necessary. Since policemen and Gestapo were on every street corner, the two of them had to look as if they had a destination in mind.

Finally, it was time to board the streetcar. Although they knew the address—Raszynska Street—neither one had any idea how far away they were from that part of town. They rode the streetcar, changing, transferring, and finally arriving in another part of Warsaw, on a clean-swept street with new houses and modern apartment buildings.

The flat where they were staying was very large and decorated, however scantily, with new, modern furniture. Lusia figured that the apartment had once belonged to Jews, for why else would it have been left empty? She did not want to think about where the owners were now.

A man named Wojciech and his wife, a pleasant older couple, had taken over the apartment with their daughter and son-in-law. Mr. Wojciech, a decent fellow, was the building's caretaker. He knew the whole Schwarzwald story and agreed to rent them two rooms in his new large living quarters. Leon, Gerdie, and Lusia slept in one room; Samek, the mother, and Krzysia had the other. The six of them pooled whatever resources they could to pay the rent. This took the last of whatever money Lusia's mother's jewelry had brought them. When there was no more money for food, Wojciech's son-in-law agreed to lend Samek the funds he needed. Samek promised to pay him back after the war.

The other inhabitants of the apartment house knew nothing about their new neighbors, not even that they existed. Anything the six of them had to do had to be accomplished during the day while everyone else was out at work. Betrayal was always a distinct possibility, so between the hours of nine and four, the secret tenants moved freely around the apartment, cooking what meager food they could buy, washing their scant items of clothing, reading over and over the few books in the apartment, and sharing any scrap of news they could scrape together.

At four o'clock in the afternoon, they removed their shoes, sat down at the table in one of the rooms, and played bridge until they were sure the building's tenants were asleep. Only then was it safe to move about. They could not go out; no one except Wojciech and his family could come in. The group never left their two rooms except early in December, when they were invited to see the family's Christmas tree. Other than that, night followed day predictably and, thankfully, without incident. Lusia and her cousins never lost sight of the undisputed fact that if the Gestapo found them, they would be killed instantly. Although it was clearly a financial arrangement for the Wojciechs, they, too, were risking their lives; the Nazis would kill anyone discovered providing aid and shelter to Jews.

The danger of their situation was made clear to them when, on the first night at Raszynska Street, Leon announced that the couple that had stayed behind on Franciszkanska Street had been betrayed by the janitor's son just as Samek had predicted. The couple was ordered from the apartment and probably killed immediately or sent to a concentration camp. Lusia shuddered audibly. Just as easily, that could have been their fate.

In spite of all that had happened to her, Lusia felt that luck had intervened to keep her safe. Somehow, at the greatest moments of despair, fortune had brought her an escape hatch of sorts: she was lucky to have met the Sonderlings who had helped her get false travel papers, lucky that her cousin Salo had provided her with Leon and Samek's address in Warsaw, fortunate to have had the presence of mind to squelch the cries of the two boys at the church, lucky that Samek had the sharp instincts that told them to leave the apartment on Franciszkanska Street just in time. It was better to think about these good things than to concentrate on all the terrible circumstances of her young life. To dwell on her parents, her brothers, her home—it raised too many questions for which she had no answers.

Early in December 1943, on a bright sunny day, Lusia and her cousins heard a volley of shots in the courtyard of their apartment building. They tiptoed to the window and looked out to see a horrifying sight: dead bodies and blood everywhere. That night, Mr. and Mrs. Wojciech called Samek aside. "You will have to disappear from the apartment," he whispered. "The Gestapo may come back again after finding Jews in the building."

Evidently, another Jewish family also had been hiding in the apartment house. Someone who knew they were there had betrayed them. Perhaps they had been spotted through the window, or perhaps one of the apartment's tenants had heard suspicious noises. The enemies were not always visible, and they were everywhere. People were capable of desperate acts during times like these, with no food, an uncertain future, and days and nights of relentless shootings and roundups on the city streets. Homeless, destitute, hungry people roamed Warsaw, begging for relief from their hopeless situations. It was an exercise in frustration to try and figure out what a panicked person would do. For a little money, some people would do anything.

Yet desperate people also performed acts of great kindness and generosity in the face of real danger. The Wojciechs were one such family. Devout Christians, they provided a safe haven for the Schwarzwald group for as long as possible, until it became evident that the safety of all involved was directly threatened. The Schwarzwalds clearly understood why they had to leave the apartment house.

They had little to pack up and carry with them, so under the safety of darkness, but before curfew—although the constant fire bombs could turn night into day—the Schwarzwald group abandoned the apartment on Raszynska Street. Leon and Gerdie knew yet another address where they could go, but Samek, Krzysia, and Lusia were left to their own devices. Samek's mother went with Gerdie and Leon, her older son.

Before they split up, Lusia, Samek, and Krzysia arranged to receive a telephone call from Leon at a certain phone booth outside a nearby restaurant. By the next day, Leon promised to have a new address where they could all reunite.

Since the other three had nowhere else to go, they went to a nearby hotel with a small bar on the ground floor. Samek, Lusia, and Krzysia sat in the bar but ordered nothing to drink—they had no money to pay for it. They remained at a corner table discussing possible plans for the night, though in truth, not one of them had any idea where to go. No one was allowed on the street after curfew, so they had to come up with something quickly.

Samek noticed the bar owner, an older woman, staring at them. "I'm going to ask her if we can spend the night here," he said to the younger women. "She'll never agree," said Lusia. "It's too dangerous to even ask. She could turn us in."

Samek prided himself on his ability to read people's faces, so he brushed aside his cousin's entreaties and approached the owner. "Could you let us stay here for the night?" he asked, without explaining who they were or showing her his false identification papers. The woman motioned for Samek, Lusia, and Krzysia to follow her upstairs, where she gave them a room with one tiny bed in which all three slept. The next morning, however, the three were outside walking the streets of Warsaw, hoping that Leon would call at the appointed time with an address where they all could go. But they did not hear from Leon.

Samek had a girlfriend named Zosia, who was also living in Warsaw with false papers. Zosia was blonde with Aryan facial features and moved freely about the city. Still, it was dangerous to offer housing, however temporary, to strangers who might or might not be Jewish. Although Lusia and Krzysia had false papers and did not look particularly Jewish, the unwritten law of false identity was this: never call attention to yourself by changing your daily habits. Inviting company to live with you for however short a time was waving a flag that could signal trouble. Still, when Samek contacted her, she agreed to let Lusia and Krzysia stay at her place that night.

Samek felt great relief that the rest of the group was safe, but he himself had nowhere to go. The woman who let them have a room the first night had made it clear that there was nothing more she could do; for him to also stay at Zosia's place would arouse too much suspicion. Zosia, Lusia, and Krzysia spent the day walking around Warsaw with him, but they had to get back to Zosia's apartment before curfew. Anyone still on the streets would be arrested or shot.

With only himself to look after, Samek went into a beer hall and sat at a table waiting for the Gestapo to come and shoot him. After all, he had no reason to be there: he had no money with which to buy a drink, no friends to meet there, and no business to conduct with anyone. In spite of his false identity papers, he looked Jewish—and if the police were truly suspicious, they could order him to drop his pants so they could be sure. Samek figured this was the end for him; he was thankful that the rest of the group had found safe places, even for this one night.

While he was wondering how his short life would end, a man in dirty work clothes sat down next to him at the table. They nodded to each other in greeting. After a minute, Samek decided to take yet another chance. He whispered, "I have nowhere to sleep tonight. Do you have a place?" The man did not flinch. Wordlessly, he got up from the table and motioned for Samek to follow him.

As they walked on silently through the darkening streets, Samek realized that the man could be taking him to the police station. It was absolutely forbidden for a Pole to harbor a Jew, and the man would be shot instantly if Samek was discovered in his home. Surely he was being led, right at this moment, to his certain death.

They walked on in silence until they came to a rundown old house badly in need of repair. The man motioned for Samek to come inside. Following him up the rickety staircase, Samek began to feel relief; he would not be denounced after all.

His host opened the door to a tiny, filthy room with a dirty mattress made from straw. In the corner stood a cobbler's bench. The man was obviously a shoemaker. He suggested that if Samek was tired, he could sleep on the mat.

Grateful for the safety offered him, Samek slept fitfully. When he awoke, the shoemaker asked if he was hungry. Samek was starving, so he gladly accepted the plate of food his new friend offered him. He took one bite and gagged; whatever it was, it was awful, foul-tasting, the worst thing Samek had ever swallowed. He turned away from the man and vomited quietly into his handkerchief. He did not want to spurn the man's generosity.

Samek stayed with the shoemaker for a few more days, sleeping on the only mattress, eating his meager food. The man never asked why he was hiding, but Samek figured that he knew he was a Jew. If angels lived on earth, this destitute cobbler surely was one.

After a few days, Samek made contact with his brother, Leon, who told him that Lusia and Krzysia were waiting for him in another flat on Leszno Street, right across from the Jewish ghetto. A crumbling wall was all that separated the ghetto from the rest of Warsaw, and Leszno Street ran alongside this wall. Lusia could look out of the window of their apartment and see the bombed and burned out ruins of the Jewish ghetto that the Nazis had destroyed after the Jewish uprising. Lusia knew that she could have just as easily been living on that side of the wall, fighting for her life alongside the Jewish resistance. Instead, luck, or God, or fate, or perseverance, or whatever-it-was had intervened to protect her from such an ending.

She was not allowed to dwell on these possibilities for very long since the group had some real challenges ahead. For one thing, all their money was spent. They had no food. Somehow, they would have to pay rent to their new landlords, Zbyszek and his wife, Irene, who owned the apartment and who lived there with their two small children and Irene's mother. Gerdie, Leon, and Leon's mother had found a place to live in another part of Warsaw known as "the new city."

The three of them—Samek, Krzysia, and Lusia—lived in one sparsely furnished room in the old apartment house. Lusia and Krzysia shared one small bed. The bed was also used for seating, since the room had only a few chairs. The kitchen was old and dark. Everyone, including Zbyszek, Irene, the two children, and Irene's mother, shared the one old bathroom with its unreliable plumbing. In a way, though, this was the best place in which they had lived, because Zbyszek and Irene made them feel so comfortable.

Sharing these close quarters, especially since their daily lives were controlled by constant tension, fear, and uncertainty, could have easily torn apart this close-knit group of relatives and friends. Yet, somehow, they managed to put their differences aside, as if tacitly agreeing to save their emotions for safer times, when giving vent to anger over whose crust of bread was bigger, whose bed was wider, and whose chores were easier would be a luxury they could more easily indulge. For now, nothing mattered but their safety and survival.

Surviving without any means to pay for the apartment and their meager meals shut out the small matters that could have led to squabbles in ordinary times. Now Samek had to go to Zbyszek and confess that they did not have any money right now but would pay the monthly rent of five hundred Polish zlotys as soon as they could. Zbyszek, a soft-hearted fellow who liked his vodka, accepted Samek's promise and told his tenant not to worry. He poured Samek a stiff drink, which Samek heartily accepted, even though it was early in the morning. In fact, every morning Zbyszek invited Samek to join him in liquid refreshment, which Samek felt obligated to accept. The man was kind enough to wait patiently for his rent; he should not have to drink alone.

In addition to the rent, they needed to buy food and medicine when necessary. Samek hit on an idea: they would make cigarettes and sell them on the black market. He waited for the usual objections: too dangerous, too risky, where would they get the tobacco and the cigarette papers, what if they got caught? None was raised. They all thought it was an excellent idea.

Samek's girlfriend, Zosia, was their main contact. Because she was able to move freely around Warsaw, it was Zosia who had the contacts to buy the tobacco and the cigarette papers on the black market. She would bring the empty shells and the tobacco to the apartment on Leszno Street, where Samek, Lusia, and Krzysia had set up production. Working day and night pushing the tobacco tightly into the empty shells with a metal tube held against their chests and then sealing the ends of the product with a hot iron, the three of them could turn out several hundred cigarettes a day. The easiest chore was packing the cigarettes, a hundred at a time, into cardboard boxes that Zosia would carry from kiosk to kiosk and sell on the black market. Lusia and Krzysia complained good-naturedly that they were getting holes in their chests from pushing on the metal tubes to secure the tobacco inside the cigarette papers, but the enterprise was bringing in the money needed to pay Zbyszek his back rent and to keep the group from starving.

While they made the cigarettes, they talked about their families and the little luxuries they once enjoyed, such as hot baths, clean clothes, the smell of baking bread. They constantly spoke of food: shopping for it, preparing it, eating it, savoring it. The conversations about food reminded them so much of their prewar lives that they could not help but think about their families. Lusia also mourned for her mother, father, and older brother and prayed that somehow her younger brother was still alive. She had never heard from Milek, but she refused to give up hope.

Their little cigarette enterprise, which sustained them through the late days of 1943, led to more production work for their cottage industry. A few days before Christmas, Zbyszek came to the Schwarzwalds' room and asked if they would like to produce Christmas stars out of silver foil. He would bring them all the materials they would need. Between cigarettes and Christmas stars, the group was kept busy, productive, sheltered, and fed.

Early in 1944, when Christmas stars were no longer in demand, Zbyszek and Irene came to the Schwarzwalds' room again. They were a handsome couple: Zbyszek was a Polish army officer, dignified with regal bearing; Irene was short and stocky, but she had a kind and beautiful face. They knew very well the problems the Schwarzwalds were facing and tried to help them as best they could. If the rent was late, Zbyszek shrugged it off: "Pay me later," he'd say. If the group had no money for food, Irene would see that they had something to eat.

"You know," said Zbyszek, "you really should belong to the Polish underground. Jews should be the first fighters." Samek agreed, volunteering the three of them for whatever jobs they could fulfill.

In their two previous apartments, the group had been in hiding, never leaving their four walls for fear they would be discovered and shot. While living with Zbyszek and Irene on Leszno Street, they became fixtures on the local scene. By now, there were many Polish refugees in Warsaw, renting rooms in apartment houses from friends or relatives, so their presence was not all that striking. Every Sunday, they would go to church together, genuflecting, saying the rosary, and singing the hymns like all good Catholics of Poland.

They tried to blend in with the neighborhood rather than call attention to themselves, so it was not unusual for them to go to the ragged marketplace in twos or threes or to appear on the streets in pursuit of some other errand. Still, they kept as low a profile as possible, trying to appear as ordinary Polish citizens caught up in the German occupation, as if they were distant relatives who had come to stay, whose presence was not exactly unwelcome, but whose departure would be a definite relief.

When Zbyszek asked them to deliver newspapers on behalf of the Polish government in exile in London, they were eager to cooperate. The papers carried real items about the war: where battles had been fought, victories by the Allied armies, news of Churchill and Roosevelt. Naturally, this product was strictly forbidden; if the Nazis caught anyone reading it, delivering it, or selling it, that person would be arrested or shot immediately. Since Warsaw was now rid of its Jews, the Gestapo was on the lookout for Poles collaborating with enemies of the Reich. The ghetto had been liquidated months earlier, and all the Jews who had inhabited it had been either killed or deported. Any Jews who remained in Warsaw were deep in hiding or living like the Schwarzwalds on false papers and borrowed time.

One day when Lusia was out on the street delivering her papers, she was caught in a German roadblock. The Gestapo would frequently descend on an area of the city, block it off with sawhorses and guards, and proceed to check everyone's identification papers. Anyone caught in the blocked-off area was stuck, because there was no escaping until you were dismissed—or shot or arrested for some infraction.

Lusia stood frozen to the pavement, the cloth bag of newspapers held close to her side. As the SS approached, she knew it was her last moment on earth. Delivering those newspapers—*reading* those newspapers—was a capital crime, punishable by swift death. So this was how her life would end. At least she would die for a noble cause.

"Papers!" the SS man demanded. Lusia could barely speak. But he meant her identification papers, not her newspapers. Flooded with relief, she handed over her false documents and watched as he gave them a cursory glance. He then moved on to the next person, never even looking in her shopping bag full of contraband. Again, she had survived a brush with certain death. Was she a cat with nine lives? How much longer could her luck hold out? Were her parents looking down on her, protecting her? It was something more than luck that she was still alive.

She hurried back to the apartment, eager to share this close call with her family. Samek had more good news for her. Now that they were officially members of the Polish underground, Zbyszek had arranged for them to be paid for delivering the illegal newspapers. Samek held up an American twenty dollar bill. What that could buy them on the black market! Food, of course—they were always hungry—not that there was much to eat. Warm clothes, perhaps. Certainly, it would help pay the rent they owed Zbyszek. The money from the outlawed Polish government was irregular, at best, perhaps two or three payments at the most, but certainly welcomed.

Lusia continued to deliver the underground papers, despite the close call of the week before. One night she and Samek were coming home from delivering some orders, and just as they drew near to their apartment house, a Pole approached them.

"You are Jews," he said. It was more an accusation than an inquiry. To show he meant business, he opened his jacket so Samek could see his gun. "I will hand you over to the Gestapo." Now this would be the end, Lusia thought. We will be betrayed. But Samek was not one to give up his position that quickly. "Come upstairs with us," he said to the man. "I have some money in my flat. Let's go upstairs and talk."

The three of them mounted the stairs to the apartment. While Samek showed the intruder into their room, Lusia grabbed Krzysia, and the two teenagers hid in the bathroom. Suddenly they heard a great commotion outside on the landing. Samek opened the door to find a dozen Gestapo lining the steps of the spiral staircase that led to their apartment.

"We have a report that someone here has a revolver," said the Gestapo captain. Carrying guns was strictly forbidden for Polish citizens. "It's this one," shouted Samek, pointing to the intruder. The men of the Gestapo rushed into the apartment, seized the man, and beat him so badly that he fell bleeding to the floor. All but two of the SS hustled the man out of the apartment building and arrested him.

Lusia and Krzysia remained huddled in the bathroom. Samek knocked on the door. "You have to come out," he whispered. "They want to see everyone's papers." The SS men sat down at the kitchen table and began to pore over their documents one by one. One of them pointed to Lusia; her turn was next. Just as Lusia handed him the papers that said she was a Polish Catholic from the city of Wilno, a small kitten, the children's pet, jumped on the SS man's shoulder. The man was immediately charmed by the cuddly animal and began patting and playing with it, totally forgetting that he was there on official business. So distracted was he by the playful cat that he picked up his machine gun, signaled for his comrade to follow him, and left the building.

Relief flooded the inhabitants of the apartment, including Zbyszek and Irene. They could have been killed right then and there. "We're not safe yet," Samek cautioned them. "The man they arrested could tell them who we are. We had better think about leaving."

"I am not leaving," said Lusia. "I am tired of running. Whatever happens will happen. Besides, there is nowhere left for me to go."

Her cousins stared at her in amazement. Who was this young girl to decide their fate? A heated discussion began among them: to resign themselves to their fate meant certain death; if they moved again, how would they know if they would be running to a better place; why didn't Lusia mind her own business, she was just a child, after all; but she did have a point. They had run enough, taken too many risks already. Anyway, it was Lusia who had bankrolled them at first, so she should have some say in their dubious future.

So they stayed on Leszno Street throughout the spring and summer of 1944, their fear of betrayal lessening with each passing week. The group continued its cigarette business. Lusia, Krzysia, and Samek were now registered members of the official Polish underground, Armia Krajowa, delivering messages and newspapers, trying not to think what was the point of it all. It did not seem that the Germans would ever give up.

Because of their underground connections, they were warned that sometime during the summer, the organization would mount an uprising. Leon, Gerdie, and Leon's mother were in another hiding place in the new part of Warsaw. Samek, Krzysia, and Lusia were told they were to reassemble in a house in the old city.

Zbyszek and Irene were prepared for the uprising, except for one main concern: their ten-year-old son was attending a summer camp on the other side of the Vistula, the river that divided Warsaw into two parts. One day, Irene announced that she was afraid that when the uprising started, they would become separated from the boy. She set out to walk to the other side of the Vistula River to bring him home.

"I'm going with you," Lusia announced. Both women could not help laughing over the absurdity of the situation: Lusia, a Jew living on false papers, was going to accompany and protect a member of the illegal Polish underground. Still, the two of them set off on foot to collect the youngster and bring him home.

The camp was many miles from Leszno Street, over several roads, across a bridge that spanned the Vistula, then through a dense forest. As they crossed the river and approached the woods, Lusia stopped short and placed her hand on Irene's arm. "Look," she whispered, pointing to a clearing in the forest. "Do you see what I see?"

What Lusia saw were Russian soldiers, with anti-aircraft guns and cannons. They were so close she could see their faces, and she was sure they could see hers as well. The two young women said nothing and hurried along. The soldiers watched them impassively.

For several nights, Lusia and the others had seen the bright flames of the anti-aircraft guns coming from the east, so they knew the Russians were close—but not that close. They figured that the Russians were preparing for a major offensive.

Lusia and Irene found Irene's son and arranged for him to accompany them back to Warsaw. It was already August, and the camp was scheduled to close in a week or two anyway. It was a good thing, though, that they did not wait until then.

Three days later, the Warsaw uprising began. Samek, Lusia, and Krzysia had been posted to an address in the old city of Warsaw, where the women's assignment was to help build barricades and carry guns and ammunition to the fighters on the front lines. Samek fought alongside the men. The Germans, of course, had heavy artillery and fighter planes, while the Poles were equipped with a few rifles and handguns. Yet, as each day went by, they refused to surrender.

The Poles fought together as one force, although two distinct Polish groups had a vested interest in a victory. Alongside the Polish nationals, who were supported by the exiled Polish government in London, were the Communist Poles, who had a government in Moscow and were hoping for a Russian takeover. Once the uprising started, the Russians stopped their offensive and continued to sit on the other side of the Vistula River, waiting to see who could hold out the longest and hoping for a defeat of the uprising so they could set up a Communist government in Poland.

Lusia and Krzysia had made contact with Samek's girlfriend, Zosia, and together the three of them joined the Polish women every morning in prayers for the fighting Polish soldiers at the barricades. At first, Krzysia refused to pray; she was tired of pretending to be Polish and subverting her religion.

"You most certainly will pray," said Lusia, adamantly. "It's too dangerous if they find out we are Jews." It was still common, despite the veneer of camaraderie, for a Pole to turn over a Jew for a few zlotys. Lusia refused to take that risk.

Like their comrades in arms, Samek, Krzysia, and Lusia were in the line of fire. Proudly, they wore the white armbands that identified them as part of the home army. Many times a piece of shrapnel or a grenade would explode nearby, and they would be covered in fragments. The Germans bombed and shot at them relentlessly, while the resistance did its best to hold out despite its shortages of everything: weapons, ammunition, food, medical supplies, nurses. Lusia was pressed into duty as a nurse, although she had had no training whatsoever in that field. American or Russian planes would drop boxes of food or other supplies in the center of the old city to aid the resisters, but too often, it fell into German hands. The Poles nicknamed the old Russian planes "clickety clack," for the sounds they made as they approached.

The underground was simply outmanned, outgunned, outbombed, outsupplied. They tried their best to hold on to their territory and their people, but the attempt was futile. They were a defeated army from the start, trying valiantly to hold its position with little ammunition, ragtag soldiers, and empty stomachs, for there was little food to fuel their depleted bodies. The resistance fighters were living on raw grain by this time, running under a hail of bullets from house to house each time their headquarters was bombed. They were simply no match for the German bombs, tanks, and heavy artillery.

After thirty days, the underground gave up the old city of Warsaw and ordered its fighters to escape to the new part of the city. Through their contacts, the underground had learned that the Germans' plan was systematically to go through the old city and blow up every building. To remain meant certain death. To escape, the resistance was ordered immediately to the new city of Warsaw, but the Germans were stationed between the two. How could they get there? The Germans were mowing down anyone they saw on the streets. There was just one escape route from the old to the new: underground, through the city's sewers.

The commandant of their post ordered everyone into the sewers. At first, Lusia, Krzysia, Zosia, and Samek could not decide what to do: should they stay in the old city and risk being killed by the Germans or run through the sewers and risk being killed by the Germans? They finally decided to leave, dashing through the streets to an open manhole near a church where they had often attended mass. They descended into the sewers through the manhole, vowing to stay together, but they knew it would be difficult. Warsaw was a huge city with miles and miles of underground pipes. It would be easy to get lost in its netherworld.

Bent low in the pitch-black darkness, with foul-smelling sewage seeping and swirling all around them, the freedom fighters tried to make their way across a German-held part of the city. Lusia clutched the person in front of her, but people kept stumbling over bodies—those who had given up or been shot by the Germans, who would lift the manhole covers and fire a round indiscriminately or toss in a grenade. Lusia often lost the person in front of her when she was forced to crawl on all fours. She tried not to think about those who were actually carrying wounded friends or relatives with them. She could concentrate on nothing but staying alive, surviving this ordeal as she had lived through so many others.

On September 2, five hours after the arduous journey had begun, the four of them—Samek, Zosia, Krzysia, and Lusia—surfaced in "New Town," where they were immediately assigned to fight at the front lines. The Germans continued their relentless bombing and shooting. As they had done in the old city, the freedom fighters ran from building to building just ahead of the tireless German artillery. Again, they lived on rationed water and two pocketfuls of raw grain. Being told over and over that they were heroes of the resistance made their tasks a bit easier to bear, but they never lost sight of the most important truth: they were Jews with false papers who could be exposed at any moment. So they had their overt fear—murder by the enemy—and their covert fear—betrayal by their "friends."

The Germans kept up their bombing, while the resistance tried to stay one step ahead. After a long day of fighting, Samek, Zosia, Krzysia, and Lusia took refuge in a school, hoping to get some sleep. As they settled into the school's basement for the night, they could hear a German plane directly overhead. Lusia reached for Krzysia's hand.

Suddenly, all was chaos as the German plane rained bomb after bomb upon the area. The school where the four had sought a safe night's sleep exploded into rubble. Lusia was nearly crushed by the weight of debris. Choking on dust, she tried to scream, to call out for someone to help her, but no sound came forth. In a few moments, however, she felt hands trying to dig her out. Finally, she was freed but bleeding and dazed. As she looked around, she could see Samek, digging through the rocks and splintered wood looking for survivors.

"Krzysia!" Lusia cried. "She was right next to me! I was holding her hand!"

Wounded themselves and covered in blood, they tried to find Krzysia, Lusia's closest friend and confidante, someone who had shared in the group's triumphs and defeats. She had never had a sister, but hours later, when they gave up their search for Krzysia's body, Lusia felt as if she had indeed lost another sibling, one who had become, through tears and adversity, a trusted and beloved soulmate.

7   *Steve: Forced Hard Labor*

IT WAS A SAD AND FEARFUL PASSOVER SEDER celebrated by the Hornstein family of Hajdunanas, Hungary, in April 1944. Although Steve had arrived home on the overnight train from Budapest, his brother Jerry had never showed up. The last time Steve had seen Shmuel was when his older brother had advised him to take Jerry and leave Budapest right away for Hajdunanas. Steve had managed to fool the Hungarian police and slip onto the train bound for home. His last glimpse of his younger brother was of Jerry standing off to the side of the railroad station in a throng of other Jews trying to escape the city.

Steve celebrated the Jewish holiday with his parents, older sister, Ann, and younger brother Henu. Soon after, he received notice of his induction into the Hungarian military. For Jews, this meant serving alongside the Hungarian army but in a forced labor camp, digging ditches, clearing roads, or doing other tasks deemed too laborious or dangerous for the regular army. It was well known—since Jewish men had been assigned to forced labor ever since the alliance with Germany—that the Jews were given meager rations and were forced to contend with the worst sort of conditions. Like his oldest brother, Joel, who died in 1941 of starvation and exposure at a forced labor camp on the Russian front, Jews were thought to be expendable. Their needs for food, clothing, and shelter were therefore the last attended to by the Hungarian army officers.

When his parents accompanied him to the station, his mother, Tobi, embraced him tearfully. "Will I ever see you again?" she asked him. "Now, don't worry, Mother," said Steve, his own voice trembling. "We will see each other again very soon."

Tobi shook her head sadly. She had borne eight children. One had died of disease at eight years of age. Joel had died in a forced labor camp. Karl was safe for the moment as a regional veterinarian in eastern Hungary. She had not seen or heard from Shmuel and Jerry for several weeks. Steve was reporting to hard and dangerous labor under the administration of the Hungarian military. Ann and Henu were still at home, but how much longer could she protect them?

Steve kept his eyes on his parents, sister, and brother as the train pulled out of the station. He had heard the same horror stories that his parents had, but as a young man, just twenty years old, his self-preservation instincts were strong. He would come back. But would his family be there?

Steve had been assigned to a labor camp in Szolnok, a city on the Tisza River between Debrecen and Budapest. His job was to dig ditches and trenches for the regular Hungarian army. He and his fellow laborers—Jews who were forced to wear the yellow Star of David—were housed in primitive barracks, where they slept on the ground covered in a thin layer of straw. Their food was the barest possible rations. They spent their days harassed and harangued by Hungarian soldiers, who taunted the Jews mercilessly. Although they were not beaten, death from malnutrition was always a possibility since the provisions were so minimal.

Even under these adverse conditions, Steve kept a cool head. He was constantly aware of his surroundings, and although he realized that escape was impossible, he tried to keep his mind as sharp as possible.

One day, Steve observed a German officer in the camp, watching the forced laborers at their chores. The next thing he knew, the camp commander, a Hungarian Nazi, motioned for him to approach. The German officer needed some workers to unload drugs and other supplies from the trucks bringing medical equipment to a nearby German field hospital. For some reason, Steve was selected for this chore.

He rode back to the hospital camp with the German and a few other officers and was immediately put to work. Steve began unloading the supplies, and while carrying a large bottle of a pink solution, he removed the stopper and sniffed at the liquid therein.

"You there!" an officer shouted at him. "What do you think you're doing?" "I was just smelling what's inside the bottle," Steve answered in German. "What for?" asked the officer suspiciously. He came menacingly near to where Steve was standing, still holding the flask. "I just wanted to know what it was," Steve said. "I was a chemistry student before the war." "Tell me," said the officer, "what do you think is in the bottle?" "Rivanol," Steve answered, praying it was true.

The German officer, who was actually the camp's pharmacist, was so impressed by Steve's quick answer that he went to the Hungarian commander of the camp and asked if Steve could be assigned to the camp pharmacy attached to the hospital. For several weeks, Steve helped set up the pharmacy and dispense drugs and medicine to the soldiers and officers. Working inside kept Steve clean and dry. The pharmacist also saw to it that he had decent rations. His position was several steps up from digging trenches, and he was grateful for the promotion.

Because Szolnok was a strategic transportation center with a hospital located close by, it was an obvious target for enemy fire. On a spring morning in June, an American fighter squadron targeted the camp and rained bomb after bomb upon it. Steve and the others ran for cover in a building's basement, but the shelling was so heavy, he was sure he would be killed.

When the bombing started, the Hungarian guards turned in fury on the Jews who were working at the railroad station. "We will all die here, because of you," they screamed. "Then let us go," the Jews begged, trying to be heard above the awful noise. "We are going to die anyway; let us at least take cover."

But the guards refused and continued to scream curses at the Jews as the American bombing continued. When the attack was over, not one Jew had been killed, but the railroad station was littered with the bodies of dead German and Hungarian soldiers. The next day, Steve was ordered back to the railroad station, and he and his fellow Jewish prisoners were assigned to dig a huge grave for the hundreds of Germans and Hungarians killed in the bombing.

As they dug the huge pit and carried the corpses to it, the Hungarian guards continued to harass them. "You'll be next!" they shouted. "You won't get out of here alive." Steve felt sure that after they finished this despicable chore, they would be lined up against the fresh grave and shot. He was shaking with fear.

Suddenly, he heard his name. "Hornstein!" someone was shouting. "Where's Hornstein?" Miraculously, it was the German pharmacist, who had gone to great lengths to get Steve back to work at the camp pharmacy. Even better, the pharmacist provided Steve with a document that said Steve was officially attached to the pharmacy and was not to be singled out for any other detail.

Gratefully, Steve worked in the pharmacy, stocking the shelves and even filling prescriptions. Like the German workers, he wore a white lab coat without a yellow armband or a Star of David. He struggled to keep a straight face when German soldiers came to collect their prescriptions and saluted him. If only they knew that a Jew was dispensing their medicine.

Steve worked at the camp pharmacy for the entire month of June 1944. On July 20, he was walking to the hospital with the German pharmacist who had rescued him from hard labor, when the German said to him, "The radio says Hitler may be dead." Steve kept on walking, trying not to show his reaction to this welcome news. Perhaps now the war would be over.

Before Steve could contemplate his freedom, the situation worsened. With the attempt on Hitler's life, the Nazis cracked down even harder. By now, the Russians had broken through to the south of Hungary, coming very close to Szolnok. Steve was ordered to return to his original outfit, which was told to evacuate immediately and march westward. The forced laborers trudged on, tired and hungry, offered only the barest of rations and rest.

By the time they reached the suburbs of Budapest, they heard that Governor Horthy had been arrested and that a notorious Hungarian Nazi had been installed in his place. Word also reached the Jews in Steve's unit that many inmates of forced labor camps had been ordered to the Danube and summarily shot on its banks.

Steve's unit marched for several days toward western Hungary, but without food or water, the men could barely walk. Finally, their guards stopped prodding them forward; they were too exhausted and depleted to continue.

Near their resting place was a huge farm of thousands of acres owned by the prominent Hungarian family of Count Albert Apponyi. The unit commander—the pharmacist, a man Steve had actually come to admire—went to the manager of the farm and asked if his men could work in exchange for food and a place to sleep. Because it was in the middle of autumn, the farmer was desperate to bring in his harvest, since all his usual workers were now in the Hungarian army. When he heard that Jewish laborers were encamped nearby, he readily agreed to accept the commandant's offer. The days were still cool and crisp, and the outdoor work was welcome. For the first time in many months, there was enough to eat.

One day while he was toiling in the farmer's field, Steve was approached by a Hungarian guard with a gun. "The commandant needs medicine for his ulcer," said the guard, "and he has ordered me to go with you to Budapest to get it. He said you would know what to buy." The guard even let Steve hold the money.

The two walked to the train station, the guard in his army uniform and Steve in prisoner's garb with his yellow armband. As they rode toward Budapest, Steve's mind was reeling with plans. Perhaps he could escape. But how? Not dressed in his prisoner's clothes; a Jew alone on the streets would be arrested immediately. Ideas tumbled in and out of his mind. He would just have to take a chance, that's all. If the guard decided to shoot him or have him arrested, so be it. At least he would not die passively.

Much depended on the guard's willingness to deviate a bit from the errand on which they had been sent. Steve decided to give his idea a try. "Would you mind," he asked politely, "if we stopped to see my aunt and uncle while we are in Budapest? I know they will give us something to eat or drink."

To save some of Budapest's Jews from deportation to Auschwitz, the Swedish and Swiss ambassadors had offered them citizenship in their countries. Many of that city's Jews were surviving that way, surrounded by the horrors of Nazi rule, yet protected from their edicts and proclamations. The Nazis continued to honor this arrangement, although the Jews still feared for their lives. Among those living in protected housing were Steve's aunt Mariska and uncle Adolph.

The thought of a home-cooked meal so enthralled Steve's guard that he readily agreed to a visit. The two mismatched travelers made their way to Steve's relatives' home. His aunt and uncle were shocked by his appearance. Haggard and drawn, their nephew had lost a great deal of weight; his skimpy clothing hung on his bony limbs. Uncle Adolph offered him a set of navy blue ski pants and jacket to keep him warm during the approaching winter. Steve accepted this largess, and after a meal and something to drink, he and the guard were on their way. If Steve's aunt and uncle were aware of their nephew's plan, they kept their suspicions to themselves.

After Steve bought the ulcer medication, he and the guard boarded the train back to the village where they were now stationed. They were to change trains at a point further on, but when they got to the station, all was pandemonium. The Russians had broken through the German front lines, and everyone was desperately trying to get away. The Hungarians hated Communism; their worst nightmare was life under the Russians when the war ended. Now it looked as if that nightmare was drawing closer.

People were rushing everywhere, trying to board trains heading north. Inadvertently, Steve lost his guard in the throngs of people, began looking for him, and then stopped. What was he doing? This was the perfect time for him to escape. Ducking into a restroom, he changed into the ski suit Uncle Adolph had given him and got rid of his work clothes and armband with the yellow star. As he rushed hurriedly from the restroom, he caught sight of himself in the mirror. He could not believe the change in his appearance. He actually looked like a man with hope.

That hope faded as soon as he took stock of his situation. What was he going to do? Wander the countryside until he was arrested? All men of eligible age were supposed to be serving in the Hungarian army. What was his excuse for being out of uniform? If he were caught, he would be hauled off to a military court, where orders would be given to shoot him if they thought he was a draft dodger, a deserter, or a Jew from a forced labor camp. This was a situation without a solution as far as he could see. He began to view his "freedom" differently now and saw that he was nearly as imprisoned as before.

Because of the confusion in the country, German troops were everywhere. Surely, he would be caught before long and marched off to the military tribunal. Where could he hide? Cautiously, he walked along the roads until dawn. Perhaps he could go back to his unit and say he had become separated from his guard and had gotten lost. That might keep him alive, at least, although he would surely be arrested along the way. While contemplating this idea, another thought, perhaps as foolish, popped into his head.

He could see a German SS tank brigade just up ahead on the side of the road. The SS was made up of elite military fighters charged with protecting the Nazi system. These men looked benign enough, though; they appeared to be eating breakfast. Catching up to them, Steve asked, in perfect German, where they were headed.

The men eyed him suspiciously. Who was he? Why wasn't he in the army? Why wasn't he in uniform?

As if anticipating their questions, Steve offered this information: he was a Hungarian assigned to a military unit that happened to be encamped just where this tank unit was headed. He had to report there immediately. Since they were going that way, could they take him along?

The men heartily agreed to help a fellow soldier. Steve climbed aboard the tank, happily accepted their offer of food and coffee, and rode along, laughing and joking with his newfound friends, as if he were not a Jewish deserter from a forced labor camp, as if he were not in fear for his life. As he bounced along in the tank, he wondered how long it would take these men to kill him if they discovered the truth.

Several miles later, when the tank brigade was going to veer off in another direction, Steve thanked his hosts and asked if the tank column could stop and let him off. The entire brigade came to a halt as Steve jumped down to the road, waved goodbye, and wished his new comrades the best of luck.

Between his camp and the road on which he stood was a large forest. He knew he would have to walk through this dense wooded area to get back to his unit. As he began the trek, he caught up to two women who were walking in the same direction. Taking care not to make eye contact with them, he stayed close by so he could listen to their conversation.

"Isn't it a shame about those poor Jewish boys?" one was saying to the other. "The guards won't let me bring them anything to eat, and they're too tired and hungry to work. How will they survive the next move? They'll probably be killed."

Steve realized this meant that his unit was probably pulling out. Where could they be headed? What would happen to him? If he could not catch up to them, it meant that he would have to continue roaming the country without papers that stated his army assignment. Nothing could be more dangerous.

He figured his only option was to reach the village and go to the farm where his unit had worked to bring in the harvest. If, by chance, the men were still there, he would rejoin them and hope that the commandant would believe his story about getting lost in the railroad station. If the outfit had already moved on, he would somehow talk the head of the farm into letting him stay. Surely, the Russians were close by now. He would be more than happy to be liberated by them.

He was too exhausted to think clearly; he could not walk another step. He would just take a short nap. He lay down in the forest to welcome a twenty-minute rest, but it was late the next day when he awakened. He realized in dismay that his unit was probably far away by now. He would have to hurry if he wanted to reach the farm before nightfall.

When he approached the campsite and saw that it was deserted, he hurried to the house of the local Protestant minister, where the commander had established his headquarters. When the minister saw him, he told Steve that the commander had waited for his medicine but had had to march the men toward the town of Cece-Nemetker.

Steve did not know what to do. Should he ask the minister for asylum? Before he could gather the courage to make such a request, the minister told him, "The commandant left an open order for you so you can catch up to your unit."

The words "open order" were the most welcome Steve had heard since the Germans had invaded Hungary. The open order was the most important document in the Hungarian military. It meant, in effect, that Steve was free to roam the country as long as he could prove he was looking for his unit. If he checked into a military headquarters every day and got the order stamped by a recognizable authority, he could wander all over Hungary until the war ended—as long as he demonstrated in good faith that he was trying to catch up to his outfit.

The minister had told Steve that the men were being marched westward toward Cece-Nemetker, so Steve headed west. But he was in no great hurry. If he could just stay a few hours behind them, then he would have a kind of freedom—no anti-Semitic guards, no fear of being arbitrarily shot, no hard labor to ravage his health.

The next day, which was December 1, Steve, still far behind his unit, dutifully stopped at the military station at Cece-Nemetker and received his stamp and a signature of the officer in charge. He was ordered to the next military station, thirty miles away in the city of Sarbogard. On schedule, December 2, 1944, Steve arrived there, exhausted and hungry, and asked for his stamp.

The guard at Sarbogard, however, was suspicious. Why wasn't Steve with his unit? Why was he wandering the countryside all by himself? Steve explained the fiasco at the Budapest railroad station, how in all the confusion he had become separated from his guard. He insisted that he was looking for his unit in good faith.

The guard at Sarbogard studied Steve's open order. Finally, he wrote on it that Steve was directing himself—not on the authority of the military police—to the city of Szekesfehervar, another thirty miles beyond Sarbogard. The guard did not want to take the responsibility of dispatching Steve, since he obviously suspected that the young man was up to no good. What if someone in authority asked the guard why he had not detained him? He ordered Steve on his way.

Steve was now imprisoned by his own freedom. He was tired and hungry, and the thought of walking another thirty miles in the cold Hungarian winter was frightening. If he died from starvation or exposure, he would be all alone. Trying to escape his military service now looked like a mistake.

As he trudged toward Szekesfehervar, Steve had yet another brilliant idea: he would go to see his brother Karl, the veterinarian. After the German occupation, Karl had been sent from Horthy's farm in eastern Hungary to work as a county veterinarian on a farm in southern Hungary, near the Yugoslavian border. Perhaps Karl would hide him there.

Although Karl was two hundred miles way, Steve was determined to see him. Karl, his favorite brother, the man he admired above everyone—Karl would be able to assess the situation and help Steve think more clearly about what to do. Maybe he would have news of their parents. Walking and hitching rides with army units heading in Karl's direction, Steve arrived on the farm in just two days. Just seeing his beloved and much admired older brother made Steve feel better than he had in a long time. Winter was approaching, and the thought of putting himself under Karl's protective wing was most appealing.

Karl agreed to house Steve for one night, but he was too afraid for the safety of both of them to allow more than that. Karl was sure he was being watched by the Gestapo and the Hungarian secret police, who suspected him of passing secrets across the border to the Yugoslavian partisans fighting against the Nazis. He was positive that his own arrest was imminent and felt that Steve was in great danger by staying with him.

The next morning Karl accompanied Steve to the train station. "Don't turn around," Karl whispered to his younger brother. "A man has been following us for several blocks." The brothers decided to duck into a restaurant to see what the man would do. Sure enough, he followed them inside and sat down at a nearby booth. The brothers determined that the man was a plainclothes policeman.

The man followed Steve and Karl out of the restaurant and into the train station. As they said goodbye to each other, Steve noticed that the man had disappeared. So when he settled into his seat in the train compartment, he was shocked when the man sat down near him.

Steve was sure that he had reached the end of whatever good fortune had blessed him during these horrible months. The two sat there in silence; when it was time for Steve to change trains, he bolted from the compartment and lost the man in the crowd of travelers at the next station.

Feeling lucky, Steve decided to take a train to Budapest to see if any friends living in protected houses could help him. The trip itself was uneventful, but as soon as he left the Budapest station, he was surrounded by military police who demanded to see his papers. He observed that the police were stopping every young man who was not in uniform. His open order was outdated by now, because it was now December 4 and his last stamp read December 2.

Steve was not alone in the group of young men who were marched to the police station where the military tribunal was located. This was the end of the line. They would discover he was a Jew, a deserter who had managed to avoid hard labor fraudulently. This was where he would be killed, on the streets of Budapest, where just last year, life had seemed so promising.

At the police station, Steve and ten other men—not Jews—who were suspected of being draft dodgers or deserters were taken to a large barracks, where more than a hundred men were awaiting a hearing before the military court. By listening to the conversations around him, Steve found out that anyone with papers stating he was a Jew was taken to prison and summarily executed.

Steve thought fast. Somehow he would have to get rid of the identification with "Jew" marked on it, but first, he had to falsify his outdated open order. Scrounging for a pen, he finally borrowed one and marked on his order that he had been sent to Budapest to rejoin his unit. He had to write down the name of a unit that he only thought was in Budapest, because he knew very well that his real outfit was miles away from the capital. Plus, the order had lapsed; it had not been signed since December 2. Also, the paper was no good unless it was signed by someone in authority. He tried to think of a name that would sound like that of a military commander. Finally, he wrote down the name of a unit that he hoped sounded plausible and signed the order with the name of a Gentile school friend; he hoped these falsehoods would not be his downfall. Since he had been arrested in Budapest—the document said he was supposed to go to Budapest—he prayed that the forgery would go unnoticed and that he would be sent on his way.

Men were being called out in groups of ten to appear before the court in another building, but since they were being summoned so quickly, Steve could tell that the hearings were short and perfunctory. Somewhere between the barracks and the courtroom, he would have to get rid of his identification papers that clearly stated he was a Jew.

As his group was marched through the courtyard to the courtroom, Steve let his incriminating identification papers fall to the ground. He hoped that the guards would not notice and that the winter winds would scatter them.

"Do these belong to you?" asked a guard, handing them back. Now he was sunk. He was a Jew and a deserter from a forced labor camp, a sure prescription for death by shooting. With guards all around him, he was stuck in line for his final sentencing.

As Steve mounted the staircase to the courtroom, he passed by a room marked "Military Headquarters of Budapest." This was not a court but the more benign official office of the army. If he could just get someone in that room to accept his forged open order and write him another genuine one, he could be on his way. But how to get into that room instead of the military court upstairs? He would have to think fast, because he was near the top of the staircase, and it was almost his turn. The door to the courtroom was opening and closing so quickly with men going in and out, Steve figured it was taking merely a minute or two for the judges to agree on their findings. In a few minutes, his name would be called and his death sentence pronounced.

Thinking was too dangerous, Steve realized; it was now time to act. Falling to the floor, he rolled down the staircase, stopping near the door to the local military headquarters. He let himself in the door, and immediately, a high-ranking officer at the front desk stopped him.

"Where do you think you're going?" the officer asked him. "If you're a Jew, you don't have your yellow armband. And since you're in civilian clothes, you must be a draft dodger or a deserter."

"Not at all," said Steve. "I am a Gentile who belongs to a labor camp. I don't have a uniform, because the Russians were so close, there wasn't time to give us any."

Hearing the name of the despised Russians distracted the officer, and he dropped his threatening demeanor. "Then show me your military passport," he said.

Steve had a military passport, all right, but it clearly stated that he was a Jew. He could not say he did not have one; he had just denied being a draft dodger or a deserter. Resigned to his fate, he handed over the passport.

The officer opened it, turning to the page where under religion, Jew was clearly marked. Wordlessly, he handed it back. "Show me your orders," he said.

Steve did not take the time to ponder the situation, but the officer could not have missed the word *Jew* in the military passport. Why hadn't he said something or called for his arrest? Was he trying to help him? Still trying not to think too much, Steve quickly handed over his falsified open order.

The officer took the paper and observed the name of the unit Steve had forged. He took a large notebook from a shelf and began poring over it, trying to find the name of the outfit Steve had written that he was trying to find.

"There is no outfit like this in Budapest," said the officer. "Actually," said Steve quickly, "the last thing I heard was that my unit was heading to the city of Komarom." "Then, I will write you an order that says I am sending you to Komarom," said the guard. "Thank you very much, sir," said Steve, flooded with relief. Then he took another chance, figuring that the officer already knew he was a Jew with a forged document. "Would you mind writing that I am being sent in the direction of Komarom?"

Never questioning the request, the officer wrote that Steve had reported in as required and was now being sent in the direction of Komarom. He now had a legitimate order, superseding all of his forged documents. If he were stopped, he could produce this fresh paper and, in effect, continue to wander toward Komarom. It would buy him some precious time. He had heard that the Russians were drawing closer; if he could just hold out without mishap until they broke through. . . .

It was December and cold in Hungary. He was still wearing the ski suit from his relatives in Budapest. The navy blue outfit actually looked very much like the one worn by the German SS. This was fine with Steve; as he traveled through the small cities and towns of Hungary in the direction of Komarom, he felt reasonably safe and protected.

One night, cold and hungry, he stopped at a local restaurant. He had been sleeping on trains and in railroad stations, and he was desperate for a hot meal and a warm place to sleep. He still had a little of the money left over from buying the commandant his ulcer medicine, but those funds were quickly dwindling. Wearily, he sat down at a table and ordered an inexpensive meal.

Soon, a man was standing at his elbow. "May I join you?" he asked. Steve gestured for him to sit down. The man looked as if he, too, had been on the run. Steve assumed that he was a deserter or a draft dodger looking for a place to hide out until the war ended.

Steve's assumptions proved correct. The man confessed that he was running from the draft and was planning to work at his uncle's mill in the town of Bicske, about fifty miles away. "If I get there safely," he said, "I know he'll let me stay there until the war is over." Since the military needed flour, Steve was intrigued. "Do you think your uncle could use another hand?" he asked his new friend.

By train and by foot, the two young men reached the mill and were immediately put to work, lifting heavy sacks of flour and carrying them to trucks for transport under the watchful eyes of the German soldiers who were supervising the mill's operations. Except for this scrutiny, the mill was a wonderful place to ride out the winter. Steve and the nephew shared a room in the miller's warm house, where they were given plenty of food to eat. Among his Hungarian coworkers, no one talked of politics or the war. Working there was a vacation for Steve after all he had been through.

By early January, the people of Bicske could hear the Russian planes and bombs as they drew closer and closer. The German army officers who were supervising the mill loaded all the flour they could onto a truck and sped away. A day later, the cannon fire grew so loud that the remaining mill workers dashed to the cellar of the house. They stayed there at least a full day, when suddenly, there was silence. It was just before noon when they heard a brisk knock on the cellar door. The door opened, and standing there were three Russian soldiers.

This meant it was over! Their liberators were there, right there at the top of the cellar steps. Steve rushed forward in such excitement that he did not even notice how his frightened fellow mill workers stayed cowering in a corner of the basement. This was freedom! He would be free!

He embraced the first Russian soldier and was about to kiss him in gratitude, when the soldier pushed him away in disgust—but not before noticing Steve's wristwatch. "Give that to me," he said in Russian, pointing to the watch. Steve understood and unstrapped it from his wrist.

"Germansky?" the soldier inquired of the men huddled in the cellar. "Are there German soldiers here?" When he was satisfied there were none, he and the other soldiers headed for the next house to see what they could find.

Steve and the others stayed behind at the mill, wondering what their fate would be now that the Russians were in Hungary. Steve realized that if the Russians were this deep into the country, they must have already gone through and liberated Hajdunanas, which was about 170 miles east of Budapest. He figured he was about 150 miles west of the capital. How could he get home? The railroad, he knew, had been bombed. What he really wondered, though, was who would be waiting for him. When he had left in May of 1944, he had said goodbye to his mother, father, brother, and sister. He hoped that they would be at home, preparing to welcome him back.

That night, still at the mill, another Russian officer came to the house and announced that this would be his military headquarters. Steve, who by now had let his fellow workers know that he was a Jew and a deserter, did not hesitate to approach the Russian. Steve knew a few Russian words, and since the man looked as if he could be Jewish, Steve used his limited Russian vocabulary to ask him point blank.

Yes, the man replied, he was Jewish. Did Steve know Yiddish by any chance? Yes, of course, Steve answered. The Russian officer saw that Steve was given extra food and protected from harm by the other Russian soldiers.

One day, when the officer was away from the headquarters on business, one of his soldiers accused Steve of being a German spy and threatened to shoot him. He was convinced of this because Steve's ski outfit looked a lot like the uniforms of the German SS. This officer did not know any language but Russian, and Steve knew only a few words in that language. Trying to convince the soldier that he was a Jew and had been oppressed by the Germans and the Hungarians, Steve relied on one of the few words he knew in Russian, the slang word for penis—meaning that if the Russian checked, he would see that Steve was circumcised. It was a well-known fact that only Jews in Europe were circumcised, not Gentiles.

Unfortunately, the soldier thought Steve was calling him a penis or a slang word for the male organ. He pointed his pistol at Steve and threatened again to shoot him, this time for leveling such an insult. Just at that moment, though, the Russian officer returned from his errand and rescued Steve from death.

Steve desperately wanted to start the long trek back to Hajdunanas, so he asked the Russian officer for a signed affidavit saying that he was a Jew who had just been liberated from a forced labor camp. The Russian officer agreed, and Steve began his last long walk. He was more than three hundred miles from Hajdunanas at this point, and he had no means of transportation, no money, and no idea what awaited him there.

The weather in January 1945 was bitter cold. Snow was up to Steve's knees as he trudged through war-torn Hungary, trying to make his way back to his hometown. He would go to farmhouses or small stores and ask for food, sometimes receiving it, often not. On he walked until he was picked up a few days later by Russian military police, who took him to a prisoner-of-war camp, full of Germans and Hungarian Nazis. It was like being in the forced labor camp all over again: hard work, little food, terrible sleeping arrangements. Steve felt as if he had survived the Nazis but would perish at the hands of his liberators.

Another Russian officer came to the camp and chose ten men, including Steve, to help him carry ammunition from one place to another. Steve was amazed by what he saw: guns, bullets, and hand grenades. He was tempted to pick up a grenade but knew he would be in serious trouble if the grenade was discovered in his possession.

Steve wondered if this Russian officer would help him get out of this prisoner-of-war camp. He approached him carefully, and in his awkward Russian, he told the man that he was a Jew who had escaped a Hungarian forced labor camp. He begged the officer for help, saying that as a Jew, he had been persecuted and that the officer was his liberator but was keeping him in the same camp as his oppressors.

Miraculously, this officer admitted that he, too, was Jewish. He took Steve out of the camp and walked with him to the nearest town, not leaving his side until he was sure he was safe. Steve was then on his own. Through the next few freezing weeks, Steve would walk as far to the east as he could during the day and then stop at a farmhouse and ask for a place to sleep. Sometimes he got a place right away; other times, he would have to go from house to house seeking shelter.

Still west of the Danube River—he wanted to be east—on the outskirts of a small town, he approached a farmhouse and asked the woman who answered the door for food and a bed for the night. The woman welcomed him warmly and fed him a hot meal, inviting him to relax and sit by the fire. Her daughter joined him there, and as they talked, Steve said that he was a medical student trying to get home to his parents.

When it was time to retire, the farmer's wife indicated that Steve was to sleep in the same bed as her daughter. Immediately, Steve figured out the situation: the woman knew that Steve would be a good catch and, since he had mentioned that he planned to be a doctor, would provide her daughter with a comfortable living. That was all he needed after what he had been through: a pregnant farm girl. Steve thanked the woman for her generous hospitality and left the farmhouse as soon as he could.

He walked some more, heading east, when he arrived in another small city. He found himself opposite a pharmacy and decided to ask if he could come in for a while and get warm.

The pharmacist was happy for the company of another learned man. He was a bachelor with a housekeeper and, upon hearing that Steve had worked in a hospital pharmacy during the first months of the war, invited him to stay in his house and work in the attached pharmacy. Steve, sick of walking and tired of being cold and hungry, accepted the offer of this generous man.

Besides, while walking eastward, he had met refugees going westward, and they had told him some shocking stories. The Jews of the small towns and cities of Hungary had been rounded up and transported to concentration camps. He heard of Jews being shot into the Danube by the Hungarian Nazis. As much as he wanted to get back to Hajdunanas, he feared that no one would be waiting there for him.

Steve stayed with the pharmacist for two weeks and then resumed his walking. At night, he would repeat his pattern: knock on the door of a farmhouse and ask for food and shelter. He was surprised at how often he was welcomed inside. For a week longer, he walked, dreading what lay ahead but anxious to get home. He felt as if he had been away for many years.

Finally, he approached Hajdunanas. It had not changed much, but Steve was surprised at how empty it seemed. Obviously, all the young men were trying just like he was to get home after the war.

He walked the streets to his house, but no one was there. He was told that after the Nazis came, his family had been ordered to move to a two-family house in another part of the city. He walked there but found no one.

The son of the owner of the apartment house came outside to greet him. It was then that Steve learned that all the Jews of Hajdunanas had been rounded up and marched to the railroad station, with a festive Hungarian band leading the way. The town had made a holiday of it. Then the Jews had been packed into cattle cars, said the owner's son, but he did not know what became of them after that.

Steve knew instinctively what had happened to them. He felt no need to ask any further questions, because he did not want to hear the answers.

8   Paul: Forced Hard Labor

FROM MARCH UNTIL JUNE 1944, PAUL ORN-
stein and the student rabbis were forced to work for the invading Germans,
helping to run the transit camp that the Nazis had set up in the classrooms
of the Budapest rabbinic school. As Paul worked, he thought about Hajdunanas, his parents, and his young brothers, Zoli, Tibi, and Lacika.
Where were they? His sister, Judith, was still in Budapest, but he had seen
her only infrequently.

Where was Anna? He hoped and prayed that she was safe. He had received a postcard from her saying that she and her parents had been
moved to another part of Szendro but that she did not know where she
would be going next. Paul had more than a hundred pictures of Anna and
his family that he carried with him everywhere. Although he worried that
they would fade from excess handling, he could not help taking them out
of the envelope and gazing at them each night. The photos helped ease
his loneliness and his fears. He was cautious, though; if the guards found
the pictures and took them away, it would be devastating.

Although Paul was an optimist with confidence in his abilities, his
mind kept going back to the German Jew who came to his home in Hajdunanas several years ago to address his father and a small group of men
about the atrocities in Germany. The man was traveling to Palestine and
trying to raise money for the trip. He remembered that although each
man made a contribution, they scoffed at his stories of impending doom
for Europe's Jews. How naive, how blind the Hungarian Jews had been to
actual events! If only they had believed the man's stories, they could have
protected themselves. Now, it was too late. Now, their best hope was that
the Russians would be able to break through, though life under the Russians was practically unthinkable.

Although the Nazis had taken over the rabbinic school, Paul and his fellow students were still allowed to live in the dormitory. The faculty also decreed that even though classes had been canceled, students could still sit for their exams. Paul was in his final undergraduate year of rabbinic school, and this exam would be the last he would have to take before commencing his actual rabbinic studies, but he could only work listlessly. What did it all mean when the whereabouts of Anna and his family were so much on his mind?

The irony of his current situation was much on his mind as well. Here he was, a Jew who did not believe in God, a young man whose real dream was to become a psychoanalyst, imprisoned because he was Jewish—and at a rabbinic school from which he was due to graduate—and he had no desire whatsoever to become a rabbi. Jewish history, philosophy, literature, and the Jewish men and women who had brought the world so many innovations in science and the arts—these he believed in and revered with all his heart. And with all his heart, he hated the Nazis, hated their stupidity, cruelty, and ignorance. Not for one moment would he allow them to rob him of his heritage. He would proceed as best he could, trying with all his might to look forward.

In May, he passed his last exam while still being forced to work for the Nazis at the transit camp. Jews from Budapest were being rounded up and sent to a town called Kistarcsa, several miles from Budapest. Paul and his friends knew that soon they would receive their induction notices to report to forced labor camps, since every male Jew from eighteen to fifty was expected to serve.

Paul and his friends weighed their options. Could they hide? Did they have to report in? Paul's plan was somehow to escape the labor unit, buy some false papers, and hide in Budapest as a non-Jew. Paul's head was always full of plans and alternatives; he was not one to sit by and let someone else make a decision for him that impinged on his future. Here, however, he saw that he had no choice.

In June, Paul received his induction notice and orders to report as a forced laborer to work alongside a Hungarian army brigade. At first, his unit was taken to a town on the west side of the Danube, where they worked for about four weeks constructing roads and building an airport. Rations were meager, and the guards were cruel. The Hungarian army—if not the entire country—was full of Nazi sympathizers, and the military was notoriously anti-Semitic. Paul watched as a friend of his totally collapsed beneath the weight of humiliation, beatings, and indignities inflicted on him by the Hungarian guards. While the man was strong enough to carry the heavy materials needed for the army's construction projects, he could not withstand the assaults against his pride. Paul thought it was because his friend considered himself a loyal Hungarian citizen and then a Jew; Paul was grateful for his strong Jewish identity and his Zionist ideals.

"Come on," he urged his friend. "Don't give up. Don't let them destroy you." "I am a citizen of Hungary," the man cried pathetically over and over. Paul was a citizen of Hungary, too, but his Jewish identification was so strong that his spirit was able to feed off this reservoir of pride when all his other systems had shut down from fear and hunger. The Germans and Hungarians could degrade him all they wanted, strip him of his Hungarian citizenship, but that still left him with a lot to live for. When the war ended, he knew he would say goodbye to Hungary and never look back. His idea was to make his way to Palestine with Anna, where they would study to fulfill their dreams of becoming doctors.

These thoughts—and the hundred pictures of Anna and his family that he still managed to carry with him—kept him from succumbing to the cruelties apportioned by the Hungarian soldiers and officers who were his masters. Luckily, his meager money, his pictures, and whatever other small items he had in his possession were not taken from him.

After a month on the west side of the Danube, the inmates of the labor camp were told to get ready to leave their encampment. They were transported to Poland and ordered to dig ditches for the soldiers who were fighting desperately against the stronger and better-equipped Russian army.

Stationed between the fighting Russians and the Hungarians, Paul and his fellow laborers alternately dug ditches and ducked for cover from the relentless shelling on both sides. At one point, because the day was warm, he removed his jacket. At that moment, the Russians opened fire with all their power, and the Jewish laborers began a hasty retreat. The Hungarians shouted at them, "Get back there!" and threatened them with their guns. But Paul and his friends were not ready to die in battle.

When he was two hundred yards away from the front lines, Paul turned in horror to a friend of his named George. "I left my jacket out there!" he cried. "All my pictures of Anna and my family are in the pocket!"

"You'll have to leave it there," said George. "It's too dangerous to do anything else."

"I'm going back for it," Paul insisted. "I have to have those pictures."

"You can't go back," declared George. "You'll be killed!"

It was too late. Paul was already crawling on his belly back to his jacket. When he looked around, he saw George crawling with him. Paul picked up his coat, and the two friends dashed to safety. Paul was depending on those pictures of Anna to keep him alive.

As the Hungarian army and the forced laborers retreated from the Russians, the Jews felt the brunt of the Hungarians' frustration at defeat. Paul was afraid that although he had survived the Russians, he would surely be killed by the Hungarian beasts. Threatened by their guns and the promises to make their lives more miserable than ever, the Jewish men feared the worst. As they retreated, they were still being shelled by the Russians; many men died as the army retreated further toward the Carpathian Mountains.

By now, Paul had formed a "family" with four other of his rabbinic classmates who were working in his brigade. They divided up their survival chores: one man was in charge of rationing food, another was responsible for cigarettes, others were charged with looking for opportunities to escape. Whatever decisions they made, they all had to agree. The only time a split decision would hold was in a life-and-death matter.

The shelling by the advancing Russians was now more serious than ever. It looked as if hiding or escaping was the only way the group of five would survive. Three of them thought the prudent choice was to escape to the Russian side and throw themselves on the mercy of the enemy of Hungary and beg for asylum as persecuted Jews.

Paul and George disagreed. They were just a few miles away from the Hungarian border, and they thought they would have a better chance of escaping once they were out of Poland and inside Hungary, where they knew the language. Besides, Paul had heard about captivity in Siberia after World War I, knew of Russian barbarism, and was afraid if he escaped into Russia, he would never be able to come back. He and George elected to take their chances on the Hungarian side of the border. The other three members of their group joined twenty other Jews and worked furiously at digging hiding places in the ground of a nearby forest, where they could hide from the Hungarian military police and await their Russian "saviors."

Paul had an ingenious escape plan. As soon as the unit crossed the Carpathian Mountains from Poland into Hungary, he would find a farm girl who would be unable to resist the charms of this half-starved, disheveled Jew, somehow fall in love with him, and hide him on her farm. So brilliant was this plan that Paul's friend George had something similar in mind.

The army unit, however, did not go deeply into Hungary for the expected retreat; they stayed where they were, cutting down trees and building passable roads for tanks and army trucks. New Hungarian guards were in charge now, and they were particularly brutal. Hungry and exhausted though he was, Paul's greatest fear was that he might freeze to death because of his skimpy clothes. It was October, and nights in the mountains were very cold. He was so worried about his inability to stay warm that he could think of nothing but escape.

But how? They were constantly watched by their Hungarian guards, and those who tried to escape were shot immediately. If he did manage to break free, where could he hide, a Jew with no false papers who did not speak the Polish language? If he gave up the idea of escape, he knew he would be doomed, because then he would be resigned to his fate. Paul Ornstein did not like to resign himself to any situation where he felt trapped and helpless. The more in control he felt—however small a portion of his circumstances he could control—the better he could handle his destiny.

Shivering under the stars one night, his mind reeled. What if he became sick from cold and exhaustion? He would have to go to sick call, and they would probably put him in the hospital or send him back to his unit. He was not sick, but what if he pretended to be sick with an illness he could fake, like . . . like what? A stomach ache of some unknown origin? No, it would have to be a specific disease, with symptoms he could demonstrate. Whatever he decided would have to merit a long stay in a hospital, something that might necessitate an operation. What would be his fate if they opened him up and found only healthy organs? He would have to think about that later.

For now, he needed a disease. Tonsillitis? No, too easy to see by looking down his throat with a flashlight. Hepatitis? He did not know anything about its symptoms. Appendicitis? That one had possibilities. He would complain of terrible abdominal pains and imagined that if they could diagnose appendicitis, he would be sent to a hospital across the Polish border and deeper into Hungary.

He did not know much about appendicitis either, so he asked some of his friends to describe the symptoms to him. Pain in the belly was all they could tell him. Armed with this skimpy knowledge, Paul signed up for sick call the next day.

When he got to the medical station, he informed the doctor on call that he had sharp pains in his stomach with terrible nausea. The doctor gave him a thermometer and told him to go outside with it and report back in a few minutes. Paul pondered how to make the mercury rise. If he failed at this attempt to convince the medics he was sick, they would punish him by withholding his food for a day.

Paul showed the doctor his thermometer, but his temperature looked normal. "I suspect you have a urinary infection," said the physician, and he sent Paul away with some medicine. Paul threw the medicine away immediately, because, of course, he did not have a urinary infection or, for that matter, any other ailment.

A few days later he returned to sick call with the same complaint, adding another element for authenticity. "I have also lost my appetite," he told a different doctor. Finding nothing wrong, the doctor sent Paul back to hauling logs, warning him that if he returned, he would be severely punished.

Paul went to sick leave four times, sticking to his story of pain and nausea. It did not occur to him that if he were really suffering from an inflamed appendix for that long, it would have ruptured, and he would be dead. Sometimes a doctor would come up with the infected urinary tract diagnosis, give him the medicine, and send him back. No one could find anything really wrong with him.

The fifth time Paul appeared at sick call, he was examined by a Jewish physician who had arrived from another camp. This Hungarian doctor actually knew Anna's family, so Paul took him into his confidence and explained what he was trying to do. The doctor agreed to help and offered Paul some hints about the course of appendicitis.

"Complain of pain *after* they pull their hands away from your stomach, not when they're pressing on it," the doctor advised. "And try as best you can to get a high fever." This doctor wrote up an order that Paul was to be admitted to the outpatient clinic attached to the field hospital. Luckily for Paul, the doctors at the outpatient clinic ordered him to the hospital.

At first, Paul was immensely proud that his ruse had worked, but lying on a hospital cot gave him too much time to think. He was scheduled for surgery the next day. What if they opened him up, saw a healthy appendix, and became so furious at having been duped that they left him on the operating table to die? What could he have been thinking when he started this story? He looked around the hospital ward at the nurses and doctors. These were very hostile Hungarians. That they had wasted their time on a Jew who had outsmarted them would not be borne lightly.

Because they were going to operate on him, Paul was given nothing to eat the day of the scheduled operation. It did not really matter; he was too frightened to swallow anything, anyway. Perhaps it was not too late to jump up and say that, miraculously, he was feeling much better.

Just then, the Hungarian commanding officer came through the hospital ward. "Who amongst you can walk?" he asked. "We must evacuate the hospital at once." Evidently, the Russians, having broken through the front lines, were coming closer.

Paul began to perspire profusely. He figured he could say he could not walk (he did, after all, have acute appendicitis) and take his chances on not being killed in the subsequent gun battle with the approaching Russians. He could also say that he could walk, but how could he walk if he had acute appendicitis? He decided he would tell the officer that he would *try* to walk. He took great care to fix a pained expression on his face.

At least half the patients in the hospital had said they could make it on foot, but just as they were leaving, a convoy of empty army trucks came by and picked up the ambulatory patients. The convoy drove them to a field hospital on the other side of the Carpathian Mountains, just over the border into Hungary. Paul was exactly where he wanted to be.

How long, though, could he keep up the fiction about his appendix? As he stood in line to get his papers stamped, he tried to look unwell. The next day, when a physician examined him and could find nothing wrong, she suggested he see doctors at another hospital, this one deeper inside of Hungary. It was just what Paul wanted to hear.

By foot and by truck, Paul traveled to the designated hospital. He had had nothing to eat for two days and was starving by the time he arrived there on the evening before the Jewish holiday Yom Kippur. The hospital was a large one, and Paul was happy to see that it housed a few thousand Jewish forced labor workers, as well as Hungarian soldiers, with various diseases and broken bones. Greeting them warmly, he rushed to the rations that had been set out for the prisoners. Grabbing the food, he ate it quickly, unaware that he was being regarded with disgust and dismay.

He immediately realized that he had behaved without sensitivity or discretion when the Jewish patients descended upon him, shouting insults and curses. Didn't he know it was Yom Kippur? What kind of a Jew was he? He was supposed to be fasting, not gobbling down whatever food he could find.

Paul turned to the shouting Jews and announced that he was a rabbinic student; they did not have to lecture him about Yom Kippur and fasting. This seemed to make the crowd even angrier, and they continued to curse him while he ate.

A Jewish doctor came to Paul's rescue and calmed the crowd. He took Paul aside to talk to him, and Paul confided his story. The doctor was appalled. The facility was so crowded that they probably would not be able to see him for a few more days. If he really had appendicitis, he would be dead by then. They would figure out that he was faking.

Paul decided to take a chance with his practiced tale of appendicitis. It had worked for him so far, and he was confident that he could fool these doctors as well. Unfortunately, Paul ran into a doctor who was quite familiar with the ailment. While he was examining Paul, he asked his age and occupation. Paul was so busy answering that he forgot to grimace in a timely fashion. The doctor figured out that he was faking, became extremely angry at the deception, and wrote on his papers that he was to return to the front lines.

This was terrible news for him. He feared he would never survive the cold autumn nights, and with winter right behind, what would happen to him? To go back to his unit in Poland would surely spell disaster. He would never be able to escape back into Hungary.

The Hungarians would not send a Jewish laborer out of the hospital on his own to make his way back to his original unit. When ten or so Jewish forced laborers were dismissed from the hospital, two armed Hungarian soldiers would accompany them back to where they were supposed to go. The soldiers carried the Jews' discharge papers. At the railroad station, the military officer would look up each laborer's unit on a large hanging map on the wall and tell the Jews where they were supposed to go to catch up with their outfits. Then the officer at the railroad station would affix the appropriate stamp to the forced laborer's papers and send him on to the next stop, where another officer would stamp his papers.

When the contingent of Jewish men and their guards were ready to walk to the railroad station, the forced laborers already had a plan. They had pooled whatever money they still had in their possession and paid a willing guard to procure some liquor for their journey. They had no plans to imbibe the spirits themselves but instead offered it to their two guards, who commenced to get seriously drunk. This was exactly what the men had hoped for. They rifled the guards' pockets for their discharge papers and decided to head for the railroad station—though not all at once.

Although Jews were not supposed to travel alone—they would be arrested and shot if caught—eastern Hungary was in such chaos by now that it was not unusual for Jews to show up at railroad stations without a guard but with the appropriate papers. The military officers referred to these men as "stray Jews," and while they often threatened the Jews who showed up without guards, they usually stamped their documents and sent them on.

When he arrived at the first station without a guard, Paul presented his discharge papers from the hospital. "Where is your guard?" the military officer asked him. "There weren't enough guards for everyone, so they sent me alone," Paul replied. "I'm trying to find unit one-oh-five over fifty-six." The military officer looked at him suspiciously. "Go ahead," said Paul. "Call the hospital. They'll confirm my story."

So many soldiers were waiting in line to get their documents stamped that the officer reluctantly approved Paul's and sent him out toward unit one-oh-five over fifty-six. Paul was grateful that he had not been detained, but the more officers he convinced of his story, the closer he was to getting sent back to his unit, which was still encamped over the border inside Poland—the last place Paul wanted to be.

When he arrived at the very last train station inside Hungary, it was late at night. He would not be able to get a military stamp until the next morning. Although he had managed to bargain for a new set of clothes from some of the other prisoners at the hospital, they were still not warm enough. Paul had a panic attack when he realized that tomorrow he would be sent back into Poland and hard labor. He would surely freeze to death in the cold mountain air.

Suddenly, he had an idea. He was supposed to be looking for unit one-oh-five over fifty-six. He knew that several of his friends were stationed in Budapest with unit one-oh-*six* over fifty-six. What if he changed his order by one digit? He would then be sent back into Hungary to Budapest, where he knew many places to hide and people who could probably help him.

Why hadn't he thought of this before? Borrowing a pen, he made a careful forgery. How hard was it, anyway, to change a five to a six? He spent the rest of the night marveling at his own cleverness. Now he was desperate to find unit one-oh-six over fifty-six. Of course, that he was so far away from Budapest and so desperate to get back there might raise some suspicion, but he would deal with that question if it arose.

When morning came, everyone at the railroad station lined up to get his papers stamped. Now in broad daylight, he checked his doctored document and recoiled in horror: he had made the five into a six with an ink of a different color. Anyone could tell by looking at it that someone had tampered with it. Now he was really in a panic. He would just have to deny any knowledge of the different inks and offer to let the officers search him to see that he did not have a pen.

He was already nearing the front of the line for his stamp. He observed the four military officers who were checking papers. Three of them took the documents and held onto them as they checked the large map behind them for the location of the units. One officer, however, took the papers, glanced at them, and then handed them back before walking over to check the map. Paul made sure that this officer would be the one to check him through.

Sure enough, the officer barely glanced at the paper before handing it back to Paul and walking over to the map. He searched and searched but returned to Paul with a puzzled expression on his face. "I can find no such unit," he announced. "But I am desperate to get back there," said Paul. "All of my belongings are with that unit." The man shook his head. "The best I can do for you," he replied, "is to send you back to a larger dispatch center where someone will know how to find this unit." He named a place that was even further inside the boundaries of Hungary. "The only problem," the officer continued, "is that the trains are so erratic these days. You can walk to the dispatch center or take your chances and wait for the train."

No sweeter words than these had Paul Ornstein heard in months. He could walk there. How wonderful! He still had to get a stamp every day—without it, he would be considered a fugitive—but he had a few days before he was scheduled to report to the dispatch center. All would be perfect if he could find some food, too. This was his chance to escape.

To keep on wandering back to Budapest, Paul walked slowly along the Hungarian roads toward the nearest train station. When he figured a train was due, he waited until he was sure it was ready to leave, then ran for the station, arriving breathlessly, just as the last car pulled out. He explained to the guard that he was desperate to get on the train but that the next one would not leave from this station for twenty-four hours. So he was given his stamp and sent on ahead to try to secure some other transportation.

As he walked, he conjured up one of his old ideas: find a farmhouse and help them bring in the harvest. He did find a farm on the edge of town, and they did need someone to help them bring in the corn. If Paul were anticipating a warm reception, though, he was rudely awakened by the hostility the farmer and his family expressed. They allowed him to sleep in their barn—not in the house. The next day, instead of helping with the corn, Paul headed for the railroad station.

This time, Paul caught the train to the dispatch center, the last point where travelers could go. The guards ordered everyone out of the trains and confiscated everyone's papers. When it was Paul's turn to appear before them, they could not locate the documents they had taken from him just minutes earlier. The officials did not have much time to spend on him, however. The dispatch center was overrun by people trying to reach one city or another, and the officers at the station knew by now that the Russians had broken through the front lines.

It was October 15, 1944, and Paul heard some more interesting news while waiting for his next assignment. The regent of Hungary, Governor Horthy, sensing the inevitable, had tried to disengage his country from its collaboration with the German Nazis and had offered to surrender to the Russians. He had been arrested immediately by the Germans and deported to Germany.

Instead of demoralizing the Germans and their Hungarian sympathizers, Horthy's treachery made them regroup with a vengeance. The Hungarians thought the Germans were bad enough, but the Russians were unthinkable. For now, the soldiers at the dispatch station rounded up all the Jews regardless of their prior destinations and ordered guards to supervise them as they marched west toward the city of Miskolc.

Thousands of men traveled by train and by foot, reaching Miskolc in a few weeks. There, even more Jews were added to the group and ordered to march to Budapest, a distance of about ninety miles. The men slept on farms and in forests, always cold, always hungry.

They had marched for nearly two weeks when a convoy of trucks transporting the food and cookware for the marching men pulled up to where Paul was trudging along. The workers on the trucks were also forced laborers who provided food service to those on the march. "Where are you from?" Paul shouted up to one group. "Szendro," they called down. "Szendro!" Paul exclaimed. "Do you know my girlfriend, Anna Brünn?" They did know Anna and even recognized Paul from his visit there. They offered him a ride on the truck, which was lucky for Paul, since he was exhausted from walking such a long way.

The thousands of forced laborers who were marching toward Budapest were directed to a route that bypassed the city. The convoy of fifteen trucks carrying the food, utensils, cookware, and Paul Ornstein headed in another direction. Paul worried that if the guards on the convoy found him, he would have some explaining to do, but for now, he was safe, warm, fed, and comfortable.

When the trucks stopped for the night, the Hungarian officer in charge did discover Paul and ordered the men to drop him off the next morning with his fellow marchers. At least this allowed Paul to spend the night with his new friends.

The next day, one of the trucks had to make a delivery at a stop at a different location from where the rest of the convoy was headed. That truck took Paul along and let him off at a point in the road where he promised to rejoin the marching men as soon as they came by. He did not wait for anyone, however, but headed out on his own to find the nearest streetcar station where he could take a train into Budapest.

He did not need a mirror to remind him how terrible he looked. He could not remember his last shave; his clothes were dirty and ragged and hung on his emaciated body. It was a Sunday, too, and Hungarians always dressed up for church. He would stick out like a frightened Jewish fugitive from a forced labor camp.

Thinking quickly, he formulated a plan. If he saw anyone looking at him with suspicion, he would approach the person and ask for directions to the nearest streetcar station, saying he needed to find the military headquarters so that he could rejoin his unit. He had fallen asleep in a barn, he would tell anyone who asked, and had been inadvertently left behind. That was why, he could say, his documents had not been stamped for a few days. It sounded like a good story to him.

Before he could try it out, he sensed that he was being watched by a nice-looking, well-dressed man in his early thirties. He turned and faced the man squarely. "I want to go to the military station in Budapest," he said, looking the man in the eye. "No you don't," the man whispered. "It's too dangerous. Come with me."

The man turned out to be a Jew who was living on false papers in Budapest. The military station as well as all the homes in the Jewish quarter of Budapest were very closely watched. The Jewish homes where Paul had relatives were locked and guarded around the clock, except between the hours of ten and noon when people could leave to do their shopping. Visitors were strictly forbidden. If Paul were caught, he would be sent to a prison, if not shot on the spot.

When Germany invaded Hungary in March 1944, it was so late in the war that the Nazis did not have time to round up all the Jews of Budapest and deport them. The Jews in the Hungarian countryside and small towns were easier to herd into ghettos and then send away; there were fewer of them, and they all tended to live on the same few streets. Some Jews in

Budapest—not all—were allowed to stay in designated housing or even in their own homes under a strict house arrest. Other Jews were lucky to have been offered "protected passes" by the Swiss, Swedish, and other embassies.

Paul told his new friend that he planned to go see his aunt and uncle, who had been allowed to remain in their own home in Budapest. Paul had frequently visited them in the early days of the German invasion when he was working at the transit camp located in the rabbinic school. His new protector kindly bought Paul a streetcar ticket but ordered him not to speak during the train ride, lest they arouse suspicion. When they arrived in Budapest and left the station, he told Paul where he could find a forced labor battalion in charge of cleaning up after the bombings in Budapest. He suggested that Paul go there directly and visit his relatives later. Paul was too frightened, though, to spend even one night with another forced labor group. He was afraid he would be closely questioned by the guards and would never have another opportunity to escape.

His new friend told him he could try the Swiss embassy, where the Zionist underground was helping people. Paul had many friends from his Zionist work during rabbinic school, and perhaps some of his old acquaintances would be there.

First, though, he had to see his relatives and his sister, Judith. But it was long past noon, and he looked so bedraggled; he had no business walking through the Jewish section of Budapest. What was his excuse for being there? He would just have to rely on his old story with a slight twist: this time he was looking for the railroad station so he could get directions from the military command station to find his old unit. The fact that he had just left the railroad station and was now walking away from it—he would say that he did not know his way around Budapest and thought he was headed in the right direction.

From the street, he could see his aunt and uncle's house. The gate was open. Impulsively, he walked quickly toward it, although he noticed an armed Hungarian soldier nearby talking to the janitor's son, whom Paul had met on previous visits to his relatives. "Stop right there," called the guard. "Who are you and where do you think you're going?" "That's okay," said the janitor's son to the guard. "He lives here." He swept Paul into the house without a further word.

As soon as Paul entered his aunt's apartment, he nearly collapsed from fear and exhaustion. His relatives were thrilled to see him; they had feared he was dead. They were appalled by his appearance, though, and what was worse, he was crawling with lice. His aunt and uncle ordered him out of his clothes, which they burned immediately, and into a hot bath. It was the first time he had cleaned himself in warm water in months.

It was dangerous for Paul to be there, because the Jews were not allowed any visitors. Even though they were allowed to stay in houses in Budapest, the Nazis conducted frequent *razzias,* or roundups, where they would order all the Jews outside while they searched their homes. If strangers without proper papers were discovered, the Jews were taken away, never to be seen again.

After his bath, Paul felt more alive than he had in months. He sat down at the kitchen table while his aunt gave him something to eat. "Have you seen my sister, Judith?" he asked between mouthfuls. Judith had been studying dental technology in Budapest, and he hoped to see her during this unauthorized trip. He watched as his aunt and uncle exchanged glances.

"We haven't seen Judith for a few weeks," said his uncle, "but Jews can only be out on the streets between the hours of ten and noon, so perhaps she's too busy to visit." "Do you think she's in hiding?" asked Paul. "Perhaps so," said his uncle. Paul was not completely satisfied with this conversation; they must be holding something back. But what he needed now was sleep, and he was grateful for his first real bed since the hospital.

The next day, the janitor's son generously offered to lend Paul his identification papers, so Paul could walk around Budapest. Paul's aunt and uncle had been very kind to the janitor's family, but letting someone borrow identification documents was extremely risky. Paul was most grateful for this show of bravery.

The first place he walked to was the building where Judith lived. In horror, he saw that it had been bombed to rubble. He remembered his aunt and uncle's evasive answers when Paul had asked about her. He knew instinctively that Judith had been killed in the carnage.

When he returned to his relatives' house, he asked again about his sister and told them what he had seen. They confessed that Judith was supposed to come for dinner the night before Yom Kippur but had never arrived. When they heard about the bombing, they ran to her apartment house and realized she could not have survived.

This was the first notification of a death in his immediate family. He feared the worst about his parents and brothers. As he sat there stunned, his aunt and uncle apologized for not telling him at once, but they were afraid the news would be too shattering.

Hearing about his sister's death strengthened Paul's resolve to remain a free man. He would not be caught by the Nazis or their Hungarian comrades, would not succumb to their cruelty and torture. The next day, at ten o'clock in the morning, he would go to the Swiss embassy and see if he could find a safe haven with the Zionist underground.

Paul was unprepared for the frenzied scene at the Swiss embassy. Hundreds of frantic people stood outside the gates, begging to be allowed inside. The noise was deafening. How would Paul find his friends from the rabbinic school? They were not even coming outside; the members of the underground were calling to people through the embassy's windows.

Finally, amid the shouting and chaos, Paul heard his name. One of his friends from rabbinic school was at the window and had noticed him in the noisy crowd. "Come quickly!" his friend shouted. "Come to the window!" Paul ran to the window, where two men grabbed him by his arms and pulled him inside. For the first time in the long months since the German takeover, Paul felt reasonably safe and secure. He was in the neutral Swiss embassy, surrounded by many of his friends.

A subdivision of the Swiss embassy was located in a building called "the glass house," because the building was made of glass. It had been built by a glass manufacturer and was a showplace in Budapest. A tunnel leading to another building just beyond the glass house also served as a refuge for many Jews who had been given protective passes in the name of the Swiss consul. Not far away, the Swedish embassy also gave protection to Jews; a diplomat named Raoul Wallenberg was often seen at the railway station handing out Swedish protective passes to Jews who were about to be deported. Some of the people were living in the embassies' safe houses with no papers at all or with false documents. Although the situation was far from ideal, it was quite satisfactory as far as Paul Ornstein was concerned.

Paul immediately began working for the Zionist underground in the embassy annex (the glass house) and was assigned to go out every day with a group of other workers to the designated safe houses to help people move in or out, to find housing for more Jews in danger of being rounded up, or to move people who felt they were being watched too closely by the Gestapo. Because he lived under the protection of the Swiss, he was able to procure protective passes for his aunt and uncle. Sometimes the Nazis acknowledged the documents; often they ignored them and deported their bearers anyway. Still, possession of a Swiss or Swedish protective pass was better than having none at all.

Paul worked for the Zionist underground from October until early January, when the Russians broke through to Budapest. Amid the shelling and bombing, Paul again feared for his life. He did not want to be killed by the Nazis or captured by the Russians. It was time to escape the city, but how? Under cover of darkness, he and a friend from the rabbinic school began walking toward the city of Debrecen, which they figured was already liberated. They knew that whatever fighting had taken place there was now over.

Paul and his friend had barely covered a few miles when they were captured by the Russians. They were ordered to load ammunition onto trucks headed to fight the Germans in Budapest. The Russians were tough taskmasters, making the captured men work day and night. They were not the least bit interested that Paul and his friend were Jews who had been persecuted by the fascists; their captors needed their able bodies for work. While the chores were difficult enough, the rumors circulating about the Russians were what really frightened Paul. He and his friend had heard that when the prisoners had completed the work, the Russians would put them on empty freight trains and ship them off to Russia. To make matters worse, Paul actually saw the empty trains waiting at a railway station.

As usual, Paul's brain was brimming with plans for escape. His first idea was to find a Russian Jew, speak to him in Yiddish, tell him who they were, and ask for his help. They actually found such a person and elicited a commitment from him, but the man disappeared the next day, leaving Paul and his friend discouraged and demoralized.

The two men continued their work, loading ammunition onto truck after truck and watching them speed off to the west. Between the arrival of empty trucks, the workers were allowed to spend a few minutes in a small hut to warm themselves. If they requested, they could visit the outhouse two at a time.

Paul noticed that only one Russian soldier was assigned to guard the waiting men. "When we go to the hut to get warm," Paul whispered to his friend, "we'll ask to visit the outhouse. Then, we won't come back. We'll disappear."

They planned their escape for the next night. When the time came, they were unable to coordinate the trip to the outhouse together, but each was able to convince the guard separately of the urgent need to use the facilities. His friend slipped away in the darkness, and then Paul, too, had the chance to break free. He could not find his friend, however, who evidently was too afraid to wait for him. Frightened and alone in the winter darkness, Paul decided to walk along the railroad tracks and hope his friend had taken the road. He knew that at one point the road crossed the tracks, and he hoped to meet up with his friend there.

Unfortunately, Paul reached a small railroad station before hooking up with his friend. At the station, Jewish laborers were helping to load furniture onto a truck. "What are you doing here?" asked a Russian officer. "Helping to load the furniture," said Paul, picking up a chair and hoisting it onto the truck. When the officer was not looking, Paul ran off, ducking for cover all the way.

Just as he reached the Tisza River, he spotted his friend. As he had thought, his friend had been too afraid to wait for Paul near the outhouse. It did not matter anymore; together, they could now face what lay ahead.

The two men crossed the Tisza on what was left of the bridge that spanned the river. The bridge had suffered too much damage to permit trains or trucks to cross, but it still held the weight of two men on foot. From there, they walked to the next railroad station where they planned to take the train to Debrecen, where they both had relatives before the deportations began.

At the railroad station were hundreds of Hungarian men trying to get home. Russian soldiers kept coming into the station and beckoning to them for work detail. Paul and his friend huddled together, afraid they would be chosen. Perhaps they should have waited outside the station, but it was January and their clothing was too skimpy.

Finally, they were able to board the train to Debrecen, the region's largest city. Both men had family there before the war, but after disembarking and walking around the city, they could find none of them. There was nothing left for Paul to do but travel further to Hajdunanas, where he hoped to find some trace of his family.

Paul trudged along, cold and exhausted. His excitement about his return to his hometown was tempered by apprehension. What he had seen in Debrecen had left him with little hope of what he might find in his own city. Judith was dead, but what about his parents and his brothers?

When he got to Hajdunanas, it was late at night. The city was eerily silent, as if the town itself had died in the war. Paul checked his own house and found it occupied by people he did not know. Wondering what to do but so exhausted from his long journey, he entered an abandoned house and slept there.

As soon as daylight broke, he set off to walk around the city; it looked desolate. He heard that a few Jews had returned from labor camps. He was desperate to see someone from the Jewish community, someone who could tell him about his family. He walked to the synagogue and found some men there, but they did not know anything about his parents or brothers. He asked about his friend Steve Hornstein. Yes, someone told him, he was back. They told Paul where Steve was staying, and Paul hurried there. The two friends embraced heartily. Steve was living with some friends of his family who invited Paul to stay there, too.

For the next few days, the two young men, although forever changed by the war, made plans for their future. Steve knew that he would finally start medical school as a regular student; the Russians were in charge now, and the hated *numerus clausus* was no longer in effect. Paul planned to attend medical school also, but he wanted to go to Palestine. He would not leave Hungary, though, until he had news of his parents, brothers, and Anna. He was aware that whole Jewish communities had disappeared, but he knew nothing about concentration camps, gas chambers, or Hitler's plan to rid Europe entirely of its Jewry. That information would be all too available to him in the coming months.

9   *Anna:*
       Inside the Gates of Hell

ALTHOUGH THE GERMANS WHO ENTERED Szendro in the spring of 1944 were considered an occupying force, the Hungarian officials of that town made no secret of their welcome, heartily collaborating with their conquerors in the harassment and roundup of their Jewish citizens. Just as they had done in the years leading up to World War II, the Szendro police and community leaders enthusiastically participated in the harassment of the Jews. For the most part, their Gentile neighbors completely turned their backs on them.

The Jews of Szendro stayed huddled in their homes when the Germans first arrived in their town in April 1944. What would happen to them? Anna Brünn's two older brothers, Paul and Andrew, had already been sent to forced labor camps. With her mother, Anna had lovingly arranged warm clothing and food in Andrew's backpack and had watched as he had walked off to the railroad station. Would she ever see him or her older brother, Paul, again?

Her father, so gentle and sensitive, had not eaten or slept well in weeks. Her mother, brave and resourceful, could not offer any workable solutions to this situation. There was nothing to do but wait to see what the Germans had in store for them next.

The Jews clung to one slim hope: the one undisputable fact on their side was that the Germans had been fighting a war since 1939, and now, it was nearly five years later. Surely their resolve and their manpower must be weakening. This theory was the only slant of light in an otherwise dark and gloomy time.

These hopes were soon dashed, however, when the Hungarian police—supposedly under duress because they were on orders from the German SS—commanded all the Jews of Szendro to pack one small suitcase each and immediately abandon their homes. As she left her beautiful house—easily the prettiest in all of Szendro—Anna's heart broke. She tried to hide the tears from her parents as she bent down by the front gate to say goodbye to her beloved dog, Zombor. The Jews were not allowed to take their pets, and Anna could not control her sobs when she looked back and saw Zombor gazing after the family, wagging his tail. She tried to pull herself together as she helped her father escort her ninety-six-year-old grandmother through the streets of Szendro, around the central market-place, to the three houses that were to serve as the residences of the Jews of Szendro until they learned what the Nazis had planned for them.

Anna's family was assigned a room in an old apartment building that now served as Szendro's post office. Ironically, the building had once been owned by her father's family, and Anna had been born in one of the building's flats seventeen years earlier. Now, with all of Szendro's two hundred Jews consigned to three small buildings, there was barely room to sit. To make room, the adults decided that the children would sleep outside in the yard, so the older people could use the beds, couches, and chairs.

From the Szendro ghetto, Anna managed to send a postcard to her boyfriend, Paul Ornstein, at his dormitory in Budapest. She gave him her new address but said that it might be temporary. She was not sure, but she thought the Nazis had plans to move them elsewhere.

A few days after she mailed the card, the Hungarian police came to the ghetto, banged on the doors of each apartment, and shouted for the Jews to get out of their beds, grab their suitcases, and line up in the street. As soon as they tumbled outside on this bright June morning, the men and women were ordered into separate lines. Anna, her mother, and grand-mother stood closely together, holding hands, trying to protect each other from whatever would come next.

The Hungarian gendarmes ordered the Szendro women—every female in the ghetto except the very youngest girls—into a shed, where a Hungarian midwife roughly searched their body cavities. As she reached the front of the line, Anna realized what was happening. To keep from thinking about this impending humiliation, she concentrated on the uniforms of the Hungarian soldiers: they wore brightly colored feather-adorned helmets, crisply pressed trousers and jackets, and shiny knee-high boots. If they had not looked so fierce and menacing, Anna could almost imagine them appearing in a childhood fairy tale. But this was no fairy tale; this was real—and when it was her turn to enter the shed, she bore the ordeal with all the dignity her seventeen-year-old soul could muster.

When she rejoined her mother and grandmother, she squeezed their hands to let them know she was all right.

After the examinations, the Hungarian guards pushed and shouted for the Jews to grab their bundles and climb into the backs of several trucks that would transport them to the train station. By now, their Gentile neighbors had gathered in silence to watch the spectacle, but not one moved to say goodbye. Anna, gripping her mother's hand, felt betrayed by this lack of emotion and by no one's willingness to try to help them.

Suddenly, she heard someone calling her family's name. She jumped to her feet and looked over the side of the truck to see her grandmother's former maid, whom the family called Mari Neni, waving goodbye and throwing kisses to them. "I love you!" she shouted up to the Brünn family. "Be careful!" she cried.

Anna knew how courageous it was for Mari Neni to come in person to wish them well. It was a show of emotion that could have gotten her arrested. That gesture of kindness gave the Brünns hope that somewhere along the line, other brave and sympathetic Hungarians would come to their rescue.

The trucks bounced along the unpaved streets, taking the Jews to the Szendro railroad station, where Anna saw a long train of freight cars waiting for them. The last two cars were empty, but surely the Nazis did not expect all the Jews to fit inside those two small wagons. Perhaps they would have to wait for another train. But there was no waiting. The Hungarian officials, pushing and shouting, herded the Jews into the two empty cars and sealed the doors and windows. Even before the train left the station, the air became stifling. Anna feared she would pass out.

In less than an hour, the train stopped in Miskolc, the next largest city. There, the Jews were ordered out of the trains and marched to the yard of a steel factory, where thousands of other Jews, gathered from the small towns and cities of northern Hungary, were milling about, talking, shouting, asking questions. The Szendro Jews were pushed into the crowd, and confusion reigned as people grasped for each other's hands, tried to retrieve their meager bundles of belongings, and attempted to hurry along in response to the prodding of the Hungarian guards' rifle butts. Everywhere, people were crying, wandering around in a daze, trying to locate family members from other towns.

That night, lying quietly on the ground under a thin blanket, Anna could hear her father's muffled sobs and her mother's consoling words. As she snuggled between them, she felt almost safe, as if her parents could figure out a way to save the family. Her mother, Sophie, had held them together during the most trying times, when her father was taken to jail on false charges and when her brothers left home for the forced labor camps. Anna could rely on her mother. She always had a plan.

The next day, chaos descended once again, as the Jews were transported back to the railroad station and ordered aboard another train. This time, instead of just the two hundred Jews from Szendro, thousands of Jews from all over that part of Hungary were stuffed into freight cars, usually used to transport livestock. As the train pulled away from the station, the hundreds of people in each car vied for breathing space. There was no room to sit, much less stretch out on the floor. The June air was sticky and close. The windows and doors had been sealed so that the Jews could not escape or even orient themselves. They had no idea which way they were going. The train could be headed anywhere.

The Brünn family—grandmother, parents, Anna, an aunt, an uncle, and cousins—found a corner for the grandmother to sit. They stood around her, protecting her so she would not be crushed by the hundreds of people jostling for a little piece of space to call their own. The train lurched crazily, its stuffed cargo of human bodies forcing it to list left or right.

Someone pointed to a barrel in the far corner that was to be used as a toilet. But the rising panic level in the railway car, the crush of bodies, babies' crying, the keening of the elderly, and the stagnant air made people lose control of their bodily functions. Soon, their sense of smell was assaulted by the blanketing odor of feces and vomit. Anna fainted, was revived by her mother, only to faint again. Everywhere she looked, people were crying or wailing in pain, throwing up, defecating, or collapsing. They were dehydrated from lack of water, faint from lack of food. Deprived of sleep, they could only lean against each other, flesh upon flesh, nowhere to move, nowhere else to look except at the degraded and suffering humanity around them.

They felt the train stop several times, but no one was allowed out. They could feel additional cars being hitched onto the end of the train, and after about an hour, they felt movement once again. Were they going to ride in these cattle cars forever? Were the Germans going to dump them in Russia?

By the time the train pulled to a stop after about a week and the doors were pried open, most of the Jews were too weak to move. Soldiers in uniform began shouting at them in German, motioning for them to hurry out. Those who could not move fast enough were roughly pulled or even beaten to make them hurry.

Beneath a hail of German curses, Anna tried to suck in the fresh air, great big gulps of it, as if somehow this would renew her, give her back all the strength she had lost in the cattle car. Her eyes were nearly blinded by the harsh sunlight, a brightness she had not seen in well over a week. Dogs barked and growled furiously, straining at their leashes as the German soldiers shouted commands: "Line up! Drop your suitcases! You'll get them back later! Move! Move! Move faster!"

The Brünn family struggled into a ragged formation. Many of the Jews were so weak they could not stand; their families tried as best they could to prop them up. Amidst the shouted orders of the guards and the ferocious barking of the dogs, Anna sagged against Sophie, waiting for the next set of instructions. She felt her mind beginning to shut down, as if her brain were trying to wall off the rest of her from the scene being enacted before her. As she waited numbly in the middle of the escalating chaos, she focused her eyes on a long line of cement poles that seemed to stretch into eternity. Between the poles was strung barbed wire—but why? To keep people from invading the place? Then, she realized: the barbed wire was there to keep people in. She would be a prisoner in this place called Auschwitz. She had never heard the name before.

With her mother, father, and grandmother by her side, she noticed people with shaved heads and striped uniforms moving about the Jews, taking their suitcases, telling them where to stand, and muttering the same litany over and over. What were they saying? When they drew closer to Anna's group, she understood. These were Jews, pressed into this distasteful service by their German masters. They were whispering in Yiddish to each group of Jewish prisoners, "Let the old people carry the babies. Mothers, give the grandparents your babies." When Anna saw that some mothers complied and some did not, she turned to Sophie. "Why should mothers give up their babies?" she asked. "So the mothers' lives will be saved," Sophie answered.

In that instant, Anna realized that Sophie understood the horrible truth: they had all been brought here to die. She recalled a young boy with whom she had gone to school asking her while they were still in the Szendro ghetto if she thought the Nazis would kill them. Without thinking, she had replied yes. But she did not really believe it then. She could not bring herself to believe it now.

The Jews who had survived the train trip were finally ordered to parade in twos past a Nazi officer sitting on a high platform. From the back of the line, Anna noticed that he motioned some people—usually young and healthy looking—to go to the right. He sent the old and frail to the left. "To go right is to live," Anna thought, as she and Sophie, hand in hand, approached the uniformed Nazi. He looked them over. "Right," he said.

Anna turned to watch her father and grandmother go through the line. When they stood in front of the platform, the Nazi officer said nothing but pointed his pen to the left. "No!" Anna cried softly. In tears, she watched as her defeated yet beloved father, William, slouched dejectedly off to the left, gently holding his ninety-six-year-old mother's hand. Anna kept her eyes trained on them for as far as she could see until they disappeared.

For a long time, the Jews sent to the right were made to stand and ponder their fate. People were looking through the crowd for relatives; everyone was crying or shouting out the names of family members and friends from whom they had become separated during the selection. Once in a while two friends or cousins might find each other and rush into an embrace. More often, though, the search was in vain. Anna clutched her mother's hand and the hand of her older cousin, whose parents and younger sister had been sent to the left.

Finally, after hours of waiting, the men and women were separated, and the men marched off to their own part of the camp. The women left behind were ordered to remove all of their clothing. "Hurry! Hurry!" the guards shouted, as the women fumbled out of their dresses and undergarments. As they stood there exposed to the elements, they were ordered into lines and marched toward some empty benches. Anna wondered if this would be a further selection, but from her place in line, she could see that Jewish camp inmates were standing by, shears, scissors, and razors in their hands. As the first group of women approached, they were pushed onto the benches and ordered to sit still while their heads were shaved. Then they were told to stand while their entire bodies were shorn of hair. If someone cried out in pain or in fear, the Nazi guards standing by immediately descended on that hapless person and commenced a rigorous beating.

When it was Anna's turn, she stoically bore the cutting of her beautiful thick plaits and the shaving of her head and pubic hair. Now, she had no hair, no clothes; her suitcase with her meager belongings had been taken away from her. She had no father, no grandmother either. Whatever had been part of her had been shorn and stripped away, leaving her exposed to the enemy. It was difficult to concentrate now. Again, she felt herself shutting down, as if a shroud of blessed ignorance had been draped about her shoulders. This could not be happening to them. It was a dream, a horrible nightmare. As she stood there naked, waiting for her mother, she looked away while Sophie removed her clothing. It was not that she was ashamed of Sophie's body; she merely wanted to respect whatever dignity and privacy her mother might have left.

When the shaving was complete, the women were herded into a wooden building with clothes and shoes piled everywhere. "Take one dress and one pair of shoes," a female SS guard ordered the women. Anna and Sophie hurried to a pile of clothes and shoes heaped in a corner. There was not too much time to choose any one item, but Anna listened carefully as Sophie advised her to pick out shoes that would not make her feet blister. She had a bit more time to choose her dress and pulled a tri-checkered one from the pile. As she slipped it over head, she realized that this dress had been worn before, but she tried not to think about the fate of the wearer. For a second she closed her eyes and wondered what hell the woman who had owned the dress must have gone through.

After selecting their clothes, the women were ordered to a barnlike structure that would be their barracks. The floor was made of dirt, and the barn had no ceiling, just a leaky roof. Anna and Sophie quickly chose a space to sit; there were no cots or beds. Though they were exhausted, sleep would have to wait.

The women were ordered out of the barracks and told to line up by fives. Anna and her mother clung to each other, of course. As they watched, the female SS guards in their tight skirts and uniform jackets menacingly brandished and cracked their leather whips. Women were pulled from the columns of five and beaten for no apparent reason. Anna felt as if she were being instructed in a lesson she had no need or desire to learn. "Pay attention or this will happen to you," the guards seemed to be saying. What puzzled Anna was that the women singled out for thrashings had not appeared to have been doing anything other than—like Anna and her mother—standing at attention.

Finally, the Nazis' demonstration of torture was over, and the women were sent back to their barracks. A meal of something that tasted like cooked grass was brought to them, but nothing else was offered. That first night, the women were too depleted to talk about their situation. All they could do was try to rest by leaning back to back against each other; they did not have the strength to speculate on what might happen to them next. Anna and her mother finally fell asleep, gripping each other's hands.

It was still pitch dark when the whistle blew, but Anna reasoned it must be early the next morning. The Nazi guards came into the barracks and prodded everyone awake with their whips. If someone did not move quickly enough, the Nazis used their fists. "Up and out," the guards shouted. "Stand at attention in groups of five!" Then the counting commenced, only to begin again. Over and over the women were counted. Anna could not understand why the Nazis were so obsessed with reconciling the numbers of Jewish prisoners. Where else could they go? The barbed wire and electrified fences stood as a taunting rebuke to all of them.

The second full day at Auschwitz was marked by lining up, being counted, and waiting for the next set of instructions. In her preworn dress, shaved head, and no under garments, Anna felt particularly vulnerable to the summer winds and rain. She hated the way the guards stared at her, as if they could see through her. She huddled as close as possible to Sophie, where she felt warm and protected. This would be the only way she could survive, to empty her mind as much as possible, cling to her mother, and not think too hard about what was happening. She had always been good at conjuring up dreams and letting her imagination run. She knew that her ability to take refuge in that safe place would keep her from thinking about the scenes of terror unfolding before her.

During the late afternoon, Anna, sniffing the air, asked her mother about the sweet, but unpleasant odor that permeated the camp. "What is that smell?" she asked, wrinkling her nose. "Is it true that they are burning Jews? That they are killing Jews in the gas chambers, then burning their bodies?" "Of course that isn't true," answered Sophie. But later that night, Anna overheard Sophie tell her cousin that the odor was, indeed, the smell of burning flesh. Still, Anna accepted Sophie's answer, agreeing to be lied to, so that for a little while longer, she could hide from the awful truth.

For a week, their days were filled with listening to shouted orders, standing in line, undergoing repeated countings and beatings, and trying to stay alive. Anna felt as if she were on a conveyer belt, automatically moving from one degrading episode to the next. At night, all they could talk about was what they longed for yet could not have: hot soup, a piece of soap, a warm bed, a man's strong arms. These yearnings and discussions at least helped to pass the hours.

One morning after the *appell,* or counting, on perhaps the sixth or seventh day after their arrival at Auschwitz, the women were kept in line for a longer time than usual. Anna turned questioningly to her mother, who motioned for her to say nothing. Soon, a Nazi officer in thigh-high boots and a gun at his hip strode to the head of the line and faced the waiting prisoners. The officer's aide ordered the women to march by in single file. Anna realized that another selection was about to take place, like the one when they had entered the camp. Again, the officer looked the women up and down and ordered them to the left or to the right. Anna approached the Nazi officer. She was young and healthy with a good strong body, so she assumed she would be sent to the right. Her assumption proved correct. When Sophie approached the Nazi officer, Anna held her breath. Miraculously, she was also sent to the right.

Sophie whispered to Anna that the selection meant they were going somewhere, perhaps to work. Why else would they have been sent to the right? This opinion was confirmed when the women were hosed down and disinfected. Soon, they were ordered into trucks and transported to the railroad station. There, the women piled into railroad cars, just like the ones that had brought them to Auschwitz in the first place. Again, they tried to find comfortable positions for what could be a long ride.

This trip took only a few hours, though. When the train stopped and the women were ordered out, they climbed into trucks that took them to another camp called Plaszow. As the women entered the gates, they could see a vast, barren expanse of land with no flowers, trees, or shrubs—just a huge stone quarry. Anna saw that here they would have work to do, unlike at Auschwitz, where they were expected to line up and wait.

Almost immediately upon arrival, Anna and the others were marched to the quarry and ordered to carry stones, seemingly without purpose, back and forth from one rock pile to another. From atop their horses, the Nazi guards made sure that each woman carried a rock large enough to pull her arms down straight. Anna tried to point out lighter rocks for her mother to carry, but one day, a guard observed this exchange and beat Sophie for several minutes. Anna could not bear to witness this cruelty, but to interfere would mean an even more severe beating for herself and further punishment for both. It was best to remain quiet.

The guards of Plaszow were notoriously barbarous. Every day brought a new round of beatings for the most innocent behavior—sharing of food, talking while at work. At night, the women were exhausted, not only from their arduous labor in the humid outdoor air but also from dodging the abuse, both mental and physical. The food was the only improvement over Auschwitz—cooked cabbage was served every day. Still, it was never enough to soothe their growling stomachs and hunger pains.

On they worked, carrying stones and rocks from the quarry to a rock pile, then from rock pile to rock pile, like Sisyphus, condemned forever to push a boulder up a hill, only to have it roll down again. The work had no beginning, no end, no meaning. Anna kept a watchful eye on Sophie, who seemed weaker every day. Sometimes her mother was too exhausted to eat.

One day, while working at the quarry, a shy girl who looked much like Anna approached them. "I heard someone say your name was Anna," she said. "Are you by any chance from Szendro?" Anna quickly confirmed this information. "Are you Paul Ornstein's girlfriend?" she asked.

Anna had not thought much about Paul since she had sent him the postcard from the Szendro ghetto. She did not want to think about anything but staying with her mother and remaining alive. Now, however, she was brought back into that unreal world of life before the war.

Yes, she said, she was Paul Ornstein's girlfriend. The girl who approached her said that she was from Miskolc and that her brother was Paul's classmate in the rabbinic seminary whom Paul had stopped to visit the time he rode his bicycle to see Anna in Szendro. The two girls embraced like old friends; it took Anna a while to realize that this girl had a crush on Paul. Still, Anna welcomed her into their little family. Sophie gathered the girl under her protective wing and treated her like a daughter.

"When the war is over, I want you to meet my sons," Sophie told her one night. "I would like you to marry one of them." All three laughed— the future was as far away and as hazy as the universe's most distant constellation.

The schedule at Plaszow was monotonous, broken only by intermittent yet severe beatings from the guards. Despite the improvement in the quality of food, Anna was just as hungry as she had been at Auschwitz. Still, she felt she could survive on less than Sophie, so she often pretended that the food was so unappealing to her that her mother would do her a great favor by finishing her portion.

One day while standing in line after returning from the quarry, a food truck piled with cabbage drove by. Just as it reached the spot where Anna and Sophie were standing, a head of cabbage fell from the heap and began to roll away. Without thinking, Anna scrambled after it while Sophie watched in horror. Stealing food was a crime punishable by swift and certain death. Still, Anna managed to grab the cabbage and hide it under her dress. She and Sophie shared it immediately, too frightened—and hungry—to save it for the comforting dark of night.

They knew that their love and care for each other would be the key to their survival. Having someone to care about and someone to care about you was as necessary to staying alive in the camps as food and shelter. Because Sophie had always been good at seeing the big picture, at taking the long view of a situation, Anna left it up to her mother to make the larger decisions of their lives. Sophie was completely aware of all the horrors in the camp, knew who had survived selections and who had not, and instinctively understood where to stand in line for the best food, the best corner in which to sleep, how to sort the facts from rumors.

Anna, petite for seventeen and gentle in manner, tended to the everyday chores and thousands of little ways to stay alive. Appealing and even seductive, Anna had an instinct for her own and her mother's survival that came as naturally to her as her winsome and helpful manner. She rubbed her mother's hands and feet when they were sore; she groomed Sophie as best she could, picking from the stubble of her head and pubic hair the crawling lice that made them so miserable. Because the Nazis had taken Sophie's glasses from her, Anna acted as her eyes, reading signs to her or the writing on any scrap of paper Anna could find. In that way, although they were not conscious of this division of labor, mother and daughter were able to ensure each other's survival.

For two months, the routine stayed the same. A few times, a selection took place, where those who were too sick to work were plucked from the ubiquitous formation by fives and, so it was rumored, sent back to Auschwitz for cremation. Anna always worried that Sophie would be selected, but her mother managed to fool the officers into thinking she was well and healthy.

One day, the Nazis informed the Jews that they would have to leave the camp. Rumors spread that the Nazis were abandoning Plaszow because the Russians had broken through the German lines at the Polish border. Encouraged by this news yet frantic about their next destination, they were consumed by speculation about their fate. It was all anyone could think or talk about.

While marching in fives to the trucks that would take them back to the railroad station, Sophie found a square of red material on the ground. She picked it up and tied it jauntily around her head. Anna realized that she was trying to look young and fit, but she could see her mother's face close up; her skin was dry and cracked, her teeth were rotting, and her eyes had a haunted, desperate look.

They boarded the same cattle wagon. The women tried to get their bearings and figure out which way the train was heading. East to Russia? Back to the interior of Poland? Anna hoped they were being sent to another work camp, because if the Nazis needed Jews to work, it meant that they would be allowed to live. She was thankful to be young and healthy, for old, sick Jews were useless to the Nazis. She put her head on her mother's shoulder. The weeks at Plaszow had further weakened Sophie. If only Anna could give her some of her own youthful strength.

Hours later, when the train finally stopped, one of the women cried out, "I can see the signs in German. We are back at Auschwitz!" Waves of fear rippled through the women on the train. Going back into the camp meant another selection. Anna faced her mother. Sophie had lost so much weight; she would not be able to hide her frailty. Sores festered on her lips; her eyes appeared to sink into her head.

When the women entered the Auschwitz gates, they lined up as usual for the selection. The same Nazi officer with the boots and gun sat at a high platform, using his fountain pen to gesture left or right. Anna overheard an assistant address him as "Herr Dr. Mengele," but the name meant nothing to her.

Sophie and Anna stood together as they approached the doctor who held their fate in his hands. Women they knew, women with whom they had shared food, secrets, fantasies, and memories, were being sent to the left. Anna looked after them longingly, knowing she would never see them again.

The line moved swiftly, and soon Anna and Sophie stood in front of Dr. Mengele. He looked them over. To Anna he pointed right. He looked Sophie up and down. She was only forty-six years old, but standing in the bright sunlight, she looked seventy and desperate. Her face was drawn, her body sagged, and she was weak from lack of food and sleep. Mengele pointed to the left.

"No," said Sophie. "I will not go left. I will go right with my daughter." "Left," ordered Mengele. "I cannot leave my daughter alone," said Sophie. "She and I will both go to the right."

Mengele turned to face Sophie, staring her down. Who was this woman, this Jew, to argue with his decision? Finally, he spoke. "Right," he pronounced, as if he no longer had time to waste on her. Mother and daughter went right to live.

≡

The autumn days were growing shorter, the nights longer. Life at Auschwitz this time was much different from their first stay here. The Hungarian women were now in a different part of the camp, with newer barracks that had actual cots to share. The buildings were huge, holding at least a thousand women in each. The food was a vast improvement over their first stay at Auschwitz and better than Plaszow, too. They received bread, margarine, soup, even cooked horsemeat.

"They wouldn't be feeding us like this if they did not expect us to live," Anna whispered to Sophie one night. Sophie nodded in agreement, but she was not nearly as optimistic as her daughter. Still, she felt that it was important to protect Anna, even though she was seventeen and no longer a child.

Anna, for her part, felt that she was protecting her mother by sharing her food—and even sharing Sophie herself. Most of the women had been separated from their mothers, daughters, or sisters, and Anna felt lucky to still have her mother. So when someone needed to talk, cry, or share a thought or a story, she would bring her to Sophie, who would listen and offer a caress of comfort. In this way, Anna enlarged Sophie's role as a mother, making her feel wanted and needed.

Auschwitz was not a work camp like Plaszow, so there was little for the women to do except line up, be counted, and wait. The Nazis still ordered selections, but Anna and Sophie survived them. Rumor after rumor circulated through the camp that the Russians were close now, but this did not seem to deter the Germans from their cruelties. Beatings were everyday occurrences, food was withheld for the slightest infraction, and many prisoners died from illness and exposure.

One morning, they were kept even longer than usual standing at *appell*. Anna did not mind too much, since the sun was brilliant and the air was cool and crisp. On perfect days like these, she was tempted to recall her old life, her school, her friends, the songs and games they played. A year ago, she was part of that old world. She wondered if she would ever get it back.

As she stood next to Sophie, she noticed five young, pretty, well-groomed girls carrying tables to the front of the lines. For a moment, Anna felt a stab of envy; the girls wore clean, blue uniforms, shoes, and socks—and their hair! Their hair was clean, brushed, and styled. The rustle of rumors shimmied down the lines of the Jewish women standing at attention.

The five girls at the head of the lines were Czechoslovakian Jews who had special privileges in the camp. Their assignment today was to give each woman in the line a tattoo that would forever brand her as a prisoner.

Instead of fear, elation swept through the crowd. If the Germans were going to all this bother to tattoo them, then surely it meant they would be allowed to live. Otherwise, why go to all that trouble and expense? On such a beautiful day to receive such wonderful news as this!

As Anna moved up from near the end of the line, she was able to observe which one of the Czech girls was the most delicate artist. She wanted her tattoo on the inside of her forearm with neat, straight letters and numbers, so she made sure that she was in the line of the most talented. When it was her turn, she told the Czech girl that she had chosen her especially for her nice work. This so pleased the tattoo artist that she took great care to be sure Anna was satisfied with her handiwork.

Anna came away from the line with the number B-71 tattooed neatly on the inside of her forearm just as she had requested. Proudly, she showed it to Sophie. This was a most thrilling day for Anna, almost a birthday, a day that foretold her certain survival. Her happiness was only briefly diminished when the Jews had to line up again the next day for further tattoos. The *B* in the tattoo had meant that they were attached to the "B" unit of Auschwitz, but the Nazis had changed their plans; now the Hungarian Jews would be part of the "A" unit. Anna was tattooed again, this time with a marking that said A-20071. These letters, too, were small and neat, just beneath the first that read B-71. As Anna left the line and took her place next to her mother, she realized that she had not noticed whether either procedure had hurt.

During this second stay in Auschwitz, Anna no longer hid the fact from her mother that she knew about the gas chambers and the crematoria. The smell, the selections, the disappearance of beloved friends told the story. Auschwitz might have been a kind of transit camp, Anna knew, but its primary function was to serve as a death camp. Before the tattoos, Anna was certain that eventually she and her mother would meet death there, but the markings on her arm gave her hope that soon they would be sent out of the camp again to work.

It was easier to face the chilly autumn days under this new illusion that they were protected from the gas chambers by their tattoos. So Anna was puzzled when, on a late afternoon, several of the barracks were ordered emptied and thousands of women told to stand at attention. The Nazi guards counted them over and over again. What could this be, Anna wondered. Too many women were lined up to be transported elsewhere. The Nazis must have had some other plan in mind.

Still puzzled by this departure from the usual schedule, the women were marched across a wide highway, through an empty field to the edge of a forest. As Anna walked, she saw a truck drive by with people lying down in the back. They seemed all crushed in together. How could they breathe like that, she wondered. As the truck passed the marching women, Anna saw that all those in the truck were naked. With a start, she realized that every one of them was dead. She turned to Sophie and gripped her hand even tighter.

By now, the sky had darkened, and the air had turned cold. The Nazi guards, brandishing their whips, ordered the women to undress and form another line. What about the tattoos that ensured their lives? Anna wanted to shout, "We're supposed to be saved for work! We have tattoos!" But women were crying softly, lunging for each other's hands, whispering and questioning.

For what seemed the whole night long, the naked women stood in line, shivering uncontrollably. The Nazi guards walked among them, shouting for quiet, pulling women out of line to beat them for whispering or not standing up straight. Anna and Sophie stood as close to each other as they could but did not dare to speak a word.

Finally, the women were ordered to march through the woods. When the outline of a low, nondescript building emerged from the shadows, they were ordered to halt. Anna could barely make out what seemed like some sort of flowers that ringed the structure. "It's the gas chamber!" someone shouted. Thousands of women now surrounded the building, and in the ensuing crush and screams, Anna lost sight of Sophie for a few frightening seconds. Finally she found her and grabbed her hand.

"Please, little girl," begged Sophie. "This place is for my daughter, Anna." "Mother," Anna whispered. "It's me. It's Anna." "Go away," Sophie hissed. "I'm saving this place for my daughter." Anna realized in horror that her mother could not recognize her. To Sophie, Anna was just another emaciated naked girl with a shaved head like the thousands of women ringing the outside of the fake shower house. Or was her mother delirious with fear?

She grabbed Sophie's hand anyway, as the Nazi guards pushed the Jews into the building. Anna was shoved roughly against a wooden beam. She cried out in pain, a cry that was lost among the thousands of voices begging for mercy. So this was the gas, and there was nothing Anna could do about it but greet the death she always knew deep down would come. At least she and her mother would die together. The worst thing that could happen in Auschwitz was to be separated from loved ones, and now that fear could be put behind them.

But for some reason, the gas was never turned on. The women waited and waited, their keening cries and prayers slowly subsiding. What had gone wrong? As usual, rumors filtered through the mass of humanity crushed into the huge room. The Germans had run out of gas, they whispered. The Germans had changed their minds; they wanted the Hungarian women for work. They did not know why, but finally the doors were opened, and they were sent back across the fields to retrieve their clothes and stand in line for the endless counting by fives. Later, they would learn that the building had been one of the barracks where prisoners waited *before* being sent to the gas chambers, but this information did not lessen their relief at having escaped death.

A week after their near-death experience, the women were again ordered out of their barracks, lined up, counted, and then led to some waiting trucks. The convoy of vehicles deposited them at the train station once again for another trip to a destination unknown. Shoved into the sealed cattle cars once more, the women could only guess where they were going, but the motion of the train told them that they were climbing into the mountains. Hours later, when the train finally stopped and the doors opened, the women knew that these instincts were correct.

It had been a long time since the women had seen beauty such as this: the snow-capped mountains, the lush green pine trees, invitingly snug-looking cabins off in the distance. Anna thought she must be in a resort of some kind—but why would the Germans send them here? She also noticed signs in a language she did not recognize. Someone said they were now in Czechoslovakia.

Elated with this good fortune, Anna and her mother eagerly marched toward the low bungalows. Anna could see inside: real cots with sheets and blankets! What good fortune! What was even better, more than she could ever ask for: as the Hungarian women stood in line, several girls from Szendro spotted Anna and Sophie and ran over to them excitedly. This was a wonderful place to work, they told them. They had real food to eat, too, and the cottages were warm and cozy. Anna could hardly believe their luck.

Their joy was short-lived, however. While some of the women in their group were ordered to the cottages, Anna and Sophie were marched to a large barn for the night and told that they would be moving to another camp the next day called Parschnitz. In a way, Anna was glad she had not had time to fall in love with this peaceful oasis among the pine trees. For here, among this beauty, she would surely wake up from her semi-somnambulant state only to think about her father and her brothers and the death all around her.

The next morning, the hundred women who had spent the night in the barn were taken to the train station, herded into the same sealed cattle cars, and dispatched on another journey. Anna never thought she would get used to standing in a stifling railroad car with no room to move, no air to breathe. But here they were again, headed to another place, with no idea what would be waiting for them.

The train trip to Parschnitz, a work camp inside Czechoslovakia, lasted only a few hours. This place was nearly as ugly as Plaszow. When the women trudged from the train, tired and hungry, they were sent immediately to their barracks, a square stone structure that looked as if it would provide some warmth against the increasingly colder nights.

The next morning, reveille blew while it was still dark outside. The women ran immediately for the latrines, then lined up outside in their thin dresses and summer shoes. If only they could have a sweater and a pair of socks, Anna whispered to Sophie. With nothing else to think about except what they did not have, the women commenced to march to another train station, where they boarded railway cars headed for a small town about an hour away. In that town was a factory where the women were to work at machines that made parts for airplanes.

Luckily for Anna, she was chosen to work at a machine inside the factory, where it was warm and cozy. She enjoyed the feeling of her fingers and toes thawing out from the long march and the unheated train. It was a pleasure she welcomed but also for which she felt a measure of guilt. The younger people were separated from the older ones, who were left outside to clean scraps of metal in the factory yard that the younger women would use inside. It was late autumn by now—the Jewish high holidays were probably long past—and the wind howled mercilessly across the factory's courtyard. Anna's mother was one of the older people assigned to outdoor duty. The separation from her daughter was hard enough, but the weather only added to her misery.

Although Parschnitz was a labor camp staffed by cruel Nazis, the conditions were much better than at Auschwitz. Selections took place only in the infirmary, so the morning *appell* no longer held the same elements of fear. The food was not so good—just bread, soup, and coffee—but they were fed regularly. They were always hungry—hungry enough to resort to stealing sometimes—and their preoccupation with food had not lessened.

Working in the factory along with the Hungarian women was a group of Polish Jews who had been at Parschnitz since the camp had opened in 1942. Because they were never sent to Auschwitz or any other death camp, they still had their hair and their health. Their bodies were in decent condition, considering the hardships of slave labor. Many of them were educated and spoke several languages, including Yiddish and German. Anna was thoroughly intimidated by these women—and a bit jealous of them, too.

The Polish women and Hungarian women shared living quarters, but they did not interact. For one thing, the Hungarian women knew no Yiddish, Polish, or German, so they could not communicate. For another, just looking at the Hungarian women was not a pleasant sight. Their heads and bodies had been shaved; their teeth were rotting; their emaciated bodies were dirty because they had never been allowed water to wash; their clothes were filthy and soiled. Most of them were covered in lice, scabies, and open sores. Anna could understand why no one wanted to come near them. Still, she envied the Polish girls who had been at Parschnitz for so long that some of them had important jobs in the kitchen or infirmary and were allowed special privileges, such as extra food.

One night, Anna was awakened by the sound of soft laughter. She could see two of the Polish women in a far corner of the barracks washing each other with water from a large pail. How lovely it would be, thought Anna, to give her mother a bath. Or to take a bath herself. She lay silently on her cot as she watched the women wash each other's backs.

Suddenly, she had an idea. She sat up on her cot and waited until she was sure the Polish women had finished their sponge baths. When Anna saw that the women were done with the pail of water, she tiptoed over to their corner. "Excuse me," she said, using the few words she knew in German, since she could not speak Polish. "Please don't pour the water out of the pail. I would so love to give my poor mother a bath."

The Polish women stared at Anna, a young girl with an ugly stubble on her head, her rail-thin arms poking out of her clothes. Yet, she seemed so innocent and sweet, certainly not threatening or intimidating in any way. The Polish women looked at each other and shrugged. Why not? They motioned for Anna to take the bath water.

Delighted with her good fortune, Anna woke up Sophie. "Mother, look what I have!" she whispered. "It will be our first bath since June." Sophie cried tears of amazement. On this cold winter night, mother and daughter took turns washing each other with a rag the Polish women had left in the pail. By the time they finished, the water was a dark gray.

The Polish women were actually pleased that Anna had asked for their leftover water and made sure to offer it to her the next time they had a bath. It was one of the few pleasures at Parschnitz, and Anna was thankful for it. Nothing like a second-hand bath would have been allowed at Auschwitz.

Because Sophie was forced to work outside in the factory courtyard cleaning bits of scrap and metal, Anna was sure that she would eventually fall ill with some disease and infection. But it was the younger, stronger Anna who came down with a sore throat and watery stools. Soon she was exhausted and dehydrated by typhoid fever.

She was so terribly ill, she had to go to sick call. This was never a choice borne lightly by the Jewish prisoners. In Parschnitz, the only time Nazis conducted selections was in the infirmary; a sick Jew who could not work was immediately sent back to Auschwitz—to the gas chamber.

Despite the way she looked—her stubble, splotches, scabies bites all over her body—Anna's gentle nature charmed the Jewish nurses and doctors from Poland who had been assigned to the Parschnitz infirmary. The medical staff was so sure that Anna was sick enough to be selected for the trip back to Auschwitz that they hid her in a closet alongside the daughter of a famous rabbi that they were also trying to protect. When the SS officers came to the infirmary for inspections—they would pull back the bedcovers and shine their flashlights on the diseased patients to check their conditions—Anna would cower in the closet and pray that she would not be discovered.

Weeks went by, and her condition slowly improved. Sophie came to visit as often as she could. On her daughter's eighteenth birthday in January 1945, she managed to smuggle in a wondrous gift: an apple core she had found on the grounds of the camp. She insisted that Anna eat it all— no need to share this time. The apple core was more than Anna could have hoped for—that and her restored good health.

By the end of January 1945, Anna was out of the infirmary and back at her job in the airplane parts factory. She was thankful to be working indoors, but she was still frantic with worry about Sophie, who was outside in the cold and dreary winter. With no undergarments to keep her warm or boots to protect her feet, Sophie was sometimes up to her knees in snow.

Yet both mother and daughter felt rich and lucky, because they had each other to care for and care about. It was a valued luxury denied to so many others, to have relatives or friends survive together in the camps. That they had made it this far—they had no idea how much longer the war would last—gave them the will to keep going as long as they could stay together.

The long, cold winter bore on, dragging the women down with typhoid fever, pneumonia, tuberculosis, and other dread diseases. Their resistance was so low and their bodies so depleted that many either died in the infirmary or were sent back to Auschwitz.

But finally, the snow and ice began to melt, turning the camp into mud. The mud wormed its way inside their shoes and squished between their toes as the women marched through endless puddles on their way to and from their barracks. Yet they felt this was a small price to pay for the soft rains and gentle breezes of spring that finally replaced one of the harshest winters Europe had ever seen.

One day, the German overseer of the factory appeared in the doorway and shouted for attention. "President Roosevelt is dead," he shouted. "Germany is sure to win the war." Although the women were not allowed to speak to one another while they were working, an unmistakable chatter of voices filled the room. What did it mean? Was all hope gone now? "It's a trick," whispered one of the women. "Don't believe him. The Germans are just trying to demoralize us even more." Anna was eighteen now, but politically naive; she had no idea what effect Roosevelt's supposed death would have on the outcome of the war. She wished she could talk it over with her mother, but Sophie was outside in the courtyard.

That was the strange thing about Parschnitz: except for working and living like slaves, the war itself was a mystery to the Jewish prisoners. Since battles were not being fought in this part of Czechoslovakia, the Jews never saw warplanes or heard cannon fire. Soldiers did not come through the town either. And, of course, they were not allowed to see newspapers or listen to radio broadcasts. Any scrap of news they could glean was overheard gossip or a snatch of conversation among the camp guards. Someone reported that the Americans had won a big battle in Germany, but it did not seem likely to them. The Allies should have defeated the Germans by now, they reasoned. What was taking them so long?

The weather took a sudden turn for the better. The sun came out, the crocuses bloomed, and the sky turned a brilliant blue. Although they were still awakened at 4:30 every morning, it was not long before the sun was warming their ravaged bodies. Anna recalled the last time she had witnessed weather like this: she was in her house in Szendro, right before the Germans had marched into town and ruined their lives forever.

One spring morning, Anna woke up to be greeted by a brilliant sunshine. She had overslept—but how? Had she missed the *appell?* She could be beaten for such an indulgence. She hurried to the window of the barracks, where she saw below her—nothing. No one was in the courtyard. The gate to the camp was wide open. Suddenly, she saw the camp commander standing next to his horse. As Anna looked on in disbelief, he mounted his steed and galloped off toward the nearby forest, tearing his Nazi insignia from his jacket.

Anna called excitedly for Sophie to come to the window. Soon they were joined by hundreds of others, all cheering and shouting. For what they had just seen, witnessed with their own eyes, were the Germans fleeing in defeat. The camp was theirs! The war must be over!

The noise in the barracks reached a deafening level, as women screamed and cried in joy. A babble of Hungarian, Yiddish, and Polish filled the air. So accustomed were they to their captivity, however, that at first, none of them dared to leave the barracks. Finally, a few ventured outside, then more, then hundreds, then thousands.

Most ran for the kitchen, squeezing in through the doors, barreling for the sacks of food. Anna was carried along by the frenzied crowd, losing sight of Sophie. The starving women found the bags of flour, sugar, and beans, tearing them open and gorging themselves, paying no heed to those among them who warned them that they would surely become sick.

Anna made her way out of the kitchen to look for her mother. She checked the latrines, where she saw a crowd of Polish Jews who had captured two of the SS women guards, shaved their heads, and dunked their faces in the overflowing toilets. Whatever vestiges of civility the Jews had managed to hold onto were now stripped away altogether by their sudden freedom.

Anna found Sophie in the barracks trying to talk calmly to some of the younger women amidst the noise and chaos brought on by their sense of victory over the Nazis. They had survived! They were alive! The hated Germans had been defeated.

But what were they supposed to do now? Where could they go? That afternoon, they heard a motorcycle off in the distance. Finally, a Russian soldier covered in dirt and dust pulled into the camp. He was their liberator. He pronounced them free and then took off down the road.

The women had no idea what to do next. The Russians may have freed them, but the women were imprisoned by that freedom. For one thing, they had no idea where to go or how to get there; for another, they had heard the stories about Russian soldiers, how they had raped women and pillaged the countryside in the last war.

After a few days, the women decided to leave Parschnitz and walk back to Hungary. They had no idea which way to go or what they would find along the way. Sophie and Anna set out with a group of about a hundred other women. They walked until hunger stopped them, and then they would approach farmhouses, where many times sympathetic Czechs would give them a meal of boiled potatoes. At night, they slept in the fields under the May sky.

The women walked and walked, asking directions of anyone they met along the way. They did not make much progress. Because they were so consumed by hunger, they stopped often to beg or forage for food in abandoned towns. In one empty building, they found hundreds of potatoes buried in the soil under a house. They stayed there a few days, gorging themselves on this bounty.

One afternoon, having walked several miles, the women stopped to nap in the warm sun. Anna actually slept peacefully, dreaming of Szendro and her comfortable home. After some time, she opened her eyes and looked at Sophie. "If Paul Ornstein is still alive," she announced to her mother, "I am going to marry him." "What if he doesn't want to marry you?" Sophie asked, smiling. "I hadn't thought of that," Anna replied. She really had not; she and Paul would be married, and he would wrap her in the safety and security for which she was longing. It would just have to work out that way.

On they journeyed in the heat of summer, dragging their exhausted bodies across fields, wading through rivers, trying to look for roads and railroad tracks, hoping a passing truck or train would pick them up. That would be a real risk; what if their only choice was to ride along with the infamous Russian soldiers or resign themselves to walking all the way back to Hungary? It would take forever.

One day, while straggling along near a set of railroad tracks, the women heard the unmistakable huffing of an approaching train. As it neared, they could discern men's voices, shouting and singing lustily. By now they were so anxious to reach Hungary, they decided to flag it down. When the train stopped, however, the women were delighted to find that these men were not Russians but Yugoslav partisans who were actually planning to go through Budapest. They welcomed the women aboard, even clearing out a railway car for their exclusive use.

A few hours later, the train stopped at a small railroad station. Anna, looking out the window, reported happily that the station had a Hungarian name. She and Sophie stepped out of the train to get some air. A man approached them, peering into Sophie's face, as if looking for a feature to recognize. "You look just like a good friend of mine who I last saw in Rumania," he told her. "Are you related to Paul Brünn?" Anna and Sophie could not believe the wonderful news that their son and brother was alive. He might even be home by now.

The two women boarded the train again, too excited to sit still. If Paul was alive, perhaps Andrew was, too. They did not mention Anna's father; it was too likely that he had been sent to the gas chambers at Auschwitz.

Soon enough, the train pulled into the Budapest station. Sophie had a sister who lived in Budapest, so they quickly took the streetcar to her apartment. When she opened the door, Sophie's sister's face lit up, then fell. Before her stood two deathlike apparitions, with shorn heads, torn clothes, and dull, sunken eyes.

Anna fell gratefully into her aunt's arms. She did not want anything to eat; she asked first for a hot bath. That wish was granted, and Anna allowed herself to be put to bed.

Sophie stayed awake longer, talking to her sister, who did not have good news. Hungary had been liberated since January, she said, and Sophie and Anna were the only two from their family to come back. Perhaps someone else would eventually return, but so far—no one.

Anna, oblivious to this conversation, fell asleep—for days. When she awoke, it was to a beautiful summer morning. She could smell the aroma of breakfast wafting into her room from the kitchen down the hall. Had it all been a dream? Was she really free? As she lay in the first real bed she had known in a year, she closed her eyes to enjoy this safe cocoon a few minutes longer. Someone, though, had come into the bedroom and was standing over her. In her line of vision, she could see a pair of breeches. As her eyes traveled upward, the wearer of those breeches bent down and kissed her cheek.

10   *Lusia: Leaving Warsaw*

THE FIGHTING BETWEEN GERMANY AND
the Allies continued in the skies over Warsaw, raining bomb after bomb
upon a city already in rubble. When the Schwarzwald group—Samek, Zosia, Lusia, and her friend Krzysia—was caught in a raid on the Warsaw
school where they had sought refuge, they were sure the war was going
to end for them right there. It did end for Krzysia, whose body was never
found. Krzysia and Lusia had been holding hands when the bombs had
started to fall, and now Lusia felt a wide range of unsettling emotions.
Why Krzysia and not her? Why had she been spared? Did she, indeed,
have nine lives?

After Krzysia's death and their own close call, Samek announced that
they would no longer fight for the Polish underground. Exhausted, starving, and emotionally spent, the three remaining members of the "family" felt that they had endured enough. Warsaw was in terrible shape; the
three of them moved from basement to basement, foraging for food and
water. In one cellar, Lusia discovered a bag filled with raw grain. She stuffed
her pockets with all that she could, and for the next few days, Lusia,
Samek, and Zosia subsisted on raw grain and water.

In the meantime, ever-resourceful Samek had reconnected with a Jewish couple he knew from Lvov that were also living on false papers as Polish Catholics. The couple told Samek that he could bring the two young
women to their apartment and that the three of them could stay there for
a while. From there, Samek got in touch with his brother and sister-in-law,
Leon and Gerdie, who were staying in another apartment in the new part
of Warsaw. Leon's and Samek's mother would die in this apartment. The
two men resumed their black market enterprise: they made cigarettes, sold
them for vodka, and then sold the vodka for flour and potatoes. Lusia, still

aching all over from the collapse of the schoolhouse, finally had something to eat. As she hid in the apartment, she could hear the waning sounds of the Polish uprising. Their valiant fight was coming to an end; they simply could not hold out against the stronger and better equipped German fighting force.

By early October 1944, the fighting fizzled to a halt, and the victorious Germans decreed that everyone had to leave Warsaw immediately. At that point, the population of the city was nearly 1.5 million people. Lusia could not imagine this mass of bedraggled humanity marching out of the city on the one road that the Germans had kept open.

More than the daunting thought of marching out of Warsaw with no destination in mind, the Schwarzwalds had other worries: they had served in the army of the Polish underground, and they were Jews posing as Polish Catholics. They could be recognized and easily denounced for either identity. Although some people were electing to stay, hiding out in basements and bunkers, the Schwarzwalds felt that their only chance at survival was to leave. Warsaw had no food, no water, no electricity; no one was left who could help or hide them.

They were allowed to carry one bag only; Lusia took a backpack she had found in a basement and stuffed it with towels and the few personal items that had survived with her—a pair of her mother's earrings, her Polish papers. She had no clothes other than what she was wearing. By now, it was October, and snow covered the ground as they marched in columns of five out of the abandoned and bombed-out city.

The group—Samek, Zosia, Leon, Gerdie, and Lusia—tried to stay together in the column of five. Sometimes, one or the other would fall behind, slowed by the cold or by exhaustion. Rumors snaked through the lines: they were being marched to a work camp. The Schwarzwalds knew that in a camp, surrounded by large numbers of Poles, they would be instantly spotted as Jews. Someone would give them away. Whispering back and forth, they knew their only chance for survival was to somehow jump out of the marching columns and run for their lives.

Hampering their plans for escape were armed German soldiers, marching beside them at intervals of about ten feet. But among them, the five decided that together they would take a chance. At the first possible opportunity, they would somehow duck out of the line, hide in the bushes, and then make their way to a neighboring farmhouse, where, it was hoped, a sympathetic Polish farmer would take them in, feed them, and give them a place to sleep.

Lusia watched warily as her cousins maneuvered one by one so that they were on the ends of the column of five. Darkness was quickly descending over the marching throng, and soon she lost sight of her family. It seemed that she was the only Schwarzwald still marching. She recognized the fear welling up in her, a rising level of panic she had felt so many times before. She had survived thus far because she had always been part of a group. She did not know if she could stand alone, but there was no time to think about that now. She had to concentrate on escape. This was the only way. She was almost nineteen years old and had to believe that one day the war would end and that she would have a future, but she also knew instinctively that if she stayed on the march, the future would be lost. Better to try to escape and die with her family than to live a few more days, only to find herself alone, as the only Jew, in a camp full of Poles who would be quick to denounce her in exchange for a few morsels of food. Lusia understood hunger and the depths people would go to in order to fill their stomachs. She had been close to that sort of desperation many times.

As she marched, she remembered the way her cousin Samek had maneuvered himself to the edge of the marching column. Lusia managed to do the same, by simply asking those who were marching next to her if she could walk on the end for a while. From this new vantage point, she could see lights off in the distance, a sure sign of a farmhouse beyond the fields through which they were passing. As soon as she could muster up her courage, she would make a break for it.

It was now or never. Holding her breath, she ducked out of line into the sanctuary of some bushes. She crawled beneath them to conceal herself even further and remained there motionless for a few hours until the only lights that pervaded the blanketing darkness were the beams from the German soldiers' flashlights.

If she was going to make a break for it, she would not be able to wait much longer. For one thing, she was shivering with cold; for another, she needed the shroud of darkness to hide her. She began crawling through the snow on her knees and elbows, aiming her sights on what appeared to be a farmhouse off in the distance. Looking back, she could still see the endless marching columns and hear the Germans shouting orders to the stragglers. It was unlikely that they would come after her now; it was all the soldiers could do to maintain a sense of order among the defeated Poles. Lusia could only think now about what lay ahead for her in the farmhouse.

It took nearly an hour to crawl to the farmhouse. When the farmer opened the door in answer to her knock, Lusia sighed in relief when he motioned her inside. As her eyes grew accustomed to the lighted interior, she could only gasp in surprise: there, among twenty other escapees packed into the tiny kitchen, were Leon, Gerdie, Samek, and Zosia. Lusia cried out in joy. At every brush with danger, she had always been able to count on her cousins to see her through.

The farmer and his wife generously cooked huge pots of potatoes for their refugee guests and handed out tomatoes they had harvested from their fields. Lusia had always hated tomatoes and, as a child, would never even allow one on her plate. Now, she bit into the red flesh greedily, finishing off about twenty of them, wondering how she ever could have disdained something so delicious. She paid for this feasting later on at night, when she had to crawl over the wall-to-wall people sleeping on the kitchen floor on her several trips to the bathroom.

The Poles who had sought shelter in the farmhouse started leaving after a day or two, when they were sure the marchers were far ahead. Many people had families in other towns and cities and would try to make their way there. Soon, they were all gone, except for Leon, Gerdie, Samek, Zosia, and Lusia, who had nowhere else to go. Samek asked the farmer if they could remain in his house, and the farmer agreed as long as they could get their own food. They were welcome to harvest all the potatoes they could eat from his fields if they dared to venture out there. The front lines were now near, and the shelling between the Russians and Germans seemed close. They realized, however, that they were safer near the front than elsewhere in Poland where the Germans had completely taken over. Here at the front, the Germans would have other things to worry about than a few Jews who might be living as Poles with false papers.

The Schwarzwalds wanted to earn a little money to give to the farmer for rent, and they wanted to eat something other than potatoes and tomatoes. When Samek, after a conversation with the farmer, learned that the name of the village where they were staying was Okencic and that the German air force had a base at the nearby Warsaw airport, he decided that the group should make inquiries about any available work.

"Work for the Germans?" Lusia asked. "What if they figure out that we're Jews?" "I'll tell them that we live here in the village," Samek assured her. "But remember: if Germans think that Poles can speak German, they get suspicious. So you have to pretend you don't understand anything."

Samek set out for the airport in pursuit of work for the five of them. When he reported back, he had good news: he had arranged for positions for all of them in the air force's kitchen. He admonished Lusia and Zosia again about keeping quiet; it was important that they pretend not to understand anything the Germans said. Gerdie could speak to them in German, because she could say with all honesty that she was from Prague. Many Czechs knew the German language, so this would not arouse suspicion.

The group reported for work every day, Lusia with a scarf tied around her head like a dutiful Polish girl. She and Gerdie and Zosia were told to peel potatoes, which they did by the hundreds. Samek and Leon were assigned to the fields to dig up potatoes and cabbage. Sometimes they were asked to help make repairs on some equipment. The Germans fed them a meal of whatever the kitchen was serving that day. What was asked of them, they did, only too happy to comply in exchange for a full stomach.

One day when they returned to the farmhouse, the farmer called Samek aside. "They say in the village that you are Jews," the farmer whispered to him. "I said you were not, but they don't believe me."

"A Jew?" asked Samek. "That's ridiculous. What would give anyone that idea?"

"I hate to even mention it," said the farmer, "but we will both be arrested, unless I can prove to them that it isn't true."

"Come into the bathroom with me," said Samek. "I will prove to you that I am not a Jew."

The others watched in horror as Samek led the farmer into the bathroom. What was Samek going to do? He could not hide the fact that, like every other Jewish boy in Europe, he had been circumcised eight days after his birth.

In the bathroom, he slowly unzipped his fly. The farmer, too embarrassed to look, turned his head away. "I knew you were not a Jew," said the farmer. "I will tell the others that you showed me, and they were wrong."

When Samek and the farmer emerged from the bathroom chatting amiably, the rest of the group knew they had been saved once again. Samek could not have handled the situation in any other way; in matters of life and death, a decision had to be made quickly and the chosen path followed. Lusia recalled the day when she and Krzysia had been accosted by the two Polish boys outside a church who accused the girls of being Jews. If she had chosen to ignore them instead of scolding them, she might not be alive right now.

The farmer went to his friends in the village, admitted that he had checked to see if his guest was circumcised, and was happy to assure the townsfolk that he most definitely was not. The Schwarzwald group continued to work for the German air force, an arrangement that, for the moment, kept them safe and fed.

On the day before Christmas, the Schwarzwalds were surprised when their German supervisors in the air force kitchen suggested that they all celebrate Christmas Eve together—at the farmhouse. Samek pretended he thought this was a wonderful idea, but Lusia, in her imposed silence, could only think of the havoc such a party could wreak: a group of German soldiers attached to the German air force were coming to the home of a Polish peasant to celebrate the holiday with five Jews who were pretending to be Polish Catholics. The very idea was preposterous!

The Germans arrived that evening already in their cups, singing holiday songs. As a gift to their Polish friends, they produced a bottle of schnapps. As they sat around the farmer's table, the soldiers told their Polish—and not so Polish—friends about some of their adventures at the front in North Africa. From where they were posted, they could see the American soldiers and were amazed at how congenial their relationships were with one another and their officers. The German soldiers had never seen anything quite like it.

Zosia and Lusia sat at the table in utter silence. When one of the Germans addressed them, they would shrug as if they could not comprehend. Samek and Leon made a show of translating into Polish for them. Lusia was so intent on staying in character that for a while she forgot that this day—December 24, 1944—was her nineteenth birthday.

On December 31, the Schwarzwald group reported for work as usual. They had barely begun their chores in the kitchen when two members of the Gestapo appeared in the doorway and called for Leon and Samek to come outside. The Gestapo accused them of being Jews with false papers and placed them under arrest.

The two men were hustled away from the airport and taken to the nearest railway station where, with two guards, they immediately boarded a train. The brothers did not dare to make eye contact, but there was no need; each knew what the other was thinking. Samek, who had always found a way out of every close situation, did not know how he would escape this one. And escape he must—because these Gestapo officers were not Polish peasant farmers, too embarrassed to look and see if he was actually a Jew. He knew that as soon as he got to where they were going, his identity, as well as his brother's, would be discovered.

"I have to use the bathroom," Samek told his guard. "Wait," said the guard. "You can use the bathroom at the prison." "I must use it *now*," said Samek. The guard shrugged and led Samek to the train's facilities. He had every intention of staying in the bathroom with Samek, but the area was barely big enough for even for one man. So he sent Samek in, warning him that he would be standing right outside.

Samek locked the door and did a quick survey. There was a tiny window, but surely a grown man could not fit through it. He would have to take a chance. He opened the window as wide as it would go, hoisted himself up, and managed to hold his shoulders together and squeeze through the opening.

When Samek hit the ground, he felt an instant searing pain. Lying in the snow, he saw blood everywhere. His pants were soaked through. In anguish he realized that the train had run over him, severing his right leg.

Samek's brain told him to get up and run, but of course he could not move. Suddenly, he saw the train reversing, all the freight cars snaking backwards. The train stopped, and he could see dozens of people running and shouting, calling his name. Before long, a Gestapo officer was standing over him, his gun pointed at Samek's head.

"No," shouted another officer. "Do not shoot him. Let's find a wagon and take him to a hospital." A few minutes later, the soldiers came back with a wagon, threw Samek into the back, and allowed Leon to ride along. They drove Samek to a German field hospital, deposited him there, and continued their journey with Leon in tow.

Doctors at the hospital amputated the rest of Samek's severed leg. He drifted in and out of a fitful sleep, waking each time to pain and anguish. At one point, he saw one of the German Gestapo officers who had arrested him standing at his bed.

"You and your brother were arrested because someone said you were spies," said the Gestapo officer. "A hearing was held in town, and a witness insisted you were innocent. The judge set you and your brother free."

This was good news for Samek, but he had other worries: he was afraid he would die at the German field hospital. For one thing, the German medical personnel were taking care of German soldiers; they were not all that interested in the travails of a Pole. For another thing, the Russian front was close. If the Russians came to the hospital, they would probably shoot him, thinking he was just another German soldier. He had to get out of this hospital, or else someone who knew his story would have to come take care of him.

"Please," said Samek to the German officer, "let my family know where I am and ask them to send someone to the hospital. They are staying at a farmhouse near the Warsaw airport."

Miraculously, the German officer sent someone to the farmhouse to inform the women of Samek's whereabouts. Shortly thereafter, Leon returned home. Together they decided that Lusia would walk the fifteen miles to the hospital and take care of Samek, staying with him in case the Russians came through. Zosia would follow a few days later.

Lusia walked in the direction of the hospital through snow up to her knees and without a map to guide her. The roads were covered in drifts, so she had to slog through fields and farmland. Gerdie had packed some food and water for her, but the trek took hours and hours. She knew only that the hospital was set up in an old farmhouse, and when she saw the lights of the building, she nearly shouted for joy. She remembered Leon's parting words: she did not know German. She could only speak Polish. She was so far from that other life, that other Lusia, who knew German, Polish, Russian, Yiddish, and Hebrew, that her cousin's admonition was not the least bit difficult to follow.

The hospital was indeed a farmhouse, with army cots filled with German wounded. Samek's cot was in a corner on the first floor. Not only did Lusia take care of her cousin, but she was pressed into service to tend the disabled Germans as well. Lusia made sure to hesitate when one of them called her—as any simple Pole who did not understand German would do—but a request for *wasser* was fairly universal. Lusia—and then Zosia when she arrived—filled many glasses of water for these desperately wounded men.

While Samek slept and the ward was relatively quiet, Lusia would look out the window or stand outside for a breath of fresh air. There was nothing else for her to do. She could not read any of the books because, supposedly, she could not understand German. She could not talk to any of the medical personnel for the same reason. She and Zosia would whisper quietly, but they had to take great care, lest they be overheard.

One day, in the middle of January 1945, she was leaning against the farmhouse doorway lost in thought when she saw a sight she never thought she would see: Germans, bloodied and bandaged, in retreat. Could it be true? First there were some stragglers with no shoes holding each other up, then more and more soldiers, their uniforms in tatters. The scene reminded her of descriptions of Napoleon's retreat from Russia. Lusia could barely contain herself; she rushed back to the ward to inform Zosia and Samek.

Zosia soon joined her in the doorway to watch the retreat. Sounds of cannon fire seemed very close; the women wondered whether to flee to the basement. The doctors and nurses had begun to evacuate the hospital. Soon, only Zosia, Lusia, and the most severely wounded were left. The cannons rumbled to a halt, and the air became still. Everyone who could had fled. Farmers in the area had all taken refuge inside their homes.

Around eleven that night, Lusia heard a motorcycle approaching. Should they run? No, she could speak good Russian. She was not afraid. She went outside to greet whoever their liberator might be.

When the soldier on the motorcycle drew near, he saw Lusia standing in the road and skidded to a stop. "Who are you?" he asked in Russian. "I am here with some German soldiers," she answered. "I am taking care of my cousin, who is Jewish, as am I." She waited to see what response this would elicit. "I am also Jewish," said the Russian soldier. "You are safe now. People are coming, and they will help you."

Lusia felt as if she could finally cry. "They are here, and I am alive," she thought. With great relief, she and Zosia ran to tell Samek and to wait for the Russians to set them free.

Soon, the area was empty of Germans, and the Russians arrived in their place—thousands of them, it seemed to Lusia, marching by the hospital, some of them stopping to make inquiries or to ask for food or water. Lusia was reminded of the autumn of 1939 when the Russians occupied Lvov— how bedraggled their army had looked and the comical way they had lashed their tea kettles to their horse's saddles. Now, they were the most welcome sight in the world. Lusia and Zosia nearly cheered when a regiment of soldiers from Mongolia with their distinctive hats marched by.

The two women were just about to decide which one of them would return to the farmhouse to connect up with the rest of the "family" when Leon arrived at the field hospital in a horse-drawn wagon. Somehow, the three of them managed to load Samek into the back of the wagon, and the group returned to the farmhouse, where Gerdie was waiting for them. Leon had already confessed their story to the farmer; now the whole group was assembled, and they could thank him for his kindness and generosity.

Zosia suggested that they leave together and travel to Lodz, where her grandparents had owned a big apartment building. The group agreed to send Zosia west on the train to assess the situation there. When she returned, they could make a decision based on her findings.

Zosia traveled about eighty miles to the city of Lodz and surveyed the area. The apartment house was still standing but appeared abandoned. Obviously, some Germans had moved in during the occupation, using it for their headquarters. Some furniture and kitchen equipment remained, and the building itself was in decent shape.

When she returned a few days later and reported her findings, the group decided that they had no other option but to go there. Warsaw was a mess. They had heard that after the Poles had been ordered to evacuate, the Germans had gone through and bombed every building. In addition, Samek was badly in need of treatment for the infected stump of his amputated leg.

That whole area of his body had become infected. Lusia had nursed him as best she could, trekking to a pharmacy and begging for morphine for her cousin. Finally, she knew that she would have to find a doctor somewhere to tend to Samek. No doctor practiced in the area, however; the best she could do was to implore a local veterinarian, who came reluctantly to the farmhouse and treated Samek's wound.

Leon, Gerdie, and Zosia left for Lodz first and secured the apartment. Leon then returned in a borrowed Russian car for Samek and Lusia. They said their final goodbyes to the farmer who had so generously sheltered them and left immediately for Lodz, where they would all be together again. Lusia had no belongings to pack; she was anxious to leave the Warsaw area and the memories of all they had endured.

Finally, they arrived in Lodz and went directly to Zosia's grandparents' apartment house. The grandparents had been taken away by the Nazis, and Zosia was sure they had not survived.

The next few days were a whirlwind of frustrating activity, since so many refugees had returned to Lodz seeking shelter. Samek needed medical treatment, but so did thousands of others. The Schwarzwalds stood in line for hours at the makeshift Jewish Community Center, where thousands of people were lined up for papers. Each person was claiming to be Jewish, a victim of the hated Nazi regime. Nazi collaborators were being arrested all over Poland, and people were anxious to distance themselves from their former masters.

When it was Lusia's turn to apply, she happily handed over her false papers that said she was Marysia Ladsienska of Warsaw. To be Lusia

Schwarzwald, to never again have to hide her identity—that would be the greatest gift she could ask for at a time like this.

"You say you are Jewish," said the man behind the desk. "How do we know that? You could be a Polish collaborator trying to hide your identity." "Of course I am Jewish," said Lusia indignantly. "Then, read this," said the man, handing her a Hebrew prayer book. Lusia opened the book and rapidly read a prayer in flawless Hebrew. The man behind the desk was duly impressed. He filled out new papers for Lusia with her real name and sent her on her way.

Lusia could not help but notice the irony. After all she had lost, after what she had suffered because she was a Jew, she now had to prove that she was Jewish, an identity she had had to conceal for so many years to save her life.

Samek may have been missing a leg, but that did not stop his brain from working overtime. Before the war, Lodz had been an important textile center, so Samek, looking to capitalize on the skills of former textile workers, decided that the family would become involved in selling fabric.

Illegally—for every enterprise was on the black market—Lusia and Leon obtained a case of wool, hid it in backpacks, and then brought it to a worker who would clean and wash it. When the wool was ready, Lusia would retrieve it in her backpack and take it to another worker, who spun the wool into yarn. Lusia would then carry the yarn to another set of workers, who would dye it. Lusia and Leon would bring the dyed wool to a weaver and then back to the apartment, where all five of them would stretch the fabric onto boards and take it to the city marketplace and sell it. With the money, they would pay off the workers and keep the rest for themselves to buy more wool.

The business grew. Soon, Samek had to hire more people to help produce the volume of fabric requested. Another Jewish man and his nephew moved into their huge apartment to help with the business. People were putting their lives back together and needed clothes to wear. The enterprise was an excellent moneymaker, and even though it was dangerous work—they would have no wool if workers did not steal it from the factory to begin with—a full stomach was a huge incentive. Necessity, Lusia realized, was not the mother of invention; the mother of invention was hunger. It made people do and say things that would have been unthinkable long ago in the civilized world. Among Lusia and her cousins tensions often arose—over food, space, money, responsibilities—but the squabbles amounted to nothing, meant nothing. The group had unimaginable worries and concerns; whose piece of bread was bigger was barely worth the fuss.

Whenever Lusia had the chance, she would walk to the Jewish Community Center and check the lists of survivors, looking for the names of her brothers and other relatives. She knew her parents were dead, but she still hoped that Julek and Milek were free and looking for her. Each time she came away disappointed.

One day, while checking a new list of survivors, someone said to Lusia, "Do you know that your cousin Dina has survived and is working as a governess in Cracow for a family from Lvov?" This was wonderful news. Dina was a few years older than Lusia, and they had not been particularly close as children—although their fathers had been first cousins and best friends—but her survival meant that another person from their family could keep alive the memories of their common past. To Lusia, Dina was yet another person among the very few left who had known her parents, her brothers, her home, just as Lusia had known everyone in Dina's family. In fact, Dina's father had died of typhus in the tiny kitchen of the ghetto apartment house where Lusia, her mother, and brother had been sent to live.

Lusia and Gerdie embarked on the five-hour train journey to bring Dina back to Lodz. The two women arrived at the house where Lusia's cousin was working, and the women embraced each other joyfully. Dina told Lusia that her mother had been taken away; that her sister had lived in Cracow on false papers, been discovered, and was shot; and that her brother had died under similar circumstances. Lusia told Dina that she and her mother had tried to save Dina's father's life, but the typhus was too far advanced. At least, he had died surrounded by loved ones. Like Lusia, Dina was the only survivor from her immediate family. She quit her job as a governess on the spot, and the next day left with Lusia and Zosia for Lodz, where she immediately went to work in Samek's fabric industry.

As winter turned to spring, the business thrived. Soon, they were selling silk as well. Every day, Samek hired more people to sell fabric in the marketplace or door-to-door in Lodz. They were so busy, so happy to have meaningful and profitable work, that the horrors of the war slowly began to recede. They were performing work meant to ensure a future for themselves. They were young, relatively healthy, and had their native wit and intelligence. No one had taken that from them.

By May, the war was officially over. Although the business was thriving, Lusia and the rest of her family began to grow restless by summer. She and Dina had been studying on their own to prepare for the high school exam, which they took that summer, passing easily. They knew that Poland was no place for them anymore—not a country in which they could live or have the kind of future they wanted, certainly not with the Communists in charge. But where to go?

Samek and Zosia convinced Lusia and Dina to go to Vienna with them. Leon and Gerdie decided to return to Prague, where they had lived before Hitler had forced them out. Leon wanted to resume the practice of medicine. Still, it was hardly a case of simply packing one's bags and buying a train ticket. The Russians were not letting anyone out of Poland. They would have to bribe an official who could arrange papers and transportation for them.

As usual, Samek had the contacts. He knew two Russian officers who were brothers, and they agreed to drive Samek, Zosia, and Dina across the borders of Poland, Czechoslovakia, and Austria to Vienna. By now, Samek had a prosthesis that he had had specially made in Lodz for a huge sum of money. The plan was for Lusia to follow in the company of a Russian officer and two men—a father and nephew—who were also from Lvov and looking to escape.

When the night came for them to leave, Lusia and the two men met their driver at an arranged meeting place. The driver handed Lusia a Russian army officer's uniform and gave soldiers' uniforms to the other men. The Russian officer also instructed Lusia to braid her hair in two plaits the way the Russian women wore theirs. Lusia carried the disguise a step further by lashing her mouth with bright red lipstick as she had seen it worn by the female Russian officers. On her head, she wore a beret with a red star; on her feet, the same kind of shiny black boots that Russian officers wore. When she caught sight of herself in the reflection of the car's window, she could hardly believe the transformation.

They were going to travel in an open truck with a canvass roof, with the two men in the back and Lusia and the driver up front. They successfully crossed the Polish-Czech border and kept on driving into the night, but the driver became sleepy and wanted to stop. By now it was November and too cold to sleep outside, so he pulled the truck up to a farmhouse, knocked on the door, and informed the farmer who answered the knock that he and his friends would like to spend the night in the farmer's warm house. The farmer, like his Czech neighbors, had a healthy fear of the Russians and could do nothing but invite them in as if overnight guests from the Russian army had been his own idea in the first place.

The men stretched out on the kitchen floor; Lusia slept on a bench that served as seating at the kitchen table. The next morning, the farmer gave them something for breakfast and watched happily as the four "Russians" piled back into their truck and drove away.

They crossed the border from Czechoslovakia into Austria without incident. By the time they neared the Danube River and the bridge that led from the Russian-occupied zone into Vienna, night had fallen once again. As they drew closer, Lusia's heart began to beat faster. The bridge was lit up by hundred of lights. Cars and trucks were being searched; Lusia could see that people were being asked to produce proper identification papers. Russian officers were everywhere. Their driver had proper identification for the truck, but the passengers could easily be found out by a suspicious guard, who need only ask a few probing questions to determine that they had never served a minute with the Russian army.

Like Berlin, Vienna had been divided into four sectors, each one controlled by one of the four Allied powers. Lusia knew that she had to get to the street address Freiung Six, where she would meet up with Samek, Zosia, and Dina. First, though, they had to fool the Russian guards and get across the bridge.

As they approached the checkpoint, a Russian guard stood on each side of the truck, shining a flashlight into its interior. Lusia tried not to look frightened, even giving one of the guards a half smile in greeting. After producing their permits, the guards waved them through.

Still, they had to endure another Russian checkpoint at the other end of the bridge. This time, a Russian officer stood on the truck's running board, shining his flashlight all over the interior of the truck's cab. He also asked for their papers. He looked at them for a long time but did not seem satisfied. At that point, the Russian driver, out of fear or impatience, pressed down on the truck's accelerator and took off, careening down the ramp and onto the streets of the city. He drove Lusia and the two men to the American sector and to the street address Freiung Six, where Lusia hopped out, handed over her Russian greatcoat and beret, said goodbye and thank you, and embarked on the Austrian chapter of her life.

Thousands of Jewish refugees had swarmed into Vienna looking for relatives or trying to go east or west. The ones who wanted to go east were trying to get home to look for surviving relatives; the ones heading west were already planning their new lives, an impossible feat east of the Danube, where the territory was under the control of the Russians. For help, many of these people converged on the Rothschild Hospital, which used to be the Jewish hospital of Vienna. Now it was being used as a transit stop for Jews looking for help, lost relatives, money, clothing, or food.

Samek had right away embarked on a new business, selling jewelry. Lusia did not have any real money worries—there was nothing to buy, anyway, and she had made herself some pretty clothes from their fabric-selling days in Lodz—so she volunteered to help at the Rothschild Hospital as a translator. She knew several languages: Russian, German, Polish, Hebrew, and Yiddish. The only language of the refugees that she did not understand—not one word—was Hungarian.

Lusia's days were filled with work at Rothschild. At night, the four of them might go to a concert or an opera, since the concert hall was close to their flat. Actually, their living arrangements were the only real source of unhappiness. Samek, Zosia, Dina, and Lusia shared two rooms on the third floor of a very old building, where an elderly baroness lived with her two maids. The two maids saw to it that the Schwarzwalds were not allowed in the kitchen, so the four of them cooked on a tiny stove in one of their rooms. Lusia hated this dark, unfriendly place. The walls of the long corridor leading to their rooms were hung with many pictures of the baroness's dour ancestors, who appeared to stare down with disapproval whenever one of the Jewish tenants returned from work or a night out.

Their two rooms were stuffy and badly lit, and the ancient furniture was ragged and uncomfortable. In one corner of Lusia and Dina's room, however, stood a piano in dire need of tuning. Lusia had not played the piano for five years—since 1941—but she loved to practice whatever pieces she could remember.

Lusia's secret dream was to attend medical school, but it would have to remain but a dream. Others ahead of her were vying for admission, and she was only twenty years old. Even though she was a survivor, mostly Austrians, whose educations had been cut off by the war, were given the first consideration. Still, Lusia wanted to continue her education, so she auditioned for the conservatory, was accepted, and began classes there in January 1946, but not as a beginner. Because of her previous experience, the audition committee placed her at the sixth level.

She spent her days engrossed in music and in her volunteer activities at Rothschild. At night, she would go to the theater, the opera, and an occasional movie. Life was proceeding quite agreeably, but still, Lusia felt unsettled, as if each day were a mere exercise in living leading to no goal. She continued to devour the lists of survivors, hoping to find her brothers' names.

Across the ocean in New York, one of Lusia's cousins who had lived in Vienna before the war was also perusing the survivor lists printed each week in the German-language publication *Aufbau*. This cousin was desperately searching for her parents, who had stayed with Lusia's family after they had been ordered out of Vienna by the Germans in 1938, and for any other relatives from Vienna or Lvov. One day, she came across Lusia's name and address and immediately sent her an affidavit to come to the United States.

Lusia was thrilled with this piece of good news. When she went to the American embassy in Vienna, however, she discovered that she was on the Polish quota list and would have a long time to wait. By now, Lusia was certain that she did not want to stay in Europe any longer. She wanted to go to either the United States or Palestine, but gaining admission to those countries was not easy.

Lusia knew that refugees in displaced persons' camps in Germany had the best chance of immigration as stateless persons. She was certainly stateless; the Nazis had effectively stripped her of Polish citizenship. Then, her cousin in the United States wrote that *Aufbau* had printed their aunt Caroline's name on the survivors' list. She had been liberated from the concentration camp Theresienstadt and was living in Deggendorf, a Jewish displaced persons' camp not far from Munich. Lusia wrote this aunt, whom she barely knew, asking if she could come to Deggendorf and stay with her. The aunt wrote back that she would be delighted. Lusia's new plan was to go to Deggendorf, stay with her aunt, and register for immigration to the United States as a displaced person.

There was one problem: to get to Germany meant leaving Austria illegally. Lusia had entered Austria illegally and was still stateless. When she let her plans be known at the Rothschild Center, though, arrangements were made for Lusia to travel across the border—again illegally—with a group of young Zionists looking for a way to get to Palestine.

She was told when and where to appear. The group left late at night on a balmy June evening, packed into a crowded, windowless freight car used to transport cattle. To many of the people on the train, it was all too reminiscent of their transport to concentration camps.

The train stopped several hours later at Einring, a transit camp in the mountains of Bavaria. They would stay there overnight before continuing their journey the next day. In the crowd, Lusia spotted an old high school friend of her brother Julek, and they spent the evening talking about the old days in Lvov and what had happened to them since.

The next day, the transport continued its journey to Munich. Lusia's aunt Caroline had instructed her which train to catch for Deggendorf, and as Lusia stood on the platform with her suitcase, she appeared to be a well-dressed, purposeful young woman with a bright future ahead. The clothes she wore were from the wool-making days in Lodz; her determination emanated from the years of hiding in Warsaw, which she could now attempt to put behind her. Although the future that lay ahead was unknown, her hopes had their origins in her Lvov roots and the intellectual curiosity, integrity, and perseverance fostered by her family. She was a free woman now, unleashed from the constraints of hunger, poverty, and persecution. She was almost twenty-one years old and felt that she had already learned life's hardest lessons. It was time to move forward.

11   Marriage, Munich, and Medicine

ALTHOUGH THE RUSSIANS HAD LIBERATED Hungary by early 1945, the country was a mess. Its large cities—especially Budapest, the capital—had been repeatedly bombed by the Nazis and Allied powers as well. Hungarian money was nearly worthless, and there was little to buy anyway. Milk, meat, bread, and vegetables were all rationed. The winter nights were long and frigid, especially since coal for heating was scarce. The fighting was over for Hungary, but its war-weary citizens still struggled every day with the most mundane chores to stay alive.

Steve Hornstein had returned to Hajdunanas in December of 1944, but all he knew about his family was what a local policeman was able to tell him: all the Jews in Hajdunanas had been rounded up and ordered to board cattle cars for transport out of the city. He did not know what had happened to them after that.

Just before he was ordered to leave Hajdunanas, Steve's father had entrusted the policeman with all the money he had to keep for his returning children. The money had little value now because of the galloping inflation, but Steve was grateful to receive it.

While he was waiting to learn the fate of his family, Steve decided not to be idle but to use the time as productively as possible. Now that the dreaded Hungarian Arrow Party was out of power, the *numerus clausus* act was rescinded, and Steve saw his chance to fulfill his dream of studying medicine. He enrolled in medical school at the University of Debrecen, just a few miles from Hajdunanas. He had earned some credits from his prewar days as a special student in Budapest. By March 1945, he was in Debrecen, taking classes in chemistry, physics, anatomy, physiology, and histology.

Although the war still raged in other parts of Europe, Steve felt a great sense of freedom, having been well received by most of the medical college faculty as well as the other students, both Jewish and Gentile. Still, the Jewish students, ever wary and cognizant of the recent past, kept to themselves, living together in certain flats and apartments and eating at their own *mensa,* or university dining hall.

He felt reasonably comfortable in Debrecen, but still, Steve could not shake the memories of the past year. One of the first decisions he made was to change his name from the German "Hornstein" to the Hungarian "Haraszti." He felt he could not, in good conscience, carry a German name any longer.

In Debrecen, Steve renewed his friendships with several students he had known before the war. One was a neighbor from Hajdunanas. Another had lived with a Jewish family in Hajdunanas so he could attend high school there, because his own hometown did not have any opportunities for higher education. The third was someone Steve had met when he was drafted into the forced labor camp in Szolnok.

This third friend was involved in a very interesting living arrangement, and he was able to secure accommodations for Steve. The friend rented a room in a student residence for women, which was actually the home of a widowed high school teacher. The teacher badly wanted to befriend some Jews who could testify to her kindness and generosity, since, right after the occupation, she had taken possession of a great deal of furniture that had belonged to the Jews of Debrecen. When the Jews had been rounded up and their furniture transported to a Debrecen warehouse, the widowed teacher asked the authorities if she could have some tables, chairs, sofas, and beds. After all, those people probably would not come back; why should the furniture gather dust in a warehouse when she could put it to good use?

Now, however, some Jews from Debrecen were returning and looking to reclaim their property. The widow feared that she might be liable for the theft of the furniture—not that she had actually stolen it, she informed all who would listen. No, she had merely looked after it for her Jewish "friends" until they returned. And, of course, she was now housing and feeding these wonderful Jewish medical students.

Steve and his friend really did not care about the woman's motives as long as she promised to return the goods. The accommodations were certainly excellent: nearly twenty young women lived in that house, the food was decent, and Steve's room was small but cozy. Under these reasonably pleasant conditions, Steve stayed in Debrecen for four semesters.

He threw himself into his studies, but as Jews began returning home, he sought them out, begging for news of his family. The first news was about his brother Shmuel; Steve and his younger brother Jerry had consulted with Shmuel on the day of the German occupation in March 1944. It was Shmuel who had advised his younger brothers to go home to Hajdunanas.

Through various organizations that were helping Jews find their families, Steve learned that after the Nazis had invaded Hungary, the Swiss Red Cross had made a bargain with the Germans to exchange imprisoned Jews for trucks bought with money obtained from American Jewish organizations. Shmuel had been among these lucky prisoners, spending most of the war in Switzerland. Then, because he was a strong Zionist, he had left there for Palestine at the first opportunity. Steve was glad to hear that he was well and safe.

Next he got word of Karl, who had returned to Hajdunanas after surviving miserable conditions in Austria's Mauthausen concentration camp. Steve rushed home to greet his brother and to hear his story. Just as Karl had predicted, he had been arrested in southern Hungary right after Steve had visited him there when he had escaped his guard in Budapest. Steve, too, would have been arrested and taken to Mauthausen had Karl not sent him away. Now, Karl was home in Hajdunanas, where he resumed his work as a veterinarian. In this position, he was able to send food packages to Steve in Debrecen. He told Steve, however, that he would leave Hungary for Palestine the first chance he got.

In time, he learned that his younger brother Jerry, whom he had left behind at the Budapest train station in March 1944, also survived. Jerry had been sent from a detention camp in Hungary to Auschwitz under the same deplorable conditions as Jews from all over Europe: the stifling cattle cars, death right before his eyes, the keening and wailing of those who had come to understand that a mere split second could separate them from life and death. It was in Auschwitz that Jerry and the other camp inmates were forced to witness a scene that reappeared in his dreams night after night: a young mother was ordered by the Nazis to throw her baby into boiling water.

From Auschwitz, Jerry was sent to Vistagusdorf, a work camp in Silesia, where he became deathly ill from tonsillitis, which he miraculously survived. From there, he and his fellow prisoners were forced to march for several months to Bergen-Belsen, where his job was to empty the crematoria of bodies and then bury them in a huge pit. It was from Bergen-Belsen that Jerry was finally liberated, suffering from typhus. He was taken to a hospital in the British zone, where he recovered, though his rehabilitation from the mental cruelties he had endured took much longer. He eventually made his way back to Hajdunanas and then left shortly for England, where he would attend school.

Finally, Steve learned the fate of his parents, his brother Henu, and his sister, Anna. The local policeman had recounted for Steve the beginning of their journey: that they had been rounded up with the other Jews and ordered to the city center, then marched, to the accompaniment of a brass band, to the railroad station, where they were forced into cattle cars. It was a cruel and final gesture toward a significant segment of the population that had, for centuries, contributed so much to the cultural and economic welfare of the city.

From returning survivors, Steve heard the rest of the terrible story. From Hajdunanas, the Jews traveled the short distance to Debrecen and then, in the dehumanizing, suffocating cattle cars, to Auschwitz, where Steve was told they had been selected for the gas chambers. His mother had been correct; when she had said goodbye to him in April 1944, she had voiced her premonition that they would never see each other again.

In time, Steve learned even more of his family's fate and how they had ended up in Auschwitz. The train carrying the Jews stopped near a stone quarry outside of Debrecen. The SS officer who was accompanying the train ordered Steve's father to select fifty families and separate them from the rest. Salomon Hornstein was told that those he selected would be transported to the west, while the others would be moved east.

Salomon Hornstein drew this unpleasant duty because he was a leader of the Hajdunanas Jewish community. Among those he selected for the journey west were his frail and aging mother, his younger sister, and the family of his uncle. It turned out that this contingent was transported to Vienna, where the Nazis had set up a "show camp" for the International Red Cross to inspect. All those who were sent to Vienna survived the war and arrived back in Hajdunanas in relatively good shape. Steve could only believe that his father must have felt that as a community leader, he, as well as his immediate family, belonged with the majority of the city's Jews. On that long and horrific trip to the east, he probably never imagined their fate.

For several months thereafter, Steve looked forward to going to sleep at night, when his mother would appear to him in a dream as a protective angel, guarding his life. It got to the point that he would desperately long for sleep to claim him, so that he could hear his mother's voice and feel her encompassing love.

As soon as Steve heard about his family's deaths, he made application to change his name back to Hornstein. He also sought out his best friend, Paul Ornstein, to make plans to leave Hungary forever. There was no longer any reason for him to wait.

Paul Ornstein had no idea about the fate of his family either when he arrived home in Hajdunanas in January 1945, but he did not want to stay in Hungary waiting for them. His plan was to go to Palestine, leaving word for them to join him there. He hoped that when Anna returned—if she returned—that she, too, would make her way to Palestine. He had told Anna in one of his prewar letters that he wanted to marry an Orthodox girl who would be willing to leave her orthodoxy as he was willing to leave his. He knew that she, too, was a committed Zionist and wanted to go to Palestine to study medicine.

But getting to Palestine was nearly impossible. The Russians were slowly taking over in Hungary and making it difficult to leave the country. In addition, the British kept the ports of entry to Palestine closed in deference to their interests there. Paul therefore decided to make inquiries at the medical school in Cluj, Rumania, where the curriculum was taught entirely in Hungarian. By February 1945, he was enrolled there.

Cluj was quite different from war-torn Budapest. Milk and meat were plentiful, and the air was clean and healthy. Still, Paul kept in touch with friends from Budapest, hoping to hear any scrap of news about his family. What he finally learned was devastating.

He already knew that his sister, Judith, had been killed in Budapest by an Allied bombing raid. Now he learned the fate of his mother and three brothers, Tibi, Zoli, and Lacika. Like the Hornstein family, the Ornsteins had been rounded up, taken to a ghetto, and sent to Debrecen. From that city, they were herded into cattle cars and sent to Auschwitz, where they were put to their swift deaths. The sting of this was muted only by the rumor that someone had seen his father in Mauthausen and reported that Lajos had survived.

His mother's and brothers' deaths were almost too much for him to bear. Tibi, Zoli, and Lacika were just young children—how terrified they must have been. Paul's only hope was that his father would come back—and, of course, Anna. How wonderful it would be to see this beautiful young girl, whose pictures he had carried into the line of fire. He hoped she had survived.

Paul had friends in Budapest who worked for the American Jewish Joint Distribution Committee, an organization that helped in the resettlement of Jews who had been deported. Paul asked these friends to let him know if they heard anything about his father or Anna Brünn.

One day in August 1945, Paul received a telegram telling him that his father and Anna were both in Budapest and had registered as concentration camp survivors. His first reaction was panic. Were they all right? How would he get there? Train travel was still unreliable. Paul did not care if he had to walk all the way to the capital city—and walk he did, at least part of the way.

He arrived on a warm, sunny August morning. He had an address for his father, and he knew that Anna would be staying with her aunt. Although he feared his father would never forgive him, he had to see Anna first, to reassure himself that she was all right. With some trepidation, he walked to her aunt's house, which had once served as a sort of prewar salon for members of the city's literary elite. Paul himself had taken part in many lively discussions there on Friday nights while a student at the rabbinic seminary.

The greeting he received from Anna's mother and aunt made the whole trip worthwhile. They hugged and kissed him, tears streaming down their faces, as they whispered his name over and over again. By now, Mrs. Brünn suspected the tragic fate of her two beloved sons, and seeing this strong young man before them restored her faith in a possible future for her daughter.

"She's sleeping," Mrs. Brünn cautioned, a finger to her lips. She pointed the way to the bedroom. Paul walked quietly down the hall and softly pushed open the bedroom door. The window was open; sunlight poured into the room. Anna lay sleeping peacefully in bed, her thin face and the stubble on her head telling Paul the story of the previous year and a half. He stood over her in disbelief.

Slowly, Anna awoke. As she opened her eyes, she saw before her a pair of brown breeches. As her gaze traveled upward, she let out a weak cry of relief and amazement. That's when Paul bent down, gathered her in his arms, and kissed her cheek.

≋

When Paul finally went to find his father later that day, he could not believe what he saw before him. Lajos looked barely alive. He had survived the inhumane cruelties of Mauthausen but was in terrible condition, his skin nearly hanging off his bones. Paul was shocked by his father's appearance and vowed to make him well.

Within a few days, Paul sneaked his father and Anna aboard a train's open wagon headed from Hungary to Cluj, Rumania, where he knew they would get well with the help of that city's plentiful food and fresh air. As soon as they were safely on the train and sure that they had escaped the guard's watchful eye, the skies opened, and it began to pour. Emaciated and fatigued though he was, Lajos stood the whole way, using his coat to shield Anna from the storm.

As she huddled in the corner of the wagon, protected from the rain by Lajos's coat, Anna thought back to the last time she had seen this man. He had walked her to the train station through the wheat fields of Hajdunanas, so that they would not be spotted by the Germans, who had just occupied Hungary. That may have been in March 1944, but it seemed a hundred years ago.

While in Cluj, Anna and Lajos stayed at an inn that had been converted for refugees. The fresh milk and meat helped make them stronger. Anna's stubble began growing out, and she began to look like the young beauty Paul had courted before the war. Lajos, too, began to heal, gaining back some of the weight he had lost in the concentration camp. The two remained in the inn while Paul finished his exams at the medical college.

Six weeks later, when Paul's exams were over, he returned with Anna to Budapest and enrolled in the medical school at the university there. Anna took the remaining courses she needed to complete her final year of high school. Coincidentally, the headmaster of the Budapest gymnasium was the same man who had run the gymnasium where she had studied in Debrecen. With Paul and Anna safe in Budapest, Lajos went back to Hajdunanas.

Anna's mother was happy to have her daughter back in Budapest, where she was still living in her sister's apartment. Then, through her contacts with several Jewish refugee organizations, including the Zionist underground, Sophie was offered a position as director of an orphanage serving forty Jewish children who had been hidden by Gentile families during the war. The parents of these children had never returned and were presumed dead.

Anna moved with Sophie into the orphanage, helping her mother with every aspect of the children's care: cooking, cleaning, teaching, and bringing them back to emotional and physical health. The orphanage, which had once been a large, spacious villa with lush grounds and gardens, was the perfect setting for these children, whose loss was almost unimaginable. As they recovered with the help of Sophie's love and attention, she, too, got back her strength, her courage, and her smile. Anna watched as her mother's personality began to bloom again. These children needed her, and Sophie was happy to oblige.

By the early months of 1946, Paul and Anna told Sophie that they planned to marry. Sophie thought back to that June day last year after their liberation when they were resting in a Czechoslovakian potato field and Anna had looked up at her and said, "If Paul Ornstein is still alive, I am going to marry him." Sophie remembered smiling indulgently at the young girl as she shared her dreams so openly. Now, Anna was nineteen years old, her husband-to-be was twenty-two—and nothing seemed more right.

Paul and Anna were married in March 1946 in the orphanage's splendid garden. Their formal engagement had been a short one—just two days—the wedding date decided on rather quickly, by Sophie's clever bargaining for a nice plump hen that would make a perfect wedding feast. The reception was small—Paul's father and a few surviving relatives who lived in Budapest—with entertainment provided by the orphans, who serenaded the wedding couple with Hebrew and Hungarian songs.

After the ceremony, Paul told Anna that they had waited in Budapest long enough. Food was scarce, and inflation was horrible. The only thing that made living in that city bearable was Paul's cousin from Pennsylvania, who was stationed at the embassy. From time to time, the cousin's family from Pennsylvania sent packages to Paul and his father in care of this cousin. The packages contained food, clothing, and sometimes money.

Paul knew that he had no future in Hungary, because he was certain that the Russian Communists would soon close the borders and no one would be allowed to leave. He badly wanted to escape with Anna and his father for Palestine, where he could study medicine. He knew that his friend Steve Hornstein had the same thoughts in mind.

Although Paul was enrolled in the necessary courses to continue his medical education, he decided not to sit for the exams. It was too dangerous to wait another month to leave Hungary. If they did not escape now, they would be stuck there forever. Any dreams they had about Palestine would have to be put aside.

If Paul Ornstein's experiences during the war had taught him anything, it was to follow his instincts, because his instincts were usually good. To ponder the alternatives forever meant getting trapped inside a web of inaction, only to become further enmeshed by doubts. So when Paul knew it was time to escape Hungary for Germany, where they could make plans to get to Palestine, he talked it over with Steve Hornstein.

"We cannot wait any longer," said Paul, nudging his friend Steve toward the thought of escape. "And if we're caught?" asked Steve, who was usually willing to try anything if it meant his future. But he was not willing to take an unnecessary risk that could land them in prison, not Palestine. "We can't think about getting caught," said Paul firmly. "Our goal is to study medicine and to become doctors. If we don't leave now, the Russians will see to it that we never get out."

Steve readily agreed. First, though, their escape plan had to be foolproof. Paul had actually tried to cross the border by train into Austria with Anna several weeks earlier, but the Russians had caught them and turned them back. Luckily, they had not been arrested. This time, they were going to succeed at any cost.

Steve and Paul traveled to Sopron, Hungary's westernmost city, to find out how an escape over the border into Austria could be accomplished. The two men registered at a hotel and planned that the next day they would make inquiries through the Jewish community, with the hope that they would help them get to Vienna.

By midnight, the two were fast asleep when they heard a loud rapping at their hotel room door. Panicked, they sat up in their beds and called for the visitor to identify himself. "We are the police, and we want to see your papers," came the voice from the other side of the door. The Hungarian police! This was not good, they knew. Trying to leave the country was a serious crime. "We have to let them in," Paul whispered to Steve. "We'll think of something to say."

When they opened the door, a policeman and a plainclothes detective asked to see their papers. Paul and Steve knew this was a routine check, because every traveler's papers were usually thoroughly examined. Before they handed them over, though, Steve spoke up.

"A former classmate of mine was a high-ranking officer in the Hungarian Nazi party, and we've come to Sopron because I know that he is a student at the College of Forestry," said Steve glibly. "We plan to seize him and turn him over to the authorities."

Paul looked at his friend with admiration, but the policemen did not. Again, they asked for their papers, which Steve and Paul warily produced.

The plainclothes detective lingered over Steve's papers, glancing up at him and then studying the documents further. It was clear to Steve and Paul that the policemen did not believe their story and that money would have to exchange hands to effect this escape.

Luckily, they had the funds they needed. Paul's cousin who worked at the American embassy in Budapest had given him some money that his parents had sent from the United States. The sum was just enough to pay a high-ranking officer of the Russian army to transport all of them—Paul, his father, Anna, Steve, and Steve's brother Karl—over the Hungarian border to the American sector of Vienna. First, though, Steve and Paul had to send a message to the others, who were waiting for word in Budapest.

The party of five would have to travel separately; it was too dangerous for them all to go at once. Five people, plus a driver, squashed into one car would surely arouse the suspicions of the border police.

When Anna, Lajos, and Karl joined Paul and Steve in Sopron, it was decided that Paul, Lajos, and Anna would undertake the first trip. They were to make their way to the American sector of Vienna and the Rothschild Hospital, where Jewish refugees had gathered from all over Europe. Steve and Karl would wait until they heard word from Vienna that all was well and that it was safe to join the other three.

When it came time for Steve and Karl to make the trip in the Russian officer's car, they embarked without trepidation. This journey, however, did not proceed as smoothly as their friends' trip had. When Steve and Karl arrived at the carefully guarded border, a suspicious guard ordered the brothers and the driver to step out of the car so that he could inspect it. The Russian officer who was doing the driving objected. The guard, unaccustomed to having his authority questioned, cocked his gun and pointed it at the officer. The officer leaped from the car, raining a hail of Russian curses upon the guard. Intimidated by this show of force from a superior officer, the guard nervously motioned the travelers on their way. It took several minutes for Steve's heart to stop racing.

Finally, Steve and Karl were dropped off in Vienna's American sector, joining the others at the Rothschild Hospital, where Paul had already made friends with the entire Hungarian population seeking refuge there. He figured that he knew half the Hungarians already; the others quickly became like old friends, since they all seemed to have the same goal in mind: getting to Palestine. Refugees usually waited at Rothschild for about six weeks before being transported from Austria to Germany, then to Italy, and finally to Palestine by the Brichah, an organization made up of members of the Jewish Brigade and others who specialized in smuggling Jews out of Europe.

Rothschild ran its center like a well-oiled machine. Steve, Karl, Paul, Lajos, and Anna sailed smoothly through the registration process and were assigned rooms and roommates. Little by little, they allowed themselves to breathe in their newfound freedom. To walk the streets without fear, to eat decent food again, to enjoy a hot shower—these small affirmations of life made them feel that anything was possible.

During their six-week stay, they learned that their dream of going to Palestine to become doctors might have to undergo adjustment. The only medical school at the time was in Jerusalem at the Hadassah Hospital, but students were not taught anatomy there because dissections were not allowed under Jewish law. Jews from Palestine had to take their preclinical years in Europe before continuing their clinical work in Jerusalem. This news forced Steve and Paul to reconsider their options. Lajos was not deterred, however, nor was Karl. Palestine was definitely a part of their future plans.

While at Rothschild, Steve and Paul attended a lecture at the Vienna medical school, in part to test their German. Steve had learned German as a child in Hajdunanas, because a German teacher had once boarded with his family. The language was more of a struggle for Paul, but he pressed on doggedly, with heavy reliance on the dictionary.

Their new idea was to find a medical school in Germany where they could earn their degrees and then go to Palestine to practice. Before they could construct a concrete plan, however, they were told to get ready for evacuation to Einring, a transit camp in Bavaria near the Austrian border. From there, they would be taken to a city in the American sector of Germany.

While Steve and Paul looked forward to exploring whatever opportunities existed for them to attend medical school in Germany, Anna concerned herself with the well-being of her new family. As the only woman in the group, she tended to the day-to-day needs of the men, as she had been raised to do. She was kept busy with many chores: the men's laundry, keeping their rooms clean, and making sure they had what they needed, especially Paul who was studying long into the night trying to improve his German. Anna was in love; she was married; she was safe now. She would do whatever her husband thought best, and if those thoughts included plans for her to become a doctor as she had always dreamt, then she knew Paul would make it happen. If only her mother could be there with them. She knew, though, that Sophie would not leave the orphanage until she could make arrangements for the continuing well-being of the forty children in her care.

The evacuation to Einring necessitated traveling in a closed wagon during the dark of night. This time, however, they were not prisoners; the smell and fear of death did not permeate the railroad car. Instead, hope filled the air, and while they were cautioned to keep quiet, they could not help whispering excitedly to one another.

When they finally reached Einring, a camp run by the United Nations Relief and Rehabilitation Administration, the group discovered other refugees there whom they already knew. One night, an acquaintance told them about Deggendorf, a displaced persons' camp just two hours from Munich. Paul, Anna, and Steve could live there and commute to the Munich medical school; from Deggendorf, Karl and Lajos could make plans to get to Palestine.

The idea of living at Deggendorf and commuting two hours to Munich became more and more appealing. By mid-April 1946, the five of them had left Einring and settled at the camp, with Karl and Steve in one room and Lajos, Paul, and Anna assigned to another. Lajos found a job in the camp, and Karl immediately began to make plans to get to Palestine. Steve and Paul rode the train to Munich and registered for classes at the medical school there.

The city of Munich—its architecture and infrastructure—was a postwar mess. Many buildings—the ones that were left standing after relentless Allied bombings—had no windows or running water and were filled with rubble. The laboratories at the medical school were in ruins, and there was not enough equipment even to share. Steve and Paul decided they would stay two semesters at the most, pass their exams, and then check the facilities at medical schools in Frankfurt and Heidelberg. They were especially interested in Heidelberg because they heard it had barely been touched in the war. Plus, the European headquarters of the U.S. Army was there.

Still, the five of them were so happy to be alive, so thrilled to put their pent-up energy into their ambitions. They constantly thought and talked about the war, but these glances into their pasts did not stop them from looking forward. They were consumed with getting something accomplished, getting another exam behind them, and learning another language. Their days were filled with setting goals, reaching them, and then reaching further.

Usually, Steve and Paul stayed with friends in Munich during the week and traveled to Deggendorf on the weekends. Of course, Paul had Anna to come home to, but Steve found Deggendorf dreary and lonely. He had become involved in several Jewish organizations, requiring his presence in Munich most of the time anyway. He had been elected to the position of secretary-general of the Jewish Student Union of the American Zone of Germany, so he was constantly in demand at meetings and lectures. In this capacity, he met Jewish students from all over Europe, which helped strengthen the ties among the generation that had survived the war.

One night in June, Steve had to stay in Munich later than usual, so he caught the train back to Deggendorf by himself. He did not really mind; it would give him a chance to do some studying and improve his German.

In the third-class car where he was sitting, some noisy Jewish teenage boys were loudly debating the pronunciation of some Hebrew words they had just learned. Opposite Steve sat an attractive, well-dressed young woman reading a German book in Gothic print. Steve opened his medical textbook, trying to ignore the noisy antics of the boys in the train, who were sitting just behind the pretty woman with the Gothic German novel.

Steve had remarkable powers of concentration and could easily tune out the boys' spirited discussion. As the boys shouted back and forth about the pronunciation of a Hebrew word, Steve noticed that the young woman across from them was listening to their conversation. He was surprised when she turned to face the squabbling youngsters and said, "You pronounce it like this." And she proceeded to tell them the proper way to say the Hebrew.

"You're Jewish?" Steve asked her in surprise.

"Yes," the woman answered. "I'm from Lvov, Poland. I'm on my way to Deggendorf to stay with my aunt."

"I thought you were German because you were reading a German book," said Steve shyly. "I'm also Jewish."

"Really?" said the young woman. "I thought you were German, because you were studying a German medical textbook. I must admit I was a little jealous, thinking how lucky you were to be studying medicine."

Steve explained that he was from Hungary, that he lived in Deggendorf, and that he was attending medical school in Munich. Then he remembered his manners and introduced himself. "Pleased to meet you," she said. "My name is Lusia Schwarzwald. I just arrived in Munich a few hours ago."

Steve Hornstein and Lusia Schwarzwald barely noticed when the train stopped at the Deggendorf station, so engrossed were they in the stories of each other's lives. Steve insisted on carrying her suitcase all the way from the station right to the door of her aunt's apartment in the camp. Before saying goodbye, he made a date to see her the next day.

After Lusia greeted her aunt and uncle (their son had been gassed at Auschwitz), Aunt Caroline had several questions for her niece concerning the young man who had accompanied her home. "A Hungarian?" Aunt Caroline said in horror. "A nice Polish girl out with a Hungarian?" "I wasn't out with him, Aunt Caroline," Lusia laughed. "He walked me here from the station. Anyway, he's Jewish." "Yes," said Aunt Caroline. "But he's Hungarian."

The next day, bearing a bouquet of flowers, Steve Hornstein came to take Lusia for a walk around Deggendorf. The displaced persons' quarters consisted of many three-storied, red-brick barracks and had recently been the site of a German military camp. Now those barracks housed hundreds of displaced persons, mostly Jews who had escaped or been thrown out of their homelands.

Aunt Caroline and her husband shared a room with Lusia. Steve and Karl shared a part of a room with two other people, as did Paul, Anna, and Lajos. These areas were separated by strung-up blankets that afforded a small semblance of privacy. Refugees were overwhelming the accommodations, but this inconvenience could be surmounted since people knew that the arrangements were temporary.

From that day on, Steve showed up at Lusia's door at every possible moment. Not only was he impressed with her good looks and intellect, but he admired her ambition and direction as well. Lusia had been in the camp only a short while when she found herself a job in Deggendorf's administrative offices, where she helped maintain files on the refugees leaving and entering the camp. By this time, Aunt Caroline had grudgingly conceded that Lusia could do a lot worse than an ambitious Jewish medical student, Hungarian or not.

"Anna," Steve asked plaintively from the hallway outside the Ornsteins' area, "could you iron a clean white shirt for me to wear today?" This was the third time that week that Steve had asked Anna to iron a white shirt for him. Not that Anna minded—she was happy to take care of the men in her life—but she had many chores to do and errands to run. With Paul, Lajos, Karl, and Steve depending on her, there was always work to be done.

"I think I am going to have to teach you to iron," Anna laughed. "Why do you need so many clean white shirts? What's the mystery?"

"I'll tell you later," Steve said shyly. Anna had become like a sister to him, and he would readily confide in her when the time was right. Anna was so intuitive, so good with people—for all Steve knew, she probably sensed that he had a girlfriend. For the moment, though, he preferred to court the pretty young Polish woman in private. Steve knew, however, that he could not keep this secret for long. He would attend classes in Munich, rush back to Deggendorf, and then disappear for a few hours somewhere in the camp. The rest of his new "family" was aware that something was up, so he would not be able to conduct this clandestine relationship much longer.

Within two weeks of the fateful train ride from Munich to Deggendorf, Steve introduced Lusia to Anna, Paul, Lajos, and Karl. They greeted her warmly, despite the language barrier, which was not an obstacle for long. With Steve, Karl, and Lajos, Lusia spoke German; with Paul, Hebrew. With Anna—well, that was a challenge. For the time being, they settled on sign language, until Anna's German skills drew equal to those of the others.

Anna had to admit that she was in awe of Steve's girlfriend, perhaps even a bit envious. For one thing, Lusia was so well-dressed. How could a refugee own clothes like that—suits and hats and proper shoes? Where had she learned all those languages? She had so much confidence that she would jump right into an ideological discussion and argue her point with such assurance. Of course, they would try to talk in a language that they all understood, trying not to leave Lusia out of the discussion if they resorted to Hungarian to make a point. Although Anna was making rapid progress learning German, a heated dialogue on the solutions to the immigration problems of Palestine was beyond her grammar and vocabulary.

Still, Anna was a young woman of many talents and abilities. An empathetic listener and quick learner, she had a way of creating a comfort zone from the barest scraps of life and the ability to welcome everyone into it. Despite her feelings of envy and awe of Lusia, Anna did her best to make her feel a part of the family. Lusia, after all, had lost everyone, and Anna had her mother and Paul.

Lusia was impressed by Anna's energy and athleticism. When she realized that Anna knew how to swim, she asked her for lessons. Every lunch hour, the two women met by the Deggendorf pool, where Anna would tie two inner tubes together for Lusia and help her swim laps.

With Lusia now part of their "family," the young people felt renewed by life and empowered with the strength to move forward. Decisions were made jointly, with the goals of the group in mind. Their first decision was to move to Munich instead of commuting two hours each way back and forth to Deggendorf. This was an easy decision to reach, since all the traveling was taking its toll. By now, Lajos had managed to get to Palestine. Steve and Karl were able to rent a small room in the apartment of a man who later admitted to his tenants that he was a former Nazi, though Karl would soon leave for Palestine. Paul and Anna also found accommodation, but in a horrible little place, where Anna had to sleep in something resembling a child's crib. Lusia was the lucky one: a Jewish couple, who were friends with a friend of Aunt Caroline, let her stay in a beautiful room with a lovely view of the river and the art museum.

Although Lusia wanted to continue her music studies, Steve was able to convince her to pursue medicine. Originally, Lusia had planned to emigrate to New York and live with a cousin there, hoping to earn a living by playing the piano. That, of course, was before she met Steve Hornstein. Now she resurrected her old childhood dream of becoming a doctor and enrolled in science courses at the University of Munich, where she could complete the requirements for medical school. Anna, who, as a young girl in Szendro, had always wanted to become a doctor, signed up for science courses at the University of Munich as well.

When they moved to Munich, Steve, Paul, and Anna decided to drop Hungarian as a language and converse and read only in German. Since Lusia was the only one of the group who knew that language well, she would often stay up far into the night to help Paul, Anna, and, to a lesser extent, Steve, who already knew the language somewhat. Paul and Steve began compiling a German-Hungarian dictionary of medical terms, writing down every word they did not know. The volume grew to more than two hundred pages. When it came time for the men to sit for their exams, they were confident that they could give their answers in excellent German—if only they could understand the questions.

By September of 1946, the four of them were too busy to look back. They had made many friends with the other Jewish medical students; they were relishing their studies and enjoying their freedom. Still, Steve and Paul were restless and ready for a change of venue.

Munich was a depressing mess. The city had come under heavy attack during the war, and while efforts were in place to restore it, the students at the university were painfully aware of its problems: not enough desks or chairs in the rubble-filled classrooms, broken laboratory equipment, too few cadavers for the anatomy lectures. Steve and Paul decided to take the train to Frankfurt and then to Heidelberg to explore opportunities in those cities.

In the summer of 1946, Steve and Paul bought train tickets for Frankfurt. If the university there would admit them as medical students and if the surroundings were just a slight improvement over Munich, they would convince Anna and Lusia to come look for themselves. When they arrived in Frankfurt around noon, however, it was raining hard, and the registrar's office at the university was closed for lunch until two o'clock.

"Let's grab a train for Heidelberg," said Paul. "It's only about an hour's ride." "That train leaves in twenty minutes," Steve explained to his more impulsive friend. "Then, let's run," shouted Paul, already several steps ahead.

An hour later, they exited the Heidelberg train station. "Are you sure this is Germany?" Steve asked. The sun was shining brightly, flowers were in bloom, and the buildings were all intact. People bustled about the busy streets, clear of broken pavement and shattered glass. "We have to move here," said Paul. "This is the most beautiful city I've seen since the war."

As refugees and as medical students, they were certainly qualified for admission to the university, but they had not counted on having to surmount several obstacles. For one thing, the Allies agreed to regulate the number of foreigners who could enroll in the university, a *numerus clausus* that stated only 10 percent of the student body could be made up of non-Germans. This was not so in Frankfurt or in Munich, but for some reason, the rule existed here. Compared with the challenges the men had faced during the war, this impediment was not difficult to overcome.

Guarding the entrance to this magic realm was a Canadian martinet who represented the United Nations Relief and Rehabilitation Administration, known as UNRRA, whose assignment was to oversee the applications from non-Germans. Steve and Paul spent the whole afternoon with her, persuading her to admit them. Having been able to outwit several Hungarian and Nazi guards and officers during the war, Steve and Paul were quite taken aback with the ferocity of this woman, who insisted that there would not be room for them at the University of Heidelberg. Steve and Paul, however, were determined that they would never miss out on an opportunity for lack of trying.

Little by little, using a combination of Yiddish and German (the woman knew only a few words in either language, but Steve and Paul knew no English), they chipped away at her resolve. First, she tried to tell them they did not have the proper qualifications. They showed her where she was in error. Then she tried to dissuade them by saying that they had not taken the proper exams. They promised to sit for those exams immediately. The day wore on, and she was getting tired. But not Steve and Paul, who, with each objection, became more energized. By the time the two boarded the last train back to Munich, they had been promised admission to Heidelberg, providing they took the necessary exams and scored well.

Steve and Paul slumped onto their seats. "We never mentioned Anna and Lusia," said Steve. "They think they're going to medical school when they finish at Munich." "We can worry about that next spring," said Paul, who did not seem worried about it at all. "When we go back to Heidelberg, Anna and Lusia will be admitted, too," he declared.

When they returned to Anna and Lusia, they spoke glowingly of the beautiful city they had just visited: its parks, the lovely intact architecture, the castle, the university. The women seemed doubtful. "Take a trip there yourselves and see," Steve urged them, which they did, returning with the same enthusiasm displayed by the men in their lives.

By the next spring, Paul and Steve had finished their exams. They had had enough of Munich and were anxious to continue their studies at Heidelberg. The two men traveled to Heidelberg alone, and the women followed a few weeks later. All they brought with them—all they had, really—were rucksacks full of textbooks.

Paul and Anna found a spacious, sun-filled room near the university, and Steve and Lusia rented separate rooms nearby. Immediately, they met some Jewish medical students who had backgrounds and experiences similar to their own and who explained to them how to arrange for a stipend. The medical students also invited them to take their meals in the Jewish

Students Union. Under the circumstances, life could not have been more agreeable.

The next day, though, when they appeared before the same woman who had promised Steve and Paul admission, their future appeared in jeopardy. "I'm sorry," she said, "but I have no recollection of ever saying that you two could gain admission to the medical school here." "But we spent an entire day here convincing you," said Paul. "Surely, you remember that!" "No, I'm sorry, but I do not," said the woman, shuffling her papers dismissively. "If you would like to come back later. . . ."

"Absolutely not," said Paul, who resolved to stand there and refresh her memory. They glared at each other across the language barrier. If she had actually forgotten about these two men, they would begin their entreaties all over again until she relented a second time. But they had barely begun to make their case again, when the woman seemed to give up. Clearly, she did not have the heart or the stomach for another go-round with these two. Suddenly, she had an awakening of sorts and remembered the two refugees who had stood before her the previous summer, meeting her every argument with irrefutable logic.

"All right," she said wearily. "Let me have your papers." She went through their grades and course work and finally found everything acceptable. Probably, she was relieved to find that all was in order so that she could send the two of them on their way.

"We have some other business to discuss," Paul began. "What now?" she asked suspiciously. "Our wives also want to enroll at Heidelberg for their first year of medical school," said Steve. Lusia was not yet his wife, but the woman in charge of admission did not have to know that.

The woman cradled her head in her hands. Where would she find the energy or inclination for another debate with them? By the end of the day, Paul and Anna Ornstein, Lusia Schwarzwald, and Steve Hornstein were all enrolled as students at the medical college of the University of Heidelberg. The women would begin their studies in medicine, and the men would finish theirs. It was June 1947, and nothing was going to stop them. The worst had already happened to them, so any challenge or problem that blocked their path would be tackled by all four and overcome.

Anna; Paul; Paul's father, Lajos; Lusia; and Steve, in Heidelberg in the late 1940s. Lajos was visiting before he left for Palestine.

Paul; Anna; Anna's mother, Sophie; Lusia; and Steve in Heidelberg, 1950.

Paul and Steve while they were at medical school in Heidelberg in the late 1940s.

Anna and Lusia while studying in Heidelberg in the late 1940s.

Lusia, Paul, Steve, and Anna at Steve and Lusia's wedding in Heidelberg on May 9, 1948.

Anna and Lusia return to Heidelberg in September 1951 to finish their medical degrees.

Steve, Lusia, Paul, and Anna in Cincinnati, Ohio, September 1993. (Photo by Lisa Souders/University of Cincinnati)

12   Healing in Heidelberg

THE FOUR YOUNG MEDICAL STUDENTS AR-
rived in Heidelberg with one suitcase each and four rucksacks full of books
but with little else except their energy and enthusiasm. The city seemed
to have been trapped in a time warp, left nearly untouched by Germany's
miseries of the decade. With its narrow, winding streets, pealing Sunday
church bells, and air free of the dust and smell of charred and ruined buildings, Heidelberg was calm, friendly, and beckoning. Because it was of no
strategic value as far as the Allies were concerned, the city was never at-
tacked during the war. Its lovely Gothic architecture and Renaissance
palaces therefore still stood amid the thriving, bustling town that was
proud to claim the university, with its four thousand students, as one of
the most outstanding in Europe. What made it even more attractive to
Steve, Lusia, Anna, and Paul was that Heidelberg was serving as the postwar headquarters of the occupying U.S. Army. With this bubble of protection, the four felt no threat from the Germans all around them.

For the first semester, Steve had to spend most of his time in Munich
to tend to his duties as secretary-general of the Jewish Student Union of
the American Zone of Germany. While this arrangement was less than
ideal in terms of his relationship with Lusia, his position afforded Steve
the chance to meet young, determined, ambitious, hard-working people
like himself from all over Europe. He was thrilled to have been named a
delegate to the first World Congress of Jewish Students held in Brighton,
England, attended by Jews from England, France, Russia, the United
States, and other parts of the world. It was these young people who would
set the agenda for the next generation of Jewish leadership.

Every other weekend, he would take the train to Heidelberg to see Lusia. She would travel to Munich once or twice a month to visit Steve, usu-

ally returning to Heidelberg at night, then walking from the train station to her flat. Never once did she feel afraid or the least bit apprehensive. She felt that the American presence in Heidelberg would shield her from any harm.

Lusia found a lovely room to rent in Heidelberg with a German family, the only Germans she had ever met who admitted that they knew what had happened to the Jews. The husband in the family had actually lost his job at the post office during the war for making derogatory remarks about the Nazis. Paul and Anna were not so lucky. They rented a room from a bitter, angry woman whose husband—an admitted Nazi—was in jail because of his activities during the war.

Admission to the University of Heidelberg was strict, yet several Jews from Poland, Czechoslovakia, Hungary, and, of course, Germany, had managed to enroll. American Jews who had served there in the army or who could not gain admission to medical schools in the United States because of quotas were also part of the student body. After the war, the Jews who returned to live in Heidelberg were given a building to use as a synagogue. Attached to it was a smaller structure with one room and a kitchen, which served as the Jewish students' *mensa,* where they could take their meals. Paul, Anna, Lusia, and Steve, when he reunited with his friends for the following semester, were happy to meet these students and join them there for lunch. The students would pool their stipends and donate any food they received in parcels from relatives in the United States. From this, a cook managed to scrape together the ingredients for at least one adequate meal a day. Soon, this arrangement attracted thirty Jewish students and their spouses or friends, and from this grew the Heidelberg Jewish Students Union.

Steve actually managed to find a family member in Heidelberg. Right after he had arrived there, he had had to sit for a German language exam. When he passed it with flying colors, the examiner seemed puzzled. "How is it possible," the proctor asked, "that your German is so good, and your brother's is so terrible?" "Brother?" Steve asked. "I do not have a brother here." The examiner looked through his papers. "Here it is," he said, showing Steve the test. "Your brother barely passed." The name on the exam was definitely Hornstein, but Steve did not recognize the first name.

The man turned out to be an American and a distant cousin of the Hornstein family. Having served in Heidelberg after the war, this cousin had remained to attend medical school. It was in ways like this that their circle of friends widened to include every Jewish student in the area.

The Jewish students decided to stick together. Steve, Lusia, Paul, and Anna did not socialize with the German students, regardless of how often they were asked. They knew that several of their classmates and professors had either actively or passively condoned the Nazis' actions during the war. The students and teachers sometimes made deprecating remarks about the Jewish students, who did their best to ignore them. In the safety and serenity of the *mensa,* the Jewish students discussed what to do and decided to do nothing. Let them say what they wanted. As soon as they received their diplomas, they would be long gone from this country. The Germans had been defeated, and the students would not be.

Steve and Paul were already well into their medical school courses, but Anna and Lusia had only begun. Sometimes, they were the only two Jews in the class. They sat together every day and studied together on breaks. In their anatomy class, they even shared the same corpse for dissections, letting it be known that they preferred to keep to themselves. When one of the German students asked where they were from, they answered, "We are Jews from Poland and Hungary." Whenever someone inquired of their hometowns, all four were always quick to say that they were Jews.

One day, as they were waiting for a professor to arrive, a classmate asked them, "Is it true what they say? About what happened to the Jews?" Lusia and Anna had frequently heard this question and always answered it with a simple yes. They did not want to know if the German students were feigning ignorance or if they were sincerely curious. Anna and Lusia kept their own counsel, even though they knew that behind their backs, their classmates referred to them as "die grosse Judin" and "die kleine Judin"—the tall Jewess and the small Jewess.

On one occasion, while Paul and Steve were heading home from class, they recognized a former Nazi official from Hajdunanas on a Heidelberg street. Debating whether to accost him, they decided to let the American authorities handle the situation of former Nazis freely walking the streets of the city. Steve and Paul almost forgot about the man until they saw him on the same street a few days later. Angry and upset, they again discussed going to the authorities or even approaching the man themselves.

"What would we do with him?" Steve asked Paul. "You're right," said Paul. "Let him go. We have our own lives to live." Later on, while relating the incident to Anna, Paul realized that by not accosting the man, they were getting some revenge of sorts. For what would have angered Hitler and his henchmen more than for two Jewish young men, supposedly beaten and demoralized by the war, to become successful doctors?

The four of them did make one exception to their nonfraternization rule: the Episcopal Bishop of Heidelberg, the beloved *Pfarrer* (Vicar) Hermann Maas, became their benefactor, father figure, savior, and confidant. A man with a soft voice, compassionate eyes, and a friendly face, Vicar Maas had been forbidden by the Nazis to speak, write, or visit anywhere in a professional capacity from 1933 to 1945 because of his activities on behalf of persecuted Jews. Many of his colleagues were hanged for these activities. In 1944, Father Maas was deported to a forced labor camp in France under Nazi guard, because the Nazis discovered that he had been involved in helping smuggle Jewish children from Europe to Palestine.

Vicar Maas was something of a legend among the Jewish survivors in Germany. From his headquarters in Heidelberg, he embraced the Jewish students, helping them get a stipend from the government of the state of Wurtenberg-Baden as a kind of restitution for their suffering. For the Jewish holidays, he would somehow find a turkey or a goose for their festive meals. Then he would join the students for services, wearing a *kepa* and prayer shawl. He would fast with them on Yom Kippur, recite the prayers, and sing the Hebrew songs. A mezuzah marked the doorway to his office. "Where would Christianity be without you?" he would ask the students as they tried to express their gratitude. Then, with a wave of his hand, he would be off on an errand to help someone else.

In addition to the kindness of Vicar Maas, the Jewish students survived on food stamps provided by the German government and the International Refugee Organization and on packages from relatives in the United States, the contents of which they either traded with their friends, donated to the *mensa,* or sold on the black market. The packages could contain coffee, cocoa, or cigarettes, all impossible to find in postwar Germany. In this way, the thirty or so Jewish students in Heidelberg had enough to eat, clothes to wear, and money to attend an occasional concert or movie. If someone was hoping for an evening out but did not have the necessary funds, he or she would borrow the money from another student, paying it back as soon as possible, in either currency or goods. No one kept records, and everyone managed to live as full a life as possible. The Jewish Students Union remained the focal point for meals, meetings, and discussions of philosophy, politics, and Zionism that would go on long into the night. Everyone who came there—except for the few American students—had survived a concentration camp, had endured a forced labor camp, or, like Lusia, had managed to get through the war on false papers. They did not need to explain themselves to one another; each knew where everyone else stood. Their goals, dreams, hopes, and fears needed no explanation either, for they all wanted the same thing: to get an education and get out of Germany.

Hungarian was now a language of the past, and their plan to work as doctors in Palestine was becoming a dream of the past as well. For a while, the four of them thought about leaving Germany to continue their courses in Palestine, but Steve's brothers, Karl and Shmuel, who were already there, were not encouraging. The country had too many foreign doctors and not enough hospitals. Steve wrote a letter of inquiry to Albert Einstein asking for his advice on the matter. Einstein wrote back that the four of them should remain in Germany and finish their educations.

Still, Palestine was not a dream they willingly let die. This was especially true for Steve and Lusia, whose future had always included studying and working in Palestine among young idealistic Jews like themselves. "It's where we belong," Lusia argued when Paul and Anna voiced the opposite opinion. "I want to live among other Jews," Lusia declared. Steve, who had never considered going anywhere else, agreed.

"We can go to Palestine later," Paul countered. "We have to get our training. If we don't make plans to go to America now, we may never get out of Europe." Steve and Lusia looked at each other. This topic was a sore point among the four of them, but they had to concede that Paul was right. What was the point of trying to get to Palestine when they could not get the training there they needed?

More important than each couple's wants and needs were the goals of the family unit that had been forged from the ashes of their experiences. When there was no longer any argument left to put forth, Steve and Lusia shifted their priorities and agreed with Paul's plans: go to the United States, get whatever training they needed, and then reevaluate.

When Steve and Lusia had first indicated their plans to go to Palestine no matter what, Paul's feelings had been hurt. His mind was always brimming with ideas for the future, and the future always included the four of them. That they would leave Germany together, work together, and live near each other was simply understood and never questioned. He was greatly relieved when the question of their leaving Germany for Palestine was resolved.

By now, Paul had definitely decided that he wanted to train as a psychoanalyst, and Anna was also leaning in that direction. He had always wanted to pursue this career path, even long before the Nazis had put a halt to his plans. Lusia, influenced by her childhood physician, was interested in pediatrics. Steve had done some laboratory experiments involving rats and their ability to break down carbohydrates, and this work had fostered an interest in endocrinology and obstetrics and gynecology.

By 1948, Anna received word to expect her mother, Sophie, in Heidelberg. Sophie had managed to escape Hungary in much the same way as the others had—illegally, without a passport. Anna felt that her life was nearly complete now—she had her husband, and soon her mother would join them. Paul had his father, although Lajos had emigrated to Palestine. Steve had his three brothers, two in Palestine, one in England. Only Lusia had survived with no one close to her except for Samek and Leon, who were now elsewhere in Europe. Because she was so alone, the other three drew her in even closer. Anna and Paul became her sister and brother.

When Sophie arrived, she took over the cooking at the *mensa,* and the quality of the meals immediately improved. With Sophie in Heidelberg, Paul and Anna moved to different—and much more pleasant—quarters, with one room for them and one for Sophie. Sophie quickly gathered her "children" around her, becoming a mother to Paul, Steve, and Lusia. Lusia, who had been "adopted" by Paul's father, was delighted to find herself taken in under Sophie's nurturing and protective wing.

"If Heidelberg were not in Germany, I could stay here forever!" Anna proclaimed one day. It was true: their schoolwork was going well; the city was most hospitable; their circle of friends was giving and caring; Father Maas looked after their needs, cutting through the daunting tangles of red tape. The four medical students really celebrated their freedom, looking forward, not back. Although they owned nothing, they felt they had everything.

All around them, their friends were planning their new lives, many hoping to leave Germany soon for the United States, Canada, or even Australia. Couples who had met after the war were deciding on their futures and settling down. Most of their friends who had met at the Jewish Students Union or elsewhere after the war were already married or planning to do so, like their friends and fellow refugees Marcel and Shoshana Tuchman.

Steve and Lusia had known each other for two years, and the time was right for them to marry as well. A rabbi of the American forces agreed to marry them in a religious ceremony in the synagogue administered by the United States Armed Forces. Steve had a few relatives who had relocated to Germany as displaced persons after the war, and they were invited to attend. The rings for the ceremony were fashioned from a gold bracelet that belonged to Lusia. The American army donated the food and beverages. Strict orders were given, however, that it be kept a secret that the rabbi was a Reform Jew, not Orthodox. Steve feared that if his uncle Adolph found out, he would refuse to let the wedding proceed.

The ceremony took place on May 9, 1948, a few days before Israel was officially proclaimed an independent state. Steve's aunt and uncle escorted him to the wedding huppah, while Paul and Anna brought Lusia down the aisle, for Lusia knew no one who was closer to her than they. With nearly eighty people in attendance—their friends from the Jewish Students Union and the army, Father Maas, and Steve's relatives—the wedding was a happy celebration.

Lusia hated to move from the apartment of the pleasant German family who had rented her a room, but it was not big enough for a married couple. The new Mr. and Mrs. Hornstein found accommodation in the apartment of two other displaced persons, a kind Jewish couple and their two children. The apartment building itself belonged to an admitted ex-Nazi. Their living arrangement neatly mirrored their world in the city of Heidelberg: surrounded by those who had vowed to wipe them off the face of the earth, they had found their own way to thrive in a protective circle inside that world.

Their room was comfortable enough, with a small bed extended by cardboard boxes for length, a bureau, and a balcony overlooking the garden. It was apparent that the parents in the family were black marketeers, trading and buying goods illegally, but they were intelligent and welcoming, inviting Steve, Lusia, and their friends for Sabbath dinners and holidays. It was pleasant to be a couple, visiting back and forth with the other members of their group, delighting in each other's triumphs, providing a shoulder to cry on when the memories of lost family and friends pushed through to the surface. They were healing and happy, concentrating on making themselves whole again.

The Jewish Students Union continued to thrive, becoming more significant in their lives with each passing season. Every holiday was celebrated here—Purim parties, Passover seders, birthdays, and anniversaries. The Purim parties were the most festive, with the Heidelberg students dressing in costumes and Sophie preparing as many treats as the meager rations could buy. Steve and Lusia became known for the most imaginative getups, with Steve coming to one party dressed as a woman and Lusia as a bridegroom, dressed in the long black robes, hat, and side curls of a Hasidic Jew.

The Jewish Students Union also welcomed the presence of American Jewish army officers. Bob Lewis, an army dentist, with his German-Jewish wife, Yochen, known as Jo, became close friends. Jo had been liberated at from Bergen-Belsen at the end of the war and then adopted by the famous rabbi Joachim Prinz, himself a refugee from Nazi Germany. Bob and Jo had actually met in the United States but returned to Germany when Bob was assigned to Heidelberg. They met the Ornsteins and Steve and Lusia when a mutual friend brought them to a New Year's Eve party held in Steve and Lusia's room. The Hornsteins, Ornsteins, and Lewises became firm friends, and, through Bob, they were able to make a few purchases at the Army PX, which was strictly off limits to non-army personnel. Bob and Jo joined in many of the activities of the Jewish Students Union, becoming a part of their big family. Because the group shared their possessions, including their intellectual property, Jo agreed to give Steve English lessons if he would try to teach her French.

Although German had become, by necessity, their common language, nothing brought the group together like the old songs from their childhoods sung in Yiddish and Hebrew. Without parents or siblings, for nearly everyone had lost most of their family to the Nazis, the songs were a common link to the past, just as they themselves were now the link to Judaism. Just being together was a rebuke to those whose master plan was to wipe out every remnant of their people. Now, they were the surviving remnant that would keep Jewry alive.

Through 1949 and 1950, the Hornsteins and Ornsteins attended several functions at the Jewish Students Union, but by late 1949, many of the parties were being held to say goodbye to people who were leaving Heidelberg for the United States, Israel, and Australia. Paul and Steve would not finish their studies until 1950, and Lusia and Anna would not receive their degrees until 1952 at the earliest. The thought of remaining in Heidelberg without the rest of their extended family became more and more difficult as the goodbye parties increased.

"We have to start thinking about leaving, too, before it's too late and we end up in Germany forever," Paul warned the other three.

"Lusia and I won't finish until almost two years after you and Steve," Anna reminded him.

"We have to leave before the displaced persons' quota runs out," Paul explained. "We're stateless. We can't leave on the Hungarian quota or the Polish quota. If the stateless quota fills up before we have a chance to leave, then we'll really be in trouble."

"You have to promise that Anna and I can come back to Heidelberg and finish medical school," said Lusia. "You know that in America, we will have to start medical school and even college all over again. That's if we could get accepted at an American medical school and if we could pay the tuition—and the chances of that are not very good."

The thought of finally getting to America and then having the women turn around and come back was less than ideal for all four of them. Not to do that, however, would be tantamount to throwing away years of rigorous education and hard work. If they could all stay in Heidelberg until 1951, it would take the women only nine months to finish. When they came back to Heidelberg, they would stay with Anna's mother. The men assured their wives that they would do all they could to help them return.

Leaving Anna's mother behind troubled all four of them. Sophie, however, was not about to stand in the way of their goals and ambitions. She had a wide circle of friends, both Jewish and Gentile—including the much-adored Father Maas, who had been the first German invited to visit the new State of Israel—so they knew she would be looked after and content until they could send for her.

Steve and Paul finished their medical studies at the University of Heidelberg, and while waiting for their wives to finish the semester, they began work on their doctors' theses, which was required of every medical school graduate in Germany who wanted to be known as both a doctor and a physician. Steve also applied to work on a Ph.D. in philosophy. He was immediately admitted and enjoyed his classes on Freud, Shakespeare, and Plato, earning the highest marks. But the men were becoming anxious: they knew the four of them could stay in Germany no longer unless they wanted to remain there forever as stateless persons. Their friends had embarked on new lives in new countries where they would apply for citizenship. Anna, Paul, Lusia, and Steve wanted to put down roots, to become citizens, to contribute to the society in which they would live. This would not be possible for them in Germany. They never would apply for citizenship there.

The stateless persons' quota for emigration to the United States, limited to 200,000 people, would soon be filled; they would have to make plans immediately and book their passage. The American Jewish Joint Distribution Committee arranged for posts as medical technicians for the four of them, the Hornsteins at a hospital in Indiana and the Ornsteins at a facility in Texas. The United States would not grant visas to foreign doctors, but it would allow medical students to come in as technicians.

The four of them had not gone through all they had and worked so hard in medical school to take positions as technicians in the United States, though. Before they left Heidelberg, their American friend Bob Lewis, who had already returned to the United States, had arranged for an internship for Steve and a job for Lusia at Newark's Beth Israel Hospital, where his brother, Sandy, was a physician. An army chaplain serving in Heidelberg named Rabbi Blumenthal had used his connections to secure an internship for Paul in psychiatry and a job for Anna as an aide at Delaware State Hospital. One of Paul's cousins in the United States had a friend who worked for the International Refugee Organization, and he was already trying to find a way for Anna and Lusia to return to Heidelberg to resume their studies. The Joint Distribution Committee had no idea about this arrangement. While the four of them did not want to deceive the committee, they could not be deterred from their plans: to emigrate to the United States, to work together, and to apply for further training in their chosen disciplines. The wives did not want to leave their husbands in separate locations while they finished their studies in Germany, but New Jersey and Delaware were a lot closer than Indiana and Texas.

Once their passage was booked on the SS *Ballou,* an American transport ship, the Hornsteins and Ornsteins set about saying their farewells. Leaving Sophie was the hardest goodbye of all, but Anna and Lusia knew they would see her again in a few months.

They had nothing more than one suitcase each, although Steve insisted on bringing with a him a rucksack full of German medical texts "in case I have to look something up," he told the others. Lusia brought her one prized possession—a camera that Steve had bought on the black market for her birthday. Anna and Paul carried their pictures of their families, some of them the same pictures Paul had nearly left at the front lines so many years ago.

The ship was scheduled to leave from the port of Bremerhaven, but before they were allowed on board, they each had to take a physical. Steve, Paul, and Anna were waved through, but the military doctor held up his hand when Lusia attempted to go by.

"Sorry," he said, "but you did not pass the physical. We cannot let you leave for America."

"What are you talking about?" Lusia demanded to know. "I am as physically fit as anyone trying to get on this boat."

"We found sugar in your urine," the doctor said. "That's a sure sign of diabetes."

"I do not have diabetes," said Lusia, drawing herself up to her full height. "I am a medical student, and my husband is a doctor. Surely we would know if I had diabetes." Yet, Lusia suspected the cause of the problem: she was menstruating and was probably spilling sugar into her urine.

"Come back tomorrow," said the government doctor. "Take the test again and if all is okay, you can go."

Fortunately, the ship was not scheduled to leave until the next day, and sure enough, when Lusia repeated the test, everything was normal.

Another shock awaited them when they boarded the SS *Ballou*. "Men down these steps, women and children, this way," shouted a crew member. Anna and Lusia followed the directions and entered a huge stateroom that had served as sleeping quarters for soldiers. Hammocks for beds were stacked in fours for the nearly three hundred women and children who would be consigned to this space each night for the ten-day crossing. A babble of languages greeted them: Ukrainian, Russian, Yiddish, and Polish. Nearly every passenger was a displaced person, seeking a new home in a new country.

The first night was almost unbearable. Almost everyone except Lusia was seasick and moaning in misery. "I can't take this much more," Anna whispered to Lusia. "We have to find the men and get out of here." What they did not know for sure, but could only imagine, was that Steve and Paul were stuck in similar circumstances. "It's just one more thing we have to get through," Lusia whispered back, trying to comfort her friend. "But it's still horrible." When dawn finally broke, Anna and Lusia rushed to find their husbands. "We spent an awful night," Paul began, but the women stopped him. Theirs had been just as bad.

"We're going to go to the ship's hospital, say that we're doctors and that you two are nurses, and ask if we can work there," said Steve. "At least that will get us out of the hold during the day."

The four raced to the ship's hospital in case some other refugees came up with the same idea. The American doctors and nurses were thrilled to have help treating the many passengers who had become sick, and they put their four new assistants to work immediately. The Ornsteins and Hornsteins treated cuts, bruises, seasickness, and the other maladies to which hundreds people crammed together on a ship plowing the Atlantic ocean were prey. One passenger even shot himself in the leg; Steve,

Lusia, Anna, and Paul watched with great excitement as the doctors operated on him right there in the ship's hospital.

That night, the four refugees decided that they would somehow manage to sleep on deck rather than go back to their sleeping quarters. They were shocked and grateful when the senior ship doctor invited them to spend the night in the quiet and privacy of the infirmary. Instead of a swaying hammock that only exacerbated a queasy stomach, the four were offered beds with clean linen and warm blankets. Lusia was so overwhelmed by the kindness of the crew that she could not bring herself to sleep under the covers that first night. She curled up at the foot of the bed with her feet propped up on a stool.

After a few days, the hospital was practically empty as the passengers became accustomed to the rolling of the transport ship. The American doctors, nurses, and technicians were happy to give their four assistants any tips they could about what to see and do in the United States. Wait until they saw the New York skyscrapers! Wait until they tasted a blueberry pie!

It was after midnight when the ship sailed past the Statue of Liberty and into the New York harbor. Anna, Paul, Lusia, and Steve had rushed up on deck when they heard that land was near. When the ship dropped anchor, they assumed they would disembark shortly, but the passengers were told to remain on board. For several hours through the night and even as a misty rain began to fall in the morning, the Hornsteins and Ornsteins stood on deck and watched in amazement as the lights of New York City flickered on and began to bring the city to life.

Finally, the SS *Ballou* chugged to Pier 42 and docked. It was June 29, 1951, but it could have just as well been a raw autumn day. A chilly rain continued to fall, casting a pall of gray over the city. Anxious and tired, bedraggled and nervous, the four of them could not hide their disappointment. "So this is the new world," Lusia whispered to Steve. "It's not at all what I expected."

The processing of passengers and documents seemed to take forever. The four of them stood in the long lines, clutching their papers and possessions. The rucksack full of Steve's German textbooks grew heavier by the minute. Suddenly, they heard people shouting their names. In the waiting crowd, they spotted some aunts, uncles, and cousins who had come to greet them, for all four of them had relatives who lived in or near New York. Frantically, they waved to each other and excitedly called out their names.

Slowly, their arrival in New York and all of its implications began to dawn on them. They had been the homeless and the tempest-tossed, the wretched refuse of Europe's teeming shores—but no longer. They were also young, healthy, well-educated, and eager for knowledge. The last decade had proved that they could overcome any obstacle bent on defeating them. Hitler had done his best to separate them from society, but they had already rejoined it with strength and vigor. The United States would become their country now; every promise it had to offer would be grasped by the four of them and paid back in full measure.

13   America—and Back

THEIR FIRST STOP IN NEW YORK CITY, AR-
ranged by the International Refugee Organization, was at a seedy midtown
Manhattan hotel. The window sills were thick with soot. Their beds were
crawling with bugs. The dirty bathroom, which they had to share with the
other hotel guests on the floor, was located at the end of a dingy hall.

Lusia was exhausted from the long wait at the pier and was now near
tears. "What are we doing here?" she asked her husband, who looked just
as miserable.

At dinner time, one of Lusia's cousins showed up to take them out on
the town. This cousin was originally from Vienna, and Lusia had not seen
him since she was four, when she had traveled to the Austrian capital for
a mastoid operation. The cousin made them feel much better. He took
them for dinner at a cafeteria, where they tasted cantaloupe for the first
time, and then for a walk around the town. Their necks ached from looking up at all the skyscrapers. New Yorkers were rushing about, to the theater, to dinner, to concerts. Steve and Lusia barely understood English, but
they could not help getting caught up in the city's excitement. They resigned themselves to put up with the hotel's bedbugs for one more night.

The next day, the four of them were to meet with a representative of
the Jewish agency that helped foreign-trained doctors find placements in
American health care, usually as lab technicians. Although Steve and
Lusia were supposed to go to Indiana, Steve had already lined up an internship at Beth Israel Hospital in Newark, New Jersey; Paul and Anna had
been assigned to a hospital in Texas, but Paul had a residency waiting for
him at Delaware State Hospital in Wilmington. The refugee organization
would not be happy with their change in plans, because it had most likely gone to considerable trouble to get them these other posts as techni-

cians. But Paul Ornstein, with his eternal optimism, was quite certain that everything would work out to their advantage.

The woman in charge of placement for foreign physicians heard their story and began to shake her head. "You cannot work as doctors because you have German diplomas," she told Paul and Steve sternly. "You have been guaranteed employment as lab technicians."

"We have graduated from medical school at the University of Heidelberg and received our diplomas," Paul told her. "Our plan is to do our internships and residencies, then apply to take the boards for our medical licenses."

"Most states will not grant a license to foreign-trained doctors," the woman pointed out.

"Ah," said Paul, "but some will. And by the time we are ready to apply, then perhaps more states will allow us to sit for the licensing exam." Of course, the four of them still had hopes of eventually going to Israel and practicing medicine there.

"Well, I am very sorry," said the woman, "but you will simply have to go where you have been assigned." Even Paul Ornstein, with his powers of persuasion, could not budge her.

Steve, with his gentler, quieter manner, took over. "I cannot change the assignments," said the woman angrily. "You have been assigned to Texas," she said to Anna and Paul, "and you," pointing to Steve and Lusia, "to Indiana, and that is where you must go."

"Thank you very much," said Steve politely. "You've been most helpful."

The four of them left the building, but once outside, they smiled at each other. "We reported as requested," said Paul. "Now we will proceed as planned." The four of them had weathered much worse than this. An intransigent bureaucrat? Nothing but a small, unfriendly storm they had to pass through to get to the other side.

Lusia and Steve took the subway to Brooklyn to visit with relatives and deposited Steve's rucksack with its hundred pounds of medical textbooks in the basement of her cousins' house.

Paul and Anna immediately set to work on trying to secure permission and passage for Anna and Lusia to return to Germany for their final nine months of medical school. Through relatives, Paul had a contact with someone in one of the relief agencies who was willing to help.

On July 1, just three days after they had disembarked from the SS *Ballou,* Steve and Lusia were to report to Newark and Paul and Anna to Dela-

ware. Their goodbyes were tearful yet hopeful; they promised to write often—phoning would be too expensive—and visit as soon as possible. Paul
pledged to keep in close touch with his contacts concerning the wives'
return trip to Heidelberg. The Hornsteins waved goodbye as the Ornsteins
left for Wilmington, and then they boarded a bus from New York for 201
Lyons Avenue, the address of Beth Israel Hospital in Newark.

Waiting for them there were the Lewises—Bob and Jo from Heidelberg
and Bob's brother, Sandy, who had arranged the internship. Sandy greeted them warmly and introduced them to the rest of the staff. Because so
many doctors had been drafted to serve in the Korean War, Beth Israel
Hospital was woefully short of interns and residents. Twenty-four were
supposed to be on staff, but the numbers were down to twelve. Steve saw
that he would be expected to pitch in right away, which was fine with him,
except that he barely knew any English.

His abilities were tested the first day on the job. The doctor in charge
of the interns had placed Steve in the emergency room, because he figured
that a doctor working in such a busy place would not have to converse all
that much. A few hours into the day, a man came rushing in with his elev-
en-year-old son whose hand was gushing blood. The boy had been chas-
ing a baseball and had crashed into a steel gate. The emergency room nurse
stood by, expecting Steve to stitch the wound.

Steve had never sewn a cut; in fact, by his own admission, he could do
nothing practical. He could make a diagnosis, he could prescribe a drug,
but stitch a wound? That was not something a doctor learned how to do
in a European medical school. It was quite obvious that American medical training was far ahead of European training. He would have learned
to stitch eventually, but at this moment, when he was expected to do it,
he simply did not know how. Still, there was no time to ruminate on this
lack of knowledge; the boy's hand was dripping with blood.

At least Steve knew to apply a pressure bandage to the wound, and he
was able to convey to the nurse that he did not know how to put in stitch-
es. He was surprised when the nurse left the room, leaving him to continue applying pressure to the boy's hand as if he knew what to do next.

When the nurse returned a minute or so later, she announced clearly,
"Dr. Hornstein, you are needed in the next room for a heart attack patient." Steve looked at her blankly. "You must go," she urged, gently pushing him toward the door. "It's an emergency. Perhaps, with your permission, I could stitch this young man's hand."

Steve did as he was told, but the adjacent trauma room was empty. Then he realized what the nurse had done. To save him from embarrassment, she had made up the story about the heart attack patient. He waited in the empty room for ten minutes, returned to check on the child, and praised the nurse for her excellent stitching. After the boy and his satisfied father left the hospital, Steve thanked the nurse profusely. She had been happy to help and offered to teach him how to stitch a cut.

Steve continued to be plagued by his lack of English language skills, especially since he had to write up case histories and the results of physical exams. Laboriously, he set to work with a dictionary at hand. His colleagues always made themselves available for help. "One person is nicer than the next," Steve said to Lusia over dinner a few nights later. "They care about us almost beyond the call of duty."

Lusia worked on the maternity floor as a nurse's aide, wrapping packages of sanitary napkins and other items to be used by women after they had delivered their babies. She was paid for this work, so with her salary and Steve's twenty-five dollars a month, they felt quite comfortable. This gave them the funds to take the bus and train to Brooklyn to visit their relatives or to see an occasional movie or play.

Actually, they had few expenses, since all meals and accommodation were provided for them. They lived in two spacious rooms in the interns' quarters of the hospital, a bedroom and a sitting room, where Steve could study and they could entertain occasional company. Everyone was most welcoming and hospitable to them. Bob Lewis's parents frequently invited the Hornsteins for dinner. Aware of the Hornsteins' lack of appropriate clothing for city life, Bob's father gave Steve his first American sports jacket, an item that Steve treasured. When Lusia admired a beautiful charcoal gray wool dress worn by Jo Lewis, Jo offered it to her. It was the first item of American clothing that Lusia owned, and when she wore it— which was quite often—she felt worldly and sophisticated.

The Hornsteins wrote to the Ornsteins frequently, expressing the hope that they could be together soon. As nice as their new American friends and colleagues were, the two couples understood each other, knew what they had gone through during and after the war. How could the men adequately explain the daily threats of working in forced labor camps? To whom could Lusia confide the terrors of her life on the run and underground, hiding for all those years behind a false identity? And Anna— people would look curiously at the tattoo on her arm, but did they really want to hear about Auschwitz and the constant smell of death? Just as Anna had known, but did not want to know, about the coming horrors of Nazism when she was a young girl in Szendro, Hungary, so did Americans in the fifties know, but did not want to hear, about the war and the terrible fate of European Jews. While they were nearly stunned by the kindnesses of their new American colleagues, no one could take the place of their "family"—each other.

Paul and Anna were experiencing the same care and thoughtfulness in Wilmington, where they lived on the grounds of the Delaware State Hospital while Paul carried out the duties of his residency in psychiatry. The hospital's clinical director was a refugee from Germany who had managed to escape that country before the war; he was extremely helpful and receptive to Paul and Anna. The hospital's superintendent, however, was a very rough and demanding individual. He knew how badly Paul wanted training in psychiatry, and his idea was to offer to train Paul for five years but not to pay him for his work. He assumed that Paul, who barely knew English, would be so grateful for the opportunity that he would grab the chance. Paul's English may have been at the rudimentary stage, but he understood enough to know when he was being exploited. They had come to this country without a penny, and to survive, Paul had to be paid in exchange for his work. He explained the situation to the clinical director, telling him that he would stay in Wilmington for three months, but he would try to go to a university hospital, where he could get the training—and pay—he needed.

Still, Wilmington turned out to be a pleasant enough experience. Their living quarters consisted of two beautiful rooms and a kitchen all to themselves. "This must be a mistake," Anna whispered. "It's much too nice." Paul even went to his supervisor to ask if they had been assigned the right apartment.

They missed the Hornsteins terribly, writing often. They had hoped to travel to Newark to visit, but a trip like that was expensive, and they did not have money to spare. They were careful to keep in touch with the relief agency that was very close to finding Anna and Lusia the means to return to Heidelberg for their final semester of medical school.

After three months in the United States, the couples were granted their First Papers, documents that indicated that they were eligible for citizenship. With these First Papers, they could travel out of the country. Shortly afterward, they learned that through the offices of the International Refugee Organization, passage back to Europe had been secured for the women on an army transport ship that would be taking three thousand American soldiers across the Atlantic.

At the beginning of September, Paul and Anna took the train to New York to meet Steve and Lusia. Paul had even more interesting news: he had secured a six-month internship in New York at Metropolitan Hospital on Welfare Island and would begin there in January 1952. He and Steve would be able to see each other frequently while they waited for their wives' return. The Ornsteins' experience in Delaware had not been as successful as the Hornsteins', and they were anxious to settle elsewhere.

"The best thing," said Steve, "would be if the two of you could come to Newark after Anna and Lusia come back." He promised to ask Sandy Lewis if he could work on such an arrangement. For the four of them to work as doctors at the same hospital would be better than anything they had ever dreamed.

The two couples met with a representative of the International Refugee Organization, who handed over their tickets and necessary papers and warned the women that they would probably be the only women on board with three thousand high-spirited American soldiers. He cautioned firmly that except for meals, they should stay in their stateroom.

On that September day in 1951, the four of them took the ferry to Staten Island, where Anna and Lusia would board the ship. All had mixed emotions about their farewells. Steve and Lusia knew the separation would be difficult, but Steve would be well cared for at Beth Israel and by his three aunts and uncles in New York, who were insisting that he come to them for every Sabbath meal. Steve's relatives were Orthodox Jews who observed all the laws and rituals of the religion, including the prohibition against travel on the Sabbath. The only way Steve could get to his relatives' house for the Sabbath was by train, but they wanted to see him so badly and believed it was so important for him to join them that they were sure God would forgive this breach of the holy laws.

Steve and Lusia knew that this nine-month separation, however difficult, would mean everything to their futures. As doctors, they would have the freedom and finances to live where they wanted, raise a family, and have the means to travel the world. Without the diploma from the University of Heidelberg, Anna and Lusia would never get to work as doctors in the United States.

Anna and Paul also dreaded the months apart, but Anna was anxious to see her mother, who was still in Heidelberg. She knew Paul would be moving to New York in January, where his relatives would provide a great deal of love and comfort. What's more, Paul and Steve would be able to see each other frequently after January. Both men would have plenty to do to keep them busy, especially the formidable task of learning English. They had been in the United States for three months but had only a modest grasp of the language.

At the last possible moment, Lusia and Anna boarded the ship. They stood on the deck and waved goodbye to their husbands, thankful that the time had finally come to begin the end of their long quest for their medical diplomas. Returning to Germany was difficult, but what were the options? There were none, as far as they could see. Steve's relatives had been horrified that the two women would be traveling alone. The United States was at war with Korea; if it somehow turned into a worldwide conflict, they could be stuck in Germany for years. Lusia tried her best to assuage their fears. By next summer, they would be back, and they would be doctors.

The two women stood on the deck waving at their husbands until they could see them no more. As the boat moved out of the harbor, the women turned their backs on the shore and made their way down to their cabin. For quarters on a transport ship, their room was quite pleasant. They unpacked their few belongings and were resting on their bunks when they heard a soft knock at the door.

"Should we answer it?" whispered Lusia, ever mindful of the admonition that three thousand American soldiers would be their traveling companions. "I think we should," Anna whispered back. With trepidation, she went to the door. She opened it barely an inch and saw, standing there, a man wearing a crisp white jacket, bearing a splendid bowl of fruit. "The doctors on board would like you to join them and the other medical personnel in their dining room for lunch," he said formally.

When it was time for lunch, Lusia and Anna cautiously threaded their way toward the officers' dining room. "The ship seems empty," said Lusia. "I thought we were traveling with three thousand American soldiers." It turned out that they were crossing the Atlantic with about three hundred men, mostly officers and crew, as well as two physicians and four nurses. The ship would be picking up more soldiers in Germany.

The ten-day crossing turned out to be a pleasant trip. Anna and Lusia knew enough English to communicate on a basic level. They listened raptly while the two physicians and four nurses discussed American medicine. The officers and crew always invited them to the movies in the lounge after dinner, but the women declined. Lusia was twenty-four, Anna was twenty-three, and except for the four nurses, they were the only women on board. They felt it was best to go for a walk on deck after dinner and then return to their cabin to read. Still, the trip was restful and restorative. When the ship arrived in Hamburg, they were presented with a bill for the entire crossing, including all their meals: $14.50.

When the two women settled on the train for their trip to Heidelberg, they could not help experiencing mixed emotions triggered by the familiar sights and sounds of Germany. This was not their country and never would be, but it was comforting, on the one hand, to understand the language. On the other hand, they were back in the land that was the root of all their troubles. The deaths of their parents and brothers could be laid squarely at the feet of these people. It was disconcerting to realize that the Germans had obliterated their pasts but were now offering them their futures.

When the train chugged into the station, Anna spotted Sophie waiting for them on the platform. Quickly, she was out of the railway car and into her mother's arms. Oh, how she had missed her! Lusia, too, hugged Sophie tightly, happy to feel her strength and warmth. Sophie had become a mother to her as well.

The three women had so much to tell each other. Anna could not wait to bring her mother to the United States to show her all that country's wonders. Lusia told her all about Steve's family, how kind they were to both of them, how worried they were about Lusia and Anna's trip back to Germany. "They think we are crazy to be here," Lusia laughed.

They were not crazy, just determined. They vowed to think about nothing except their studies. Sophie still lived in the same two rooms she had shared with Anna and Paul; she was happy to give up the bedroom to Anna and Lusia, while she slept on a couch in the living room. Sophie took over their care, cooking some of Anna's and Lusia's favorite foods to nourish their bodies and their minds.

During the day, Anna and Lusia attended the required lectures, sitting together as usual and avoiding contact with the German students. Some of their friends from the Jewish Students Union were still in Heidelberg, which was of great comfort to them. At night, they returned to the apartment and wrote letters to their husbands. Sometimes, they would turn on Sophie's radio and dance to the music from the Armed Forces Network. Mostly, they would outline their notes and study together, quizzing each other on medical terms and procedures. Sophie helped them study; she had raised three children and was an expert on treating their illnesses. "Are you sure that is the correct incubation time for scarlet fever?" she would ask them, and they would research further and find that Sophie was correct.

As the months flew by, a word, a song, the way someone laughed would often force them to face the irony of their return. Because of Germany, they were refugees. Because of Germany, their families had been torn apart. Because of Germany, they had had to remain there after the war and could go nowhere else. Now they were back, sitting in lectures by the same anti-Semitic professors and brooking the same snide comments of their fellow students. Some of their instructors and classmates were sincerely curious about them, but Anna and Lusia kept to themselves. They had a plan and a goal and tried not to dwell on the paradoxes.

At night, they would get into bed with their books and read the material, trying to commit it to memory. They both knew that the sooner they fell asleep, the sooner it would be one day closer to their return to their husbands. The enormity of their task was daunting, and sometimes they both lay awake contemplating what they had accomplished and the challenges that lay ahead. When Lusia's mind reeled and she could not sleep, she would pick up her dermatology textbook and begin to read about skin conditions. Every rash had a name; she would never learn them all. Still, she found dermatology the most sleep-inducing of all her subjects, and it was better than a glass of warm milk or counting sheep. Many mornings she awoke, still clutching her dermatology text.

Anna admired Lusia's perseverance and stamina, but the old feelings of envy would often well up when it came time for tests and exams. Not only could Lusia remember the smallest details of diseases and symptoms, but she had a vast knowledge of other topics as well. Lusia knew several languages, could discuss philosophers and writers Anna had never read, and could grasp the intricacies of mathematics. Anna wondered if Lusia knew how she felt. Lusia had street smarts, too; she knew how to navigate around red tape and the University of Heidelberg bureaucracy. Anna was not pleased about having to be so dependent on Lusia to help her study or to surmount the university's arcane regulations.

Still, Lusia had lost so much during the war; she had all but been orphaned as a teenager. How terrible, Anna thought, never to know again a mother's loving embrace. While she missed her husband terribly, it was so comforting to be back where Sophie could take care of her. For that reason, Anna was happy to be able to share Sophie with her.

One evening, late into the night, Anna heard the sound of heartbroken, heartbreaking sobbing coming from the living room. She had never heard her mother cry like that. Quietly, she crept into the other room and onto the couch. She put her arms around Sophie and held her tightly. Just as she had done in the camps, Anna could comfort Sophie as well. "What is it, Mother?" she whispered. "I was thinking about your father," Sophie whispered back. "He would have been so proud of you."

Mother and daughter talked quietly about the past few years, each one weeping softly as they spoke of their losses. Anna waited for her mother to mention her sons she had loved so dearly. But Sophie never said a word about them. Much later, when Anna slipped back to her own bed, she regretted that she had not opened the conversation about her brothers, Paul and Andrew. She missed them terribly and knew their loss had to be even worse for her mother—she had doted on them so. Anna knew now that she was becoming a doctor, she was also taking the place of those beloved sons.

Between attending classes, studying for exams, and writing letters home, Anna and Lusia did not have time for much else. Their study method was simple. They would review thoroughly the material for a course— surgery, for example—take that exam and then begin studying for the next one.

At the medical college of the University of Heidelberg, students took courses, studied the material, and then arranged with the professor to take the exams, both written and oral. Sometimes, a professor would find himself testing four students at the same time, sometimes only one or two. For the surgery exam, for example, Anna and Lusia were the only students to be tested that day.

"I understand you are going to America," the professor said, eying them warily. "I have to make sure you know everything." For several hours, he drilled them, not letting up until he had covered the smallest details.

"It's a good thing we had the blessing from your mother," said Lusia as the two exhausted women headed back to Sophie's apartment. Before each exam, Sophie would gather Anna and Lusia in her arms and recite a special Hebrew prayer over their heads. It must have worked, because they received high marks on every exam, including surgery, a testament not just to Sophie's heavenly connections but to their own quick minds and diligent study habits.

After nine months, they were awarded their medical diplomas. It was June 1952, and time to leave Heidelberg. But how to get home? They could not count on any more transport ships offering them free passage, nor could they afford to buy a ticket themselves.

Steve and Paul turned to their relatives for help. Anna had a wealthy uncle who gave Paul money to buy Anna a ticket on the *Queen Elizabeth,* sailing from Cherbourg, France. Steve's brother Jerry, who was working at an optical firm, sent Steve the money for Lusia's ticket aboard the same ship. Both men had mailed their wives money from their weekly pay-checks for living expenses in Heidelberg, keeping about five dollars a week for themselves.

In addition to the tickets for their passage on the *Queen Elizabeth,* Steve and Paul sent their wives a surprise graduation gift: forty dollars each to spend on four days in Paris, a city neither woman had ever visited. The trip would help heal the pain of a wrenching farewell to Sophie.

With their new diplomas, Dr. Anna Ornstein and Dr. Lusia Hornstein said goodbye to the university, to the Jewish Students Union, to Father Maas who promised to look after Sophie, to a special few of their profes-sors, to the landlords of their various residences over the years, and to the beautiful city itself, which had offered the four young medical students a warm, safe haven that since 1947 had nourished their minds, bodies, and souls. Leaving Sophie was the hardest of all. She was a loving mother to both women, and now they would be so far away. Anna vowed to bring her to the United States at any cost.

By train they traveled to Paris, anxious to see its parks, museums, monuments, and nightlife but apprehensive about navigating the city by themselves. Anna knew a little French, but Lusia did not speak a word. They were worried, too, about the money. What if they ran out?

The two of them found a cheap hotel on Place de la République and, for-tunately, noticed an open-air market nearby. Every morning they would go to this market and buy their food for the day: bread and cheese most-ly, and perhaps one piece of fruit each. For dinners they ate frugally at a nearby coffee shop or at a kosher restaurant in Paris's Jewish quarter.

Like any two avid tourists, they crammed in as much sightseeing as possible: Notre Dame Cathedral, the Louvre, several smaller museums, shops along the Champs Elysée, and walks by the Seine, through the Tui-leries, and along the Bois de Boulogne. At night they attended the opera and visited the Folies-Bergère—twice. On the last day, they had a little money left, so they decided to treat themselves to a real Parisian lunch. With great trepidation, they entered a charming restaurant, were shown to a table, and proceeded to examine the menu. Neither one could under-stand a word.

When the waiter appeared, Lusia pointed to an item that she thought she recognized. When their lunch was served, they saw that they had ordered French sausages and eggs. The lunch smelled heavenly and tasted delicious.

When they arrived in Cherbourg from Paris to meet the ship, the harbor city reminded the women of Munich after the war. It was in such disrepair that they had to ride in a kind of hovercraft from the harbor to the ship. They finally boarded and made their way down to their cabin located on the lowest deck.

The *Queen Elizabeth* was a grand luxury liner, all gleaming wood and shining brass. The decks looked as if they were painstakingly polished every night. The passengers were lively and beautifully dressed, looking as if they had just stepped from the pages of a fashion magazine. Lusia and Anna were shocked when they heard some of the best-dressed people speaking German. The English passengers looked as if they had trotted out their old tweeds for the crossing.

"Who won the war and who lost it?" Anna asked Lusia. Anna admitted to some resentment of the German passengers, the way they swept into the dining room trailing their fur stoles, laughing, talking, and ordering champagne. It was only 1952, and Germany was already back in business.

In spite of their fellow passengers, Anna and Lusia had a marvelous time until a terrible storm came up when they had been at sea for only two days. Again, Anna was stricken with seasickness and confined to the cabin. The storm did not bother Lusia at all. She made her way to the dining room for dinner and was surprised to find it totally empty except for a group of six young Englishmen and the waiters. Evidently, the storm was affecting everyone. Lusia felt very special, indeed, as all the white-coated servers hovered over her.

After dinner, she went for a walk and watched through the glass doors as the storm raged on, waves crashing over the topmost deck. As Lusia stood there, contemplating the angry sea, she thought about her parents and what they would have said about her life. How proud they would have been that she had married a man like Steve, that she had completed her M.D. degree, that she had survived the war by depending on her wits, her good judgment, and luck. Although she thought about her family every day, it was almost a luxury to have these spare moments to dwell on the past, to examine those events, to turn them over and over in her mind. That was one thing that neither she nor the three others had the time or the inclination to do: to concentrate on all that had happened to them and think about how their lives could have so easily turned out another way.

Lusia turned and went back to her cabin to see if there was anything she could do for Anna. Luckily, the storm soon subsided, and the rest of their journey was uneventful. When they docked in New York, their papers were processed in the first-class dining room; Anna and Lusia were in awe of its gleaming splendor. When they could finally disembark, they saw their husbands waiting for them on the dock, waving excitedly. They were home.

Paul had wonderful news: thanks to Sandy Lewis, all four of them would be working at Beth Israel by July 1, 1952—Steve and Paul as residents and Anna and Lusia as interns. They would be together in the same place! This was the beginning, he told them excitedly. All four of them would begin their training there, and if they had to separate for further residencies, they would do it. But their goal was to live in the same city and work together in a hospital-based program where they could teach, research, write, and see patients.

Paul still had to continue his internship at Metropolitan Hospital on Welfare Island for a few more weeks. Anna found it a sad and depressing place, infested with mice and rats. She felt all alone on that island in the middle of the East River and, as the only woman on the interns' floor, at a loss for companionship. Even using the bathroom posed a challenge, for she did not have a women's restroom to use. When he was available, Paul was willing to stand as a lookout in the hall, but Paul was gone all day at the hospital.

Fortunately, they were on Welfare Island for only a few more weeks. Soon enough it was July 1, and Anna could not have been happier. She and Paul were given rooms on the same floor as Steve and Lusia and were amazed by their light and airy ambience. Anna felt her old spirit returning, that same spark that had made her want to sing and dance whenever she could.

Steve and Paul were busy as residents and in a year had already made great headway with the quirky English language. Anna and Lusia were trying their best, but neither of them had progressed beyond the most basic conversation. They were not worried, though; the English would come, they knew, but they would just have to be patient.

In the meantime, the doctors at Beth Israel were extraordinarily helpful to them. One of the older physicians was especially proud of Anna and the progress she was making. Day after day, they sat together at a table, as he took her through the steps of giving a physical exam, instructing her how to conduct the exam itself and then how to write up her notes for the charts. He stood by proudly as she attempted as best she could to talk to the patients she was serving.

"You are doing so well," he commented one day. "You deserve a nice gift. I am going to take you out for your first banana split." Anna had never eaten a banana split and had certainly never ordered anything quite so extravagant. She accompanied the doctor to a nearby soda fountain and slid into a booth. He ordered coffee for himself and a banana split for her. When the dessert arrived, Anna could not believe her eyes. She had never seen such a concoction, with all the whipped cream and the cherry on top. She knew she could never eat it all, but this man had been so nice to her, so understanding, that she devoured as much as she could.

Lusia found everyone at the hospital extended the same kindness to her. When she returned to Beth Israel from Heidelberg, she still had a month before her internship began. The resident who was to be her supervisor asked if she would like to get a head start on her program. He took her onto the wards with him, patiently instructing her and helping her with her English.

The first patient he gave her was a Polish man, thinking that she would find this an easy assignment since Polish was her native tongue. The patient was happy to see a doctor who knew his language, and he began quickly to rattle off his ailments. Unfortunately, Lusia did not know any medical terms in Polish, so she wrote up the case in German, ran to her room where she grabbed a dictionary, and translated her notes into English.

Lusia also found that her knowledge of Latin came in handy. She would often work on the floor until two in the morning, translating her cases from German into English, using many Latin tenses. The other interns and residents were so kind and helpful, always offering to come to her aid.

The four doctors had not been on staff at Beth Israel very long when a reporter from the *New York Times* called and asked if he could come to the hospital and conduct an interview with them. He had heard from a friend that the hospital had four Jewish war refugees on its staff—two married couples, all physicians who had graduated from a German medical school with honors.

When the article was published on July 4, 1952, a picture of the four of them in their hospital whites appeared over the headline and the two-column, two-page story. Although the reporter had confused some of the facts—he wrote that all four had been in concentration camps, when, actually, only Anna had been an inmate of Auschwitz—his description of the enormity of what they had accomplished was incontestable.

"In their crisp white uniforms," wrote the reporter Charles Zerner, "smiling and cheerful and at ease in their surroundings, it was difficult to visualize them as survivors of the macabre drama of genocide in which sixteen members of their immediate families were among the millions of Jewish victims of the Nazis."

The article's prominent display in the *Times* brought them even more attention. Soon, everyone at the hospital knew them and wanted to hear their stories. Word of their experiences spread, and one day, Steve got a call from a lawyer in Washington. "My name is Hornstein," said the man, "and I read about you in the *New York Times*. I believe we are cousins." Later that month, Lusia and Steve took the train to Washington, where Steve's cousin showed them all the sights of the capital.

Still, most of their time was spent at Beth Israel Hospital, where, as in Heidelberg, they developed a close-knit circle of friends. Nearly everyone on staff knew about the four refugees and what they had endured before coming to the United States. The four young doctors were so overwhelmed by the generosity and help they received from the staff that their pasts were becoming an ever-present shadow rather than a hovering cloud.

Working at Beth Israel provided them with many light-hearted moments. The hospital had a paging system to call doctors to come to the telephone or to a certain floor. The hospital was still understaffed, with only twelve interns and residents, and now four of the twelve had the same sounding last name. When the loud speaker paged Dr. Hornstein, they were never sure which Dr. Hornstein the operator was paging—or had she called Dr. Ornstein? And which one? Consequently, all four of them would run to the phone to answer the page. A patient once asked Lusia, "Why are they always calling you? You must be terribly busy." Lusia could only laugh. They were still very friendly with Jo and Bob Lewis, and, in a bow to their close relationship, they had nicknamed them "the Born-steins."

To alleviate the mix-ups, the hospital decided to page them by their first names. "Calling Dr. Anna," the operator would announce or "calling Dr. Steve." This helped take care of the confusion.

One night, Anna and Lusia noticed that they were receiving an inordinate number of pages. Every other minute, it seemed, the operator was calling one of them to the phone. Anna went to the office to look into the matter and emerged laughing. It was October and something called the World Series was being played. All of the other doctors in the hospital had signed out to the two women and were gathered in the doctors' lounge around the television.

One of the residents refused to believe that Lusia did not know anything about baseball. "You're in America," he told her. "Baseball is the American pastime." He stood in one of the hospital corridors with her, trying to explain the complicated game. The more puzzled Lusia looked, the louder he talked. Finally, Lusia had had enough of balls and strikes. "Just because you're yelling doesn't mean I'm going to understand it any better," she told him. The same doctor also insisted on explaining the American electoral system to her, but with similar results.

Everyone at Beth Israel went out of their way to make the four refugees feel needed and wanted. Most of the other doctors had cars, so when Lusia, Steve, Anna, and Paul were on call and could not leave the hospital, the other doctors always made sure to bring them something back for a snack. The four were always excited to see the take-out containers and taste the wonders within: Chinese food, pizza, and even shrimp. They had been kosher all their lives and had never tasted this forbidden food.

Whoever made out the work schedules for the interns and residents was kind enough to give the couples the same days off whenever possible. They would take a bus to New York City and buy the cheapest theater tickets available. That way they were able to see some memorable theater: *Mother Courage, The Seven Year Itch,* and *Carmen* at Carnegie Hall with Richard Tucker and Rise Stevens. Bob Lewis's parents gave them tickets to see *South Pacific.* Anna could not help thinking that her parents' dream was to attend the theater or an opera, and now she could go every weekend if she wanted.

Soon, Anna had other things on her mind than the theater. In the fall of 1952, she discovered she was pregnant, due in May. The staff at the hospital was so kind and solicitous during her pregnancy, always willing to help her with her English and her duties, constantly on the lookout for her well-being. Anna tended to her tasks as an intern with her usual energy and vigor; pregnancy did not slow her down a bit.

Everyone on staff waited excitedly for the birth of the Ornsteins' first child, making bets as to which doctor would have the distinct honor of taking Anna up to the maternity floor when she went into labor. All the doctors wanted to be part of the excitement. They told Anna they wanted to chip in and buy her a special gift; money was no object. She should choose something she wanted but would never buy for herself.

"You know what I would really like?" she said one day. "A baby carriage just like the one Queen Elizabeth is using." The Queen of England, who was the same age as Anna, had recently had a baby, and the newspapers were full of stories and pictures of the new young royal and the fantastic baby carriage. Paul and Anna were deeply touched when the interns delivered the same model carriage to their door.

Sharone Beth Ornstein was born on a warm May day in 1953. Her middle name was given to her in honor of the hospital that had provided her parents with their first real American home.

"Have you ever known so much love?" Anna asked Paul one day after their fellow interns and residents had come by to see the baby. "I never knew people could be so nice."

Sadly, Lusia's and Anna's internship and Paul's residency at Beth Israel were finished in June. Steve still had six months left on his residency at Beth Israel, where the Hornsteins continued to live, and Lusia had taken a six-month residency in infectious diseases at another New Jersey hospital. Paul, Anna, their baby daughter, and the fantastic carriage moved to Brooklyn, where Paul had taken a residency at Kings County Hospital. After three months at Kings County, Paul was told that to take the licensing exam that would allow him to practice in the state of New York, he would have to sign up for a postgraduate course in general medicine at New York University. This dismaying news derailed his internship at Kings County, but his main goal was to pass the licensing exam. He called Steve immediately and relayed to him what he had learned. Steve agreed that the postgraduate course would have to take precedence: doctors without a license to practice were useless in the United States.

Anna was not working at first; she was at home taking care of the baby. What would the family do for money if Paul went back to school? As they talked over their finances, fate intervened in the form of a wonderful gift to the six-month old Sharone: the arrival in New York of her grandmother Sophie. At last, Anna felt complete. She had her husband, her mother, and her daughter. Sophie was thrilled to stay home and take care of Sharone while Anna worked at Brooklyn State Hospital to earn money for the family.

In the winter of 1954, Steve began the course at Bellevue Hospital. He and Lusia rented an efficiency apartment—one large room with a built-in kitchen and tiny bathroom—on New York's Second Avenue, although Steve, still completing his residency in New Jersey, commuted to New York only on weekends. While at Bellevue, Steve also signed up to take the same postgraduate course as Paul at New York University to prepare himself for the New York licensing exam. Often, Steve, Paul, and Marcel Tuchman, their friend from Heidelberg, would use the apartment during the week to study. When Lusia, who was now a pediatric resident at Beth El Hospital in Brooklyn, came home at night, she would find their lovely apartment strewn with papers and the sink piled high with plates and coffee cups.

Lusia was on call every other night and every other weekend, but at least she could live with her husband at the little apartment they had furnished so painstakingly together. Lusia had made all the curtains, and she and Steve had bought unfinished furniture. Lusia spent all her free time sanding and varnishing. With an inexpensive rug to make it even cozier, the apartment was warm and welcoming.

Lusia would take the train from the Third Avenue subway station to the hospital in Brooklyn, managing to finish the entire *New York Times* on the long ride there. She spent several nights a week at the hospital, as well as every other weekend. Her frequent absences actually turned out to be a blessing, since Steve was busy studying, usually with Paul and Marcel. The Hornstein apartment was so small that if Paul and Marcel wanted to move on to a different subject, Steve would take his books and lie down to read in the bathtub.

At the Beth El Hospital in Brooklyn, Lusia was assigned to work with the highly regarded Dr. Bela Schick, inventor of the famous Schick diagnostic test for diphtheria. Although he was by now quite elderly, he was a respected and world-famous physician. He took Lusia under his wing, inviting her home to dinner with his wife and to conferences and seminars. It was unusual for a man of his stature to lavish such attention on a resident, but Dr. Schick was quite taken with this charming refugee who worked so hard. He assured Lusia that wherever she and Steve settled, he would write her a glowing recommendation.

One spring morning in 1954, Steve went out to get the mail and came back both excited and alarmed. "You will not believe this," he told Lusia. "I have been drafted into the air force." Paul had received a similar letter.

"If we go into the air force now," Paul said, "we'll never get the training we need to practice. Let's see if we can get them to let us put it off."

Steve and Paul took the train to the air force recruiting office, discussing strategy along the way. When it came time to meet with the air force officer in charge, Paul began by presenting a solid case. "You know," he told the air force officer, "American soldiers deserve the best. You want the cream of the medical crop to take care of them." The officer nodded. Paul was, of course, correct. "We do not have our American medical licenses yet," Steve continued. "We have not even sat for our boards." The officer listened and gave the men permission to put off the military until they became licensed—if not, indefinitely.

Toward the end of the postgraduate course at New York University, Steve and Paul felt ready to sit for the New York state licensing exam. A doctor from Albany, the state capital, would come to the city on weekends to test the readiness of the applicants, but each time he met with Paul and Steve, he hinted that although they were ready to take the exam, it would cost them each three thousand dollars. It finally dawned on the two young doctors that they were being asked for a bribe.

"Maybe we can borrow it from our relatives," said Paul, who desperately wanted the four of them to stay in New York. In the end, though, neither man liked the idea of having to give the corrupt official any money, nor did they have any money to give him. They decided not to sit for the New York exam after all.

That summer, Steve and Paul took jobs in the Pocono Mountains as summer camp doctors to earn some money. Lusia, Anna, Sophie, and Sharone commuted to the mountains on weekends. By August, Lusia had some interesting news for her husband: she was pregnant with their first child. Everyone was thrilled for the couple, but Steve knew he would have to put off the final months of his residency and try to find a place where he could earn a real living.

Steve's younger brother, Jerry, was working for an optical firm in Chicago and told Steve and Paul that Illinois would let them take the licensing exam. If they passed, they could practice medicine there. Both men traveled to Chicago, sat for the Illinois medical boards, and passed first time around. With Jerry in Chicago and a baby on the way, Steve and Lusia decided they could do a lot worse than to move there. Jerry was sure he could arrange a job for his older brother. Jerry's best friend was an obstetrician-gynecologist who had a friend—a general practitioner—who needed another general practitioner in his private clinic. If Steve took this position, he would earn fifteen thousand dollars a year, which he and Lusia considered a small fortune.

In November 1954, the Hornsteins said goodbye to the Ornsteins and moved their possessions from New York to Chicago. They rented a downstairs flat in a two-story house on the South Side, near the clinic where Steve would work. The couple that lived upstairs owned the apartment building. The wife was wonderful to Lusia, cheerfully giving her new tenant friendship and moral support, showing her where to shop, and introducing her to the neighborhood. For social life, though, Jerry and his friends were the only people they saw on weekends. Unfortunately, they lived on Michigan Avenue, a world away from the blue-collar neighborhood where Steve and Lusia lived. The Hornsteins' main goal, however, was to save money so that Steve could finish his residency in ob-gyn somewhere and Lusia could complete hers in pediatrics. Lack of a social life seemed a small price to pay.

In April 1955, their son Mark was born. "It's like falling in love all over again," said Steve, cradling his new baby. Lusia, however, felt isolated and alone, except for the couple upstairs. Although the Ornsteins had visited earlier in the year and Sophie had come with Sharone for a brief stay, Lusia's days on the South Side of Chicago were long and lonely. She missed work terribly. Mark was an adorable, loving, but colicky baby. At least Jerry Hornstein appeared every Friday after work, full of good cheer. He always helped Lusia by vacuuming her floor.

The Hornsteins desperately missed the other part of their "family," though—the Ornsteins. Lusia thought about them constantly as she bundled Mark into the carriage the doctors had given Anna to use for Sharone. Anna had sent the carriage to Chicago just before Mark's birth. Lusia would walk for hours pushing that carriage, since it was the only time she could count on the baby to sleep.

After Steve and Lusia moved to Chicago, Paul and Anna had moved to Boston with Sharone and Sophie to take up residencies in psychiatry at Metropolitan Hospital. They found the city quite hospitable and, with Sophie to help care for Sharone, thought seriously about making Boston their home—if they could convince the Hornsteins to move there as well. Massachusetts, however, would not allow foreign-trained doctors to take the medical boards.

To become psychoanalysts, Paul and Anna needed money for the training. Part of the course of study was to undergo an analysis by a trained psychoanalyst—a process that could last from four to seven years—but this step was prohibitively expensive. If they wanted to pursue their dream of becoming psychoanalysts, they would have to find a way to make more money. To make more money, they would have to be licensed to practice medicine.

The Ornsteins had some friends who were in residency in Cincinnati, Ohio. These friends wrote glowing letters to Paul and Anna about the wonderful training program in psychiatry at the University of Cincinnati's medical college and at its affiliated hospital. While Cincinnati did not have a psychoanalytic institute for training, four analysts who belonged to the Chicago Institute for Psychoanalysis practiced in Cincinnati. When they saved enough money, Paul and Anna could undergo the rigorous psychoanalysis in Cincinnati and then commute to Chicago on weekends for their training. Even better news: Ohio allowed foreign-trained doctors to take the licensing boards. Their friends also suggested that Paul and Anna attend a psychiatrists' meeting that spring in Atlantic City, where they could meet the head of the psychiatry department, Dr. Maurice Levine.

Dr. Levine was most encouraging. "I think you will both like Cincinnati," he told them. "Why don't you come for an interview?"

Paul and Anna talked it over. Moving to Cincinnati—if they were both offered residencies—would be expensive, but they could take the licensing exams there. Once they received their licenses, they could practice psychiatry and earn money for their analyses. Then, if they were accepted for further training at the Chicago Institute for Psychoanalysis, Paul would commute there on weekends. When he was finished with his training, Anna would begin hers. All the while, they would continue to work. Thankfully, Sophie was thrilled to be able to help her children by looking after Sharone while Anna and Paul completed the necessary steps to reach their goals.

By the summer of 1955, both Drs. Ornstein had been accepted for residencies in psychiatry at Cincinnati General Hospital. They moved their family into an apartment not too far away from the hospital and the university. So desperately were they saving money for the future that they did not even own beds—they slept on mattresses on the floor.

Now it was time to convince Steve to query Cincinnati's ob-gyn department about a residency so that the Ornsteins and Hornsteins could be together once again. From Chicago, Steve wrote to the head of the ob-gyn department and said that he would be visiting Cincinnati in the spring. Could he set up an interview for a position as a resident?

He received a very curt reply from Dr. Stanley Garber, the director of obstetrics, written on the stationery of the Cincinnati General Hospital: "Dear Dr. Hornstein," said the letter. "We have not entirely completed our selection for residents for July 1, 1956. We are looking for men for the top positions only. We are not considering you a candidate for chief resident. Yours very truly, Stanley T. Garber."

"It's useless," Steve said to Paul. "It sounds like the door is completely shut." Paul Ornstein, however, knew how to open doors, even doors to departments that were reputedly inhospitable to foreign-trained doctors. When he and Anna sat for the Ohio licensing exam, Paul passed first in the state—not first among the foreign-trained doctors but first among all the doctors in Ohio who had written the exam.

The day after the results were posted, Paul encountered the dean of the medical college in the hall. "Congratulations!" said the dean. "Passing first is quite an achievement, and we're very proud of you. If there is anything we can do for you here at the university, just let me know."

"Actually, there is something you could help me with," said Paul. He told the dean about his best friend, Steve Hornstein, a brilliant doctor in Chicago who wanted very much to come to Cincinnati for a residency in obstetrics and gynecology but could not seem to arrange an interview. The dean promised to look into it. As far as Paul was concerned, Steve, with his brilliant mind and unimpeachable resume, was as good as in.

A few months later, when the Hornsteins came to Cincinnati for Passover with the Ornsteins, Paul suggested that Steve try to contact Dr. Garber by phone to set up an interview. After a good deal of prodding, Steve called Dr. Garber for an appointment, but his secretary told Steve that the doctor was not available to see him.

Paul, sure of himself and as optimistic as ever, insisted that Steve call back and say that he was willing to meet with Dr. Garber any time, any place. The secretary took Steve's phone number and called back a few minutes later. Dr. Garber had no appointments available, but if Steve wanted to come in while Dr. Garber ate his lunch, he could.

Steve jumped at the chance. When he arrived at the office, Dr. Garber told Steve that he could only have a few minutes of his time. "So, what are your interests?" Dr. Garber asked, biting into a sandwich.

An hour later, Steve was still talking about a paper he had had published in the highly respected German journal *Experimental Medicine* on his experiments with diabetic white rats and their ability to break down carbohydrates. Dr. Garber had an interest in the problems of diabetes during pregnancy and was most intrigued by Steve's findings. By the time the interview ended, Steve knew that an offer would soon be forthcoming.

Shortly thereafter, Steve received the following letter: "Dear Dr. Hornstein, After your interview . . . we of the obstetrics/gynecology department are glad to extend to you an appointment on the obstetric-gynecology service beginning July 1, 1956."

In June 1956, the Hornsteins moved to an apartment in Cincinnati upstairs from the Ornsteins. Geography would never separate the four doctors again.

14   *At Home*

SEATED IN THE LIVING ROOM OF THEIR SPA-
cious new home in one of Cincinnati's most desirable residential areas, the
Ornsteins were a perfect picture of family togetherness on this Sunday afternoon early in 1962. Anna, perched on the couch, watched lovingly as
her two daughters, Sharone, age nine, and Miriam, age four, played with
their baby brother, Rafael, who had been born in June 1960. The little boy
giggled delightedly as his two sisters tussled with him and applauded his
every attempt at words, sounds, and actions. Across the room, Paul looked
up periodically from a book he was reading to gaze with affection at the
tableau being enacted before him: his daughters, singing, dancing, and
urging their baby brother to join in their fun and games, and his wife,
Anna, serenely close by, laughing with her children, reaching down to
give them a hug. Their lives seemed so rich, so full.

On that peaceful Sunday in his own home, Paul recalled a recent conversation with a colleague about the effect of his time in the forced labor
camps, his escape, and the news of his family's demise in the Holocaust.
"I had always wanted to become a psychoanalyst," Paul remembered saying, "so I cannot credit my Holocaust experiences with that. I could not
even say that the Holocaust shaped my intellectual development." His
friend was well-meaning, as were so many of the Americans with whom
they had become acquainted. Yet Paul noticed that nearly everyone expected him to say that his intellectual development and drive for success

were the results of the Holocaust. "The Holocaust did not shape or form me," he told his colleague. "What formed me was my strong attachment to Jewish intellectual life and the ideals of my childhood, my prewar plan to become a psychoanalyst, and my love for Anna. That's what really got me through the forced labor camps. The pictures I carried of her and my plan to find her after the war and marry her."

When he thought about this conversation with his friend, he realized that he had forgotten to say something important: "The Holocaust was the biggest tragedy of my life, because I lost so many members of my family, but I would not even call it the central experience of my life. I have not lived my life since with the idea that the Holocaust destroyed me."

Yet he understood how it could have destroyed someone who had survived a concentration camp like Auschwitz or Mauthausen, where his father had been imprisoned. A systematic regimen of beatings, starvation, indiscriminate killings, the gas chambers, the torture—that was another matter. Paul did not have to endure these daily assaults. If that had been his fate, he knew that only luck would have enabled him to live.

"Do you believe," Steve had once asked him in one of their long, philosophical discussions about the Holocaust, "that in order to survive you have to do away with part of your moral self?" "Are you talking about the rabbi?" Paul had asked him. Steve had known which rabbi Paul meant. Everyone who had survived the war and ended up in Budapest knew the story of the Hungarian rabbi who had stolen bread from his own son. It had become a famous, hurtful touchstone of Holocaust lore.

"I hope I would not have to give up part of my moral self, and I am grateful not to have been in that situation," Paul had replied. It was an easy answer, but he could give no other. He had heard of situations in which such breaches had occurred but had seen none firsthand. Anna, who had survived much worse circumstances, had not witnessed such behavior either—but she had been a young girl in Auschwitz, and Sophie had shielded her from many dramas.

Steve and Paul, who had not endured the hardships that had been perpetrated on their wives, knew that they had been lucky: they had survived with their selves intact. If anything, they agreed that the Holocaust had made them see how important, yet how difficult it was, to live a civilized life.

While the Ornsteins and the Hornsteins lived in the present, the past was forever with them. Paul, in particular, found that there was one hurdle he could not overcome: his painful and overwhelming sense of loss during any Jewish ritual or holiday celebration. Although those feelings were only transient, he initially found it nearly impossible to celebrate the Sabbath or a Passover seder, to join in the songs and prayers. To do that, to chant the blessings and sing the old melodies, evoked all those memories, the wonderful Sabbath meals and holidays with his father and mother, sister and brothers. While nothing, not even the Holocaust, could destroy Paul's strong identification with Judaism's three-thousand-year-old history and its artists and philosophers, leading the prayers on Friday nights or reading from the Haggadah at Passover had been an arduous trial when they had first come to the United States. He later did it for the children, of course, but during that period, he would have to force his mind and heart elsewhere.

Yet everything else in their lives was proceeding most agreeably. The children were bright and healthy; Paul's father, Lajos, was happily a citizen of Israel, remarried, and a surrogate grandfather to the children of Steve Hornstein's brothers Shmuel and Karl. Lajos had visited Paul and Anna in the United States, and they had plans to travel to Israel in the next year or so.

Missing from this scene of family contentment was Anna's mother, Sophie, who had died of a particularly virulent lymphoma in 1960 at the age of sixty-three. Anna and Paul missed her terribly, as did Sharone, the only Ornstein grandchild who had come to know her. Miriam was only a toddler when her grandmother died, and Rafael just an infant. At least Sophie had lived long enough to see her grandchildren, to watch Paul and Anna establish their first real home, and to be there as their dreams of becoming psychoanalysts began to come true.

Her mother's death had been so quick, such a staggering blow, that Anna had been filled up with the pain of that particular sorrow. She tried to isolate the event, without allowing herself to mourn the loss of the rest of her family, her hometown, her way of life. It was best to push that to the back, to keep it locked in the mind's vault. Trotting out those images, examining them, and poking at them with her vivid imagination would only lead to unspeakable agony.

So on this sunny winter Sunday, with everyone exactly where they were supposed to be, doing exactly what they were supposed to do, Anna appeared content, bending down to retrieve a toy for Rafael, fixing the ribbon on Sharone's hair, and promising to read aloud from Miriam's favorite book. Peace and joy seemed to reign in this home, as if sorrow had been banished elsewhere.

Suddenly, without warning, Anna was engulfed by a pain of sadness and loss that was so real, so palpable, that she could feel her heart racing. She gave a soft cry, but fortunately, her children, absorbed in their play, took no notice. Her husband, lost in a book and sitting across the room, did not hear her either. She knew then, as she observed the tranquil scene before her, that she was feeling the pain of loss for her father, who had never known the joy of her own happiness and that of her precious children. The image of the last time she had seen William—stoop-shouldered and defeated, holding the hand of his tiny mother as the two of them walked to their certain deaths—welled up before her. How cruel that he could never know that his daughter had survived to become a wife, a mother, and a doctor.

Sophie had known, had seen it with her own eyes, had watched as Anna had grown and developed from a loving, giving, beautiful young girl into a sought-after teacher and psychiatrist known for her empathy and understanding of her patients. While she did not credit the Holocaust with shaping her life, Anna could speak and write with authority about how the Holocaust experience drew out the personality that had been formed earlier.

"As you all know," Anna would tell her students, "trauma does not create a personality—personality is created in the first three years of life." "I was not born in Auschwitz," she would say. "My personality was developed long before that experience. I am who I am because my parents gave me and my brothers a strong Jewish upbringing in a home filled with books, learning, and laughter."

But now, today, the pain of the memory of that upbringing bore down on her with the intensity of a heart attack. She understood why Paul had to turn away from some of the most beautiful memories of his early life. Remembering could bring not only tears but also a profound physical reaction.

Within a few hundred yards of the Ornsteins, the Hornsteins were relaxing in their new, airy home. How fortunate they had been to find such a lovely place to raise their family, and it was practically across the street from their very best friends, the Ornsteins. Steve and Lusia, the newspapers spread before them, loved to relax in the living room with its wide windows overlooking their back garden and watch their sons, Mark, age seven, and Frank, age three, as they played with their favorite toys. Lusia leaned back happily in her chair. In May 1962, she would have another child.

Earlier, before their second son, Frank, was born in September 1959, Lusia had lost a baby when she was eight months pregnant. She had been working part-time as a physician, visiting clinics throughout the county, seeing mostly sick children, and giving them inoculations and vaccines. With the new polio vaccinations, she had had plenty to keep her busy. She had been proud of herself for learning to drive, since the lack of a license—not to mention a car—had kept her pretty much housebound in Chicago. The job had been more rewarding than demanding, and she had been quite content being a working mother, especially since Sophie had been happy to watch both Mark and Sharone while their mothers worked.

In her eighth month, however, Lusia had known something was wrong when she no longer felt the baby move. She was a pediatrician and her husband an obstetrician, but she had still clung to some hope until her doctor had confirmed what she had already known. The loss had devastated her; had she not suffered enough tragedy already? Steve, seeing the miscarriage's effect on Lusia, had quickly called for a conference with the Ornsteins to discuss what would be best for his wife.

"Why not go back and finish your residency?" Paul had suggested. Anna had agreed. "Now is the time to do it when you only have Mark," she had advised. "It will be too difficult when you get pregnant again." Lusia had noticed that everyone nodded when Anna had said "when you get pregnant," not "if."

Lusia had known her husband and friends were right. She could have sat home and brooded, too, and no one would have begrudged her. But that was not like Lusia, who knew that to survive, she had to move ahead. She had wanted to finish her residency in pediatrics, which had been interrupted when they had moved to Chicago. With little time to mourn, Lusia had arranged for a four-month residency in the pediatrics department at Jewish Hospital and another six months at Children's Hospital. Sometimes, after thirty-six hours on call, Lusia would come home, drop directly to the floor to play with her son, Mark, without even removing her coat—and promptly fall asleep.

When she had completed the residency, she had been offered a position with the outpatient department at Cincinnati's acclaimed Children's Hospital. The letters of recommendation from Dr. Bela Schick, with whom she had worked when they lived in New York, had been an added plus to the strong recommendations she had recently earned during her residency in Cincinnati. During those heady days of beginning a new position and buying a new home, she had discovered that she was pregnant again. Their second son, Frank, had been born in September 1959.

Sophie's death the next year had been a great loss to the Hornsteins as well. Sophie not only had been a second mother to Lusia but also had served as a grandmother to Mark and, briefly, Frank. Sophie had had her own sorrows and tragedies, yet she had gone out of her way to make sure that Lusia felt loved and cared for in Heidelberg and again in the United States. With Lusia's miscarriage, then Sophie's death, all the feelings of loss had been reawakened for both Hornsteins.

In the meantime, Steve had become an assistant professor of obstetrics and gynecology, largely because of the support of Dr. Garber, the same man with whom Steve had had such trouble getting an interview several years earlier. Dr. Garber had made Steve chief resident of the obstetrics service, entrusting him to take over several of his classes and responsibilities. Like Paul in the department of psychiatry, Steve was making a name for himself in obstetrics. He had introduced the first course in sex education for the hospital's residents and had designed a program where the ob-gyn residents were to rotate through the psychiatry department to learn more about the psychosomatic aspects of their specialty.

Life had not been all work and study, though. Friendly, affable, generous, and anxious to become a part of the community, the Hornsteins and Ornsteins had continued to make new friends and keep up with their old ones. They had opened their homes for holidays and for Friday and Saturday evening dinners. Their children's birthdays had been occasions for great celebrations with other families. They had continued to correspond by letter and telephone with their Heidelberg friends, even the ones who had moved to Australia. Now, because they lived so close to one another, it was still the most natural thing to visit back and forth, borrow a book or a sweater, drop off a child for a play date, and make plans together for family vacations.

The birth of Ruth Ann Hornstein in May 1962 was a happy occasion that offset the recent losses that had affected both families. As the years progressed, both families kept on moving forward, refusing to dwell on the circumstances that could slow their development. Happiness and triumph were also part of their lives. The couples traveled to Israel to visit Paul's father and Steve's brothers. In 1964, the Ornsteins returned to Hungary with Paul's father and his new wife. They rented a huge Mercedes in Budapest, and all seven of them crowded in for the drive to Hajdunanas.

The Ornsteins were dismayed by what they found or did not find there: almost every remnant of the lively, prewar Hajdunanas Jewish community had been either destroyed or abandoned. Most of the Jews who had decided to remain in Hungary had moved to Budapest; others had dispersed to the United States, Canada, Israel, or elsewhere. The Jewish cemetery was still standing but was weed-choked and unkempt. No graves were marked for those Jews who had died at the hands of the Nazis. It was too sad to stay there and look for the names that had once led the vibrant and thriving Jewish community. Paul and Lajos left the cemetery dejectedly and concluded the visit by showing the family the places for which they still harbored fond memories. For the most part, though, Hajdunanas—and they themselves—had changed.

"It sure was a lot smaller than I remember it," Paul said to Steve when the Ornsteins returned to Cincinnati. Steve would discover this for himself when, a few years later, he took his own family to Europe to visit the places he and Lusia had known so well.

The four adults had been so busy with work and rearing their families that they were caught short when one of the children had asked earlier, "Where are they, all the cousins and aunts and uncles?"

"Steve and Lusia are your substitute aunt and uncle, and Mark, Frank, and Ruth are just like cousins," Anna replied. "The Hornsteins are our best friends, but they have also become your relatives because we do not have any others."

The children of both families had been studying the Holocaust in Sunday School and wanted to know all about their parents' families. Slowly, Steve and Lusia began to talk about the war and the tragedy it had wrought. Anna, they knew, had been very open with her children, who were curious about her tattoo and all the pictures of her family that had survived with her aunt in Budapest. Paul, however, was still reluctant to talk about those years.

In 1971, the Ornsteins took their children to Europe again, traveling through several countries by rail. On one lengthy leg of the journey, they had a train compartment all to themselves. Sharone got up and shut the sliding door to ensure the family some privacy. "All right, Dad," she said. "We want you to tell us everything about what happened to you and your family during the war."

"The kids really nailed me," Paul later told Steve. "They asked me question after question and would not let up until we had arrived in the next city. If the trip had lasted any longer, they would have wanted to know even more."

The children had begged Anna for information about her past, and so, on this trip, they traveled to Szendro, just as they had visited Hajdunanas nearly eight years earlier. Anna wanted them to see her house, the river where she had learned to swim, her one-room school. She even wanted to show them where the Jews had been herded into a ghetto while waiting for deportation. Mostly, though, she wanted to introduce them to Mari Neni, her mother's and grandmother's beloved maid with whom Anna still corresponded. Only a dozen Jews from Szendro had survived the war, and Mari Neni, the Ornsteins' only Christian friend who had come to say goodbye when the family was being deported, was really the last link to Anna's prewar life.

The children were teenagers now and old enough to understand the place of importance this wizened old woman held in their mother's life. Although they did not share a language with which to communicate, the touch of Mari Neni's hands on their faces spoke volumes.

Sometime after this trip to Europe, the tenor of the Passover seders held alternately at the homes of the Ornsteins and the Hornsteins began to change. Since Passover celebrates the freedom of the Jews from slavery, Sharone Ornstein suggested that each year one of the children write a brief story, poem, or essay on the theme of freedom. Paul noticed that he was becoming more amenable to joining in the celebration of the seder, agreeably singing the songs from his childhood seder table with his friend Steve, who knew all the old melodies.

Around this time, Anna began to write and tell stories of her own. For each Passover, she retold the story of her own freedom, with descriptions of her hometown, her childhood memories, her family's deportation, her experiences in Auschwitz, her liberation, and the day Paul found her at her aunt's house in Budapest. Sophie had been an excellent storyteller and had evidently passed this talent along to her daughter. Writing the stories, then reading them out loud, was liberating in itself, perfectly in sync with the holiday that celebrated the escape from bondage.

A few years after the Ornsteins took their children to Europe in 1964, the Hornsteins embarked on a similar journey with Mark, Frank, and Ruth. Steve had not been back to Hungary since he left there in 1946. The family first visited Munich, then Dachau, a notorious concentration camp preserved by the German government. Lusia and Steve wanted to show the children Heidelberg, the city where they married, attended medical school, and began the important healing process from the wounds of the war. They also found time to visit Lusia's cousin Samek and his wife, Zosia.

It was with some trepidation that Steve drove his family to Hajdunanas. He was not sure he could bear the pain of revisiting his old home, where he had last seen his parents, younger brother, and sister. He recalled the day at the railroad station in April 1944 when his mother cried because she feared she would never see her son again. He had reassured her that he would be back. He had come back, but his mother had been right.

Now, in 1968, pieces of the puzzle of their father's life became clearer to Steve's children as they walked with their parents from place to place—the Protestant gymnasium, the tower where he had searched the skies for enemy planes, the railroad station where he had bid his family goodbye. On a sad visit to the Hajdunanas cemetery, Steve was able to show his children the name Hornstein on several headstones in the overgrown burial ground, but there were no markers for the Hornsteins who had been taken away after the Nazi occupation in March 1944.

In 1984, the Hornsteins embarked on another European trip, this time to Hungary, Czechoslovakia, and Poland. Accompanying them were Steve's brothers, Karl, Shmuel, and Jerry, and Jerry's wife. The trip was especially meaningful for Lusia, who had not been back to Poland since her escape from Warsaw. Now it was time to show her family what she had endured. In Warsaw, Lusia was able to point out her hiding places and the various apartments that were the landmarks of her life on the run. In a taxi to the square in Warsaw where, on September 2, 1944, Lusia, her friend Krzysia, and her cousins had made a last-minute escape down a manhole to thread their way through the city's maze of sewers to a part of Warsaw still held by Poles, the cab driver turned to the children and said, "Do you realize that your mother is a hero of Warsaw?" The Hornstein children looked at their mother in awe. She was a mother, a doctor, a professor—but a war hero, too?

While in Poland, they traveled to Auschwitz, a place they had already heard about through Anna's stories. As they stood in that quiet place of hate and death, Steve and Lusia could not help reaching the same conclusion: Hitler had not succeeded, really. Here were their children, undeniable proof of a strong, new Jewish generation.

The more the children heard about their parents' lives, their war experiences, and their lost families, the more they wanted to know. It was all so confusing, so unbelievable. How could they possibly have survived all that? What part did luck play? How could all those coincidences occur? What if they had made this decision instead of that one? Weren't they hungry? Weren't they tired? Why didn't they fall apart from grief?

These were the kinds of questions the Ornstein and Hornstein children had asked their parents on the trips through Europe. This was the information imparted to them every Passover through Anna's stories. Still, every time they asked, a new memory would surface, and Anna, Paul, Steve, and Lusia would find that they would have to begin at the beginning and retell their story, adding the new material that the questioner had brought to the surface.

Frank Hornstein wanted to document his family's history and war experiences. When he was a student at Macalester College in St. Paul, Minnesota, and contemplating a topic for his senior thesis, he decided to interview his parents, his uncles, and his surviving cousins for an oral history of his family. Because they were considered relatives, he also interviewed Paul and Anna for their perspective and recollections. In the summer and fall of 1979, Frank traveled to New York to talk to some cousins of Steve and Lusia; to Israel to interview Steve's older brothers, Karl and Shmuel; to Los Angeles to speak with Steve's younger brother, Jerry; and to Frankfurt, Germany, to interview Lusia's cousin Samek and his wife, Zosia. At length he recorded the memories of his parents and Anna and Paul. Frank's four-hundred-page thesis turned out to be a fascinating oral history of his family's life in Hungary, Poland, Germany, and the United States. That he included the lives of Paul and Anna Ornstein is a testament to the closeness of the two families and the love between them.

The decades of the seventies and eighties proved a time of great joy and productivity for the Hornsteins and the Ornsteins. Steve and Lusia became sought-after speakers on the Holocaust and in their professional fields. Steve became known for his work on infertility and the psychosomatic aspects of pregnancy, labor, and delivery. He was also the physician of record in a most unusual case of a woman with two uteri who conceived in both several weeks apart and gave birth to "twin" girls, who technically were not twins at all. In addition to his private practice, Steve maintained his position as clinical professor of obstetrics and gynecology at the University of Cincinnati's College of Medicine. Lusia was appointed director of pediatrics at the Cincinnati Center for Developmental Disorders at Children's Hospital and continued to fulfill the duties of a full professorship at the College of Medicine.

The Ornsteins began speaking and writing on many clinical and theoretical aspects of psychoanalysis, especially self psychology, based on some new ideas about narcissistic personality disorders. Paul became interested in brief therapy, where patients see a psychoanalyst for six to sixteen sessions rather than the hundreds usually recommended. He was also named a professor of psychoanalysis, one of the few people in the country with this title. Anna became well known for her work with trauma survivors, especially children. She wrote widely about aging Holocaust survivors and their children and often spoke to local, national, and international groups on the subject. The more she wrote, the more she found herself in disagreement with established theories on Holocaust survivors and children of Holocaust survivors. Anna believed that survival and recovery from disasters depended a great deal on the personality of the victim before the event and the kind of family or support developed after the event. She presented these theories at several scientific meetings.

At one lecture, an audience member asked Anna about conflicts among inmates at the concentration camps, where one's survival often depended on securing the largest ration of food, the best sleeping arrangement, and the easiest work detail. Surely these situations must have brought about a great deal of life-threatening tension that could forever change one's world view and personality. "Of course there were tensions," Anna answered. "There was a lot of hostility, rivalry and aggression, too, but that's all part of family life. People tend to attribute these things to the Holocaust. That's really an outmoded view, to look to the Holocaust in terms of personality and behavior."

Both Anna and Paul were invited to present lectures in prestigious forums. Paul, in particular, was invited to give the Fortieth Annual Sando Rado Lecture at Columbia University Psychoanalytic Institute, a testament to his success and respect among the world's psychoanalysts. He also edited four volumes of the work of the noted psychoanalyst Heinz Kohut. He and Anna were both invited to give the distinguished lecture at the American Psychiatric Institute.

As the years have gone by and the four of them have moved into their seventies, they have begun retiring from their active professional lives. Steve has given up his private practice. Lusia now works only two or three days a week at Children's Hospital. Paul retired in 1996 from the university but not from private practice. Anna, the youngest of the four, still sees a full complement of patients, although she, too, retired from the university in January 1997.

In 1995, amidst their writing and speaking engagements, seeing patients, working on volunteer projects, and visiting with children and
grandchildren, they looked up from their busy lives and realized it had
been fifty years since the establishment of the Jewish Students Union in
Heidelberg, Germany. Now those students could be found in the far-flung
corners of the world, from New York to Canada to Melbourne, Australia,
all making important contributions to the world's advancement. Although they had kept in touch all these years and had even visited back
and forth, meeting the Australians in Hawaii, for example, or getting together with the New Yorkers on trips east, they had never all assembled
in one place—certainly not in fifty years, not since Hitler's plan to murder the Jews of Europe found them, ironically, in the only country that
would accept them and provide them with an education.

Marcel and Shoshana Tuchman, who were among the very first mem-
bers of Heidelberg's Jewish Students Union, offered their summer home
in the Berkshire Mountains of western Massachusetts as a reunion site if
Anna would organize the gathering. Steve and Lusia were immediately
interested, as were the Zarnowitzes from Chicago and the Shenitzers from
Toronto. The Zajacs from Australia promised to be there. Jo Lewis, now Jo
Seelmann, was delighted to accept the invitation. Jo's first husband, Bob
Lewis, the army dentist in Heidelberg who had helped Steve and Lusia
obtain their very first positions at Beth Israel Hospital in Newark, had died
several years earlier. In all, more than twenty members of the Heidelberg
Jewish Students Union agreed to meet at the Tuchmans' home over Me-
morial Day weekend for a reunion and a celebration.

As at any reunion, they bragged about their children and grandchildren, showed off their pictures, and studied everyone's old photos of
Heidelberg that they had brought with them. They talked about where
they would travel next. Since they were last together, some had changed
cities or professions, developed new business or academic interests, or
renewed their zest for life in other ways. The hugs, tears, and incessant
chatter rose to a feverish pitch as each person exclaimed how wonderful
it was to see one another.

The reunion was a chance to celebrate their successes and their triumphs, but it was also a time to remember, beginning with their old lives.
Hard as it was to believe, for all their past togetherness and for all the tragedy they had in common, they knew little about how each had survived
the Holocaust. The Poles among them, the Czechs, the Hungarians—each
had experienced the Holocaust in his or her unique way. Before they for-

got, before the rest of the world could forget, they told their own stories as they sat in the memorial garden the Tuchmans had created on their property, a bucolic arrangement of trees, boulders, and stones, marked with a Star of David and the dates 1939–1945.

Their very survival had been a transcendent act—they had managed to stay alive while at the fire's center. They had demonstrated through the achievements in their lives that although they could never put the Holocaust behind them, they would not carry it as cumbersome baggage wherever they went either. It was as much a part of them as the color of their eyes or the dates of their births, an immutable fact they could never change. They had melted down their tears and wounds into an invisible second skin, a definite presence but never a burden to wear.

In Heidelberg, it was natural that the Jewish students would band together, leaning on and supporting one another, immersed in what Anna called "that small island in turbulent waters." They had been reared to value knowledge and learning, had suffered losses of unknowable magnitude, and were looking for that warmth and unconditional love lost in the extermination of their families.

"I believe that something very life-affirming survived in all of us," said Anna. "The need to belong to a family is so strong, that sooner or later, you will find a family for yourself composed of brothers and sisters and all the love and jealousies you'd find in any family. Steve is my brother, and Lusia is my sister, and our children are cousins for each other."

"People ask me how we survived, intimating that to survive you had to be inhuman somehow, fighting over every piece of bread," said Lusia. "That wasn't true, at least not in my case. I was raised to help people who were less fortunate. When my mother, brother, and I were in the ghetto and I was washing windows for that Nazi, all I thought about was smuggling food in for my mother and brother so that they could survive. Later on, when I was in hiding with my cousins, the important thing was cooperating so we could survive. We had to depend on each other."

When the four are together, they are often asked what helped them survive. In unison, they recite the answer: Each one came from a solid, religious family with strong beliefs and ideals on which they could rely during their darkest hours. Anna had her mother to care for and to care about her. Lusia could rely on her cousins and her friend Krzysia. Paul depended on his strong beliefs in Zionism and the hundred or so pictures of Anna and his family to give him strength. Like the others, Steve was blessed with strong ties to Judaism and a presence of mind that enabled him to choose the correct path at each dangerous intersection of life and death. His fortuitous visits to his aunt and uncle and his brother Karl also shored him up in times when he was near breaking.

Yet surviving the war itself was just the beginning. Left with no one and nothing, they still had to go on. That was possible because the four of them had each other, and together they formed a new family.

Still together now, still moving forward, glancing back to gather strength from the past but not dwelling there, Steve Hornstein, Lusia Hornstein, Paul Ornstein, and Anna Ornstein relive their memories to keep their stories alive. They are all in their seventies; the Ornsteins and the Hornsteins have both celebrated their fiftieth wedding anniversaries. They are not old, but they are getting older. Their families are grown, but they are still growing. They have witnessed death, but they have also witnessed life renewing itself again and again. They have seen humanity at its most depraved, but they have been the beneficiaries of extraordinary kindnesses, sometimes performed at great risk. They have not unraveled the mysteries of the human heart, but they wear their own hearts openly for all to see the hope, sorrow, pain, triumph, love, and courage that lie within.

Index

American Jewish Joint Distribution Committee, 173, 195, 196
American Psychiatric Institute, 233
Anti-Semitism: in Hajdunanas, 3, 4; in Hungary, 9, 63, 68, 69; in Nazi Germany, 9; in Szendro, 10, 12, 40. *See also Numerus clausus*
Apponyi, Albert, 97
Armia Krajowa (Home Army), 89
Arrow Party (Hungary), 69, 168
Aufbau (newspaper), 166
Auschwitz: Brünn family in, 132, 204, 214; daily regimen of, 135, 140, 224; female guards in, 134, 148; food rations in, 134, 140; gas chambers and crematoria in, 135, 138, 141, 224; Hornstein family in, 170, 171; Hornsteins' postwar visit to, 231; Hungarian Jews in, 98; mothers forced to sacrifice babies in, 132, 170; selections in, 133, 136, 139; shaving and tattooing in, 133-34
Australia, 39, 194, 234
Austria, 16, 34, 63

BBC news broadcasts, 34, 39
Bellevue Hospital (New York City), 217
Belzec death camp, 48
Bergen-Belsen concentration camp, 170, 194
Beth El Hospital (Brooklyn, N.Y.), 217
Beth Israel Hospital (Newark, N.J.), 186, 200, 212, 234; gift to Anna, 216; kindness of staff, 202-3, 213, 215; paging Ornstein/Hornstein incidents, 214
Bicske, Hungary, 105
Blumenthal, Rabbi (U.S. Army chaplain), 196

"Bornstein" (nickname of Bob and Jo Lewis), 214
Bremerhaven, Germany, 196
Brichah, 177
Brooklyn State Hospital (Brooklyn, N.Y.), 216
Brünn, Andrew (Anna's brother), 11, 209; forced labor of, 13, 75, 128; in Miskolc gymnasium, 40; personality and temperament of, 13
Brünn, Anna. *See* Ornstein, Anna Brünn
Brünn, Paul (Anna's brother), 11, 209; in labor unit, 13, 75, 128; in Miskolc gymnasium, 40; personality and temperament of, 13
Brünn, Sophie (Anna's mother): and Anna, 124, 135, 138, 146, 226; in Auschwitz, 131-36, 139-43; in Budapest, 173; death of, 225, 228; and grandchildren, 216, 219, 225, 227; in Heidelberg, 192-96, 205, 207-10; and Lusia, 208; and Mengele, 139; as orphanage director, 174-75, 179; in Parchnitz, 144, 145-46, 147; and Paul, 65, 149; personality and temperament of, 12, 40, 42, 64, 128, 130, 135, 137, 175, 230; in Plaszow, 136-39; prewar life of, 11-13, 40-41; and sons, 13, 128, 209; in U.S., 216, 220, 227, 228; weeping episode of, 209
Brünn, William (Anna's father): arrest of, 42; death of, 133, 149, 226; personality and temperament of, 11, 13, 42; prewar life of, 11; psychological deterioration of, 42, 63, 128, 130; Sophie's grief over, 209
Budapest: American Jewish Joint Distribution Committee in, 173; German occu-

JEAN M. PECK has written for newspapers, magazines, and television and was the editor of *Horizons,* a magazine published by the University of Cincinnati, where she also taught writing and broadcast journalism. A native of Portland, Maine, she has lived and worked in Norwich, England; Hamburg, Germany; Cincinnati, Ohio; and Houston, Texas. She is currently writing a novel and a textbook about the Holocaust.